JUST CONSERVATION

Loss of biodiversity is one of the great environmental challenges facing humanity but unfortunately efforts to reduce the rate of loss have so far failed. At the same time, these efforts have too often resulted in unjust social outcomes in which people living in or near to areas designated for conservation lose access to their territories and resources. In this book the author argues that our approach to biodiversity conservation needs to be more strongly informed by a concern for and understanding of social justice issues.

Injustice can be a driver of biodiversity loss and a barrier to efforts at preservation. Conversely, the pursuit of social justice can be a strong motivation to find solutions to environmental problems. The book therefore argues that the pursuit of socially just conservation is not only intrinsically the right thing to do, but will also be instrumental in bringing about greater success.

The argument for a more socially just conservation is initially developed conceptually, drawing upon ideas of environmental justice that incorporate concerns for distribution, procedure and recognition. It is then applied to a range of approaches to conservation including benefit sharing arrangements, integrated conservation and development projects and market-based approaches such as sustainable timber certification and payments for ecosystem services schemes. Case studies are drawn from the author's research in Rwanda, Uganda, Tanzania, Laos, Bolivia, China and India.

Adrian Martin is Professor of Environment and Development at the School of International Development, University of East Anglia, UK.

Earthscan Conservation and Development series

Series Editor: W. M. Adams, Moran Professor of Conservation and Development, Department of Geography, University of Cambridge, UK

Conservation and Sustainable Development
Linking practice and policy in Eastern Africa
Edited by Jon Davies

Conservation and Environmental Management in Madagascar
Edited by Ivan R. Scales

Conservation and Development in Cambodia
Exploring frontiers of change in nature, state and society
Edited by Sarah Milne and Sanghamitra Mahanty

Just Conservation
Biodiversity, wellbeing and sustainability
By Adrian Martin

For further information please visit the series page on the Routledge website:
http://www.routledge.com/books/series/ECCAD

'Can nature be protected without harming local people? *Just Conservation* argues that it must, and shows how it can be done. Eloquently and clearly, Adrian Martin makes a powerful case for placing the issue of social justice at the heart of bio-diversity conservation.' – *Professor Bill Adams, University of Cambridge, UK*

JUST CONSERVATION

Biodiversity, Wellbeing and Sustainability

Adrian Martin

LONDON AND NEW YORK

from Routledge

First published 2017
by Routledge
2 Park Square, Milton Park, Abingdon, Oxon OX14 4RN

and by Routledge
711 Third Avenue, New York, NY 10017

Routledge is an imprint of the Taylor & Francis Group, an informa business

© 2017 Adrian Martin

British Library Cataloguing-in-Publication Data
A catalogue record for this book is available from the British Library

Library of Congress Cataloging in Publication Data
A catalog record for this book has been requested

ISBN: 978-1-138-78858-9 (hbk)
ISBN: 978-1-138-78859-6 (pbk)
ISBN: 978-1-315-76534-1 (ebk)

Typeset in Bembo
by Swales & Willis Ltd, Exeter, Devon, UK

CONTENTS

FIGURES AND TABLES

Figures

Tables

PREFACE

In principle this should have been quite an easy book for me to write. The idea was to pull together work that I have already done, rather than to start from scratch and collect new materials. But of course it has been far from easy. It has taken several years to complete and during that time I have constantly been learning new things, being inspired by new people, starting new projects and teaching new classes. As time has gone by, the evidence has moved on, my views have evolved and I have found myself having to rethink chapters which I once considered complete.

However, whilst my views have moved on, the motives for writing the book remain much the same. On the one hand, the struggle to conserve nature appears more urgent than ever and at times more forlorn. A couple of recent news items exemplify this. Firstly, on 31 August 2016 there was a press release from the Great Elephant Census. Between 2007 and 2014, 144,000 African savannah elephants were killed, reducing the population by 30%. In Tanzania, where I visit quite frequently for work, 60% of elephants have been killed in a mere five years. Here, of all the elephants spotted during fly-over surveys, 26% were carcasses. In northern Cameroon, 83% were carcasses. Secondly, on 4 September 2016 the International Union for the Conservation of Nature issued a press release about its new 'Red Book' data on species threatened with extinction. The Eastern gorilla had been moved from 'endangered' to 'critically endangered', a status that they describe as being 'one step from extinction'. Already in this category are the Western gorilla, Bornean orangutan and the Sumatran orangutan. Four out of six of the great ape species are now one step from extinction, whilst the chimpanzee and the bonobo are classified as 'endangered'.

Such news is appalling. Are we really going to allow the current era in human history to be stained forever by the legacy that we allowed Africa's elephants to be massacred? Or that we allowed our closest animal relatives to be killed off entirely? I find myself thinking of Gandhi's belief that 'the greatness of a nation and its moral progress can be judged by the way its animals are treated'. But this is only half of the motivation for this book because our morality must equally be judged by how we treat our fellow humans. Who would really be happy visiting a park to view elephants or gorillas, knowing that their survival had been achieved through injustices to those people living nearby? And yet that is sadly often the case: attempts to save the Eastern gorilla have involved the dispossession of Central African pygmy tribes of their ancestral forests; and attempts to save the Savannah elephants have sometimes trampled over the rights of local pastoralist peoples. My motive for writing this book has therefore been to demonstrate that we *should* combine conservation with social justice and, moreover, that we *can* successfully combine these two objectives.

I owe a lot of thanks for support with writing the book. I will begin with immediate colleagues in the School of International Development at the University of East Anglia. The various research projects that underpin this book would not have been nearly as fruitful or as fun without this group of co-researchers, travel companions and friends. In particular I have worked together on research projects with Vasudha Chhotray, Neil Dawson, Roger Few, Nicole Gross-Camp, He Jun, Bereket Kebede, Shawn McGuire, Iokiñe Rodriguez, Oliver Springate-Baginski and Mark Zeitoun. Our collaboration has in no small way been facilitated by the existence of the Global Environmental Justice research group and a special thanks goes to Thomas Sikor who had the vision to establish this and who is such a generous and inspiring colleague and friend. During the later stages of preparation I am thankful to Carole White for expert assistance with digging out some final pieces of information and to Eric Opou who helped restore my bibliography after a last minute IT catastrophe.

A lot of the ideas for this book have taken shape during a project on 'Conservation, Markets and Justice' which involved field sites in Bolivia, China and Tanzania. In Bolivia, many thanks to Mirna Inturias, to her colleagues at NUR University and to leaders of the Chiquitano people including general chief Anacleto Peña. In China, my thanks mainly to He Jun. In Tanzania, we own much to our partners, the Mpingo Conservation and Development Initiative and especially to Glory Massao, Jasper Makala and Steve Ball. Additionally, some of the work on Tanzania reported in this book is indebted to previous work undertaken with a good friend and colleague, Esteve Corbera.

I should also thank the UK's Economic and Social Research Council who funded the Conservation, Markets and Justice project. The joint research council programme on Ecosystem Services and Poverty Alleviation (ESPA) supported a number of related projects in which we have developed ideas about environmental justice. This began with the 'Just Ecosystem Management' project led by Thomas Sikor that included a case study that features in this book: a study of Bwindi Impenetrable National Park in Uganda undertaken with Anne Akol.

Most recently, ESPA have funded work to advance equity in protected area management, and I am grateful to Kate Schreckenberg and Phil Franks for involving me in that work which has been influential in the latter stages of this book.

Finally, I should offer my greatest thanks to those who have most directly put up with me writing this – the love and support of your family cannot be over-emphasised. My love and thanks to Jules and my two wonderful daughters, Lydia and Tamsin. Additional thanks to Jules for proof-reading a draft. The mistakes are of course, all mine.

Adrian Martin
14 September 2016
Norwich

1

INTRODUCTION

Why we agree about conservation

Readers of this book are probably already convinced that biodiversity is important. Some may value biological diversity in its own right, celebrating the wealth of life on earth as something inherently desirable or as something that can enrich our lives through direct encounters or media images. Others may place greater stress on the role that biodiversity plays in producing and safeguarding things that are essential to human survival, such as food. They may know that biodiverse ecosystems tend to produce more of the things we like to consume, such as fish or arable crops; or that they are more consistent in producing these things, for example because they are more resilient to climate change. Even if we have different reasons for doing so, we might still share the idea that conserving biodiversity is generally a good thing.

For a social movement to gain widespread traction, it needs such a convergence around a foundational idea. It needs a clear and compelling idea about the right way to think and act, such that its membership is attracted by the moral high ground it occupies. In recent decades calls to conserve nature's rich diversity of species and landscapes have generated increasing support from various quarters, including not only a recreation-hungry minority based in the world's centres of affluence, but also the many whose day-to-day lives are more directly dependent upon the farms, forests and waters that surround them. Such a breadth of appeal is not born from a single conception of 'the right thing to do', but rather from a constellation of reasons that lead us to pursue a shared goal, but for different purposes.

In many Western societies, membership of environmental groups is very large, making the environmental movement greater than other sectors of civil society and rivalling for size the membership of political parties (Dalton 2005). In the UK, for example, 139 environmental organisations reported just over 4.5 million supporters, amounting to about 10% of the adult population (Cracknell et al. 2013).

Furthermore, the funds received by these environmental organisations has grown rapidly, including a fivefold increase in revenue between 1995 and 2008 and only modest retrenchment following the 2008 financial crisis (Cracknell et al. 2013).

Data on membership and funding of environmental organisations would suggest that support for conservation is strongest in more economically prosperous Western democracies, and much weaker in the global South. But this focus on group membership can give a misleading impression about the geographical distribution of conservation advocacy. Sarah Fredericks compares environmental ethics across different cultural traditions with particular attention to Western sustainable development agendas, Christian and Islamic theologies, and deep ecology (Fredericks 2013). She finds a sense of responsibility towards other species to be almost universal, although the reasons behind this sense of responsibility can vary. One form of reason is awareness of ecology and in particular the consequences of species extinctions in a world in which everything is connected; another reason is belief in the virtue of caring for God's creation or doing God's will; another still is a recognition of the intrinsic value of nature. Casting an even wider net, Baird Callicott catalogues different traditions of environmental ethics around the world, from major religious traditions to smaller-scale tribal ones, many of which justify some form of responsibility towards non-human nature (Callicott 1994). In summary, a large range of belief systems are able to support care for the environment. The prominence of such care is less a matter of underlying beliefs and more a reflection of prevailing social-economic conditions, conditions that are more often present in economically better off democracies (Dalton 2005).

Care for the environment may also appear more prominent in wealthier societies simply because some ways of expressing care are more visible than others. Membership of environmental groups is one way of expressing environmental concern, but there are other, less well examined forms. In particular, the 'environmentalism of the poor' is different to that of the environmentalism of the affluent, but is found globally at sites where local people seek to protect the ecological basis of their livelihoods from those who would dispossess them of it (Guha and Alier 2013). 'Poor' environmentalists struggle to save their forests from timber and mining concessions, to preserve their water from agro-industrial over-extraction or pollution from oil wells and, more generally, to protect their right to control their environments (Martínez Alier 2014). These environmentalists often put everything on the line in attempts to prevent state or corporate incursion of their natural resources. In the early 1970s, the Chipko movement in India saw local farmers face up to the timber industry, with women using their bodies to shield trees from bulldozers; in the mid 1970s Chico Mendes and others formed the rubber tappers' unions and also put themselves in front of chainsaws and bulldozers to protect Amazonian forests from ranchers and loggers. Today there are many such struggles at commodity frontiers across the globe (see e.g. www.ejolt.org/). For example in Odisha, India, those struggling to protect their forests from bauxite mines and steelworks have been met with brutal suppression, standing strong even after several had been murdered (Kumar 2014a). Such struggles might not be signified with the contemporary metaphors of Western environmentalism: 'biodiversity', 'ecosystem services', 'resilience', 'planetary limits' or 'the anthropocene', but they are undoubtedly at the frontline of protecting nature and society against extractive capital.

Superficially at least, the motives for conserving nature can appear highly divergent. For example, there seems to be a big difference between advocating conservation out of a pragmatic concern for human welfare, and advocating conservation based on spiritual insight into the place of humans in the rest of nature.

For some, the 'rightness' of conservation flows from social and cultural practices, from religious doctrine, the vision of artists or philosophers, and associated spiritual insight into the place of humans in the rest of nature. In practice, however, the division between cultural and pragmatic motives for caring about biodiversity may not be so terribly distinct. We might bridge art and science in arriving at a sense of our environmental responsibilities. For example, the famous American environmentalist Aldo Leopold believed that environmental understanding was best pursued through art and science in tandem. His advocacy of a 'land ethic' was influenced by the emerging science of ecology but also by cultural revelation about the place of humans in nature. In his essay 'Thinking like a mountain', Leopold draws on his ecological understanding of how the elimination of wolves resulted in over-grazing by deer and ecological destruction. But he clearly signals that this scientific awakening is connected to a spiritual one.

> We reached the old wolf in time to watch a fierce green fire dying in her eyes. I realized then, and have known ever since, that there was something new to me in those eyes – something known only to her and to the mountain. I was young then, and full of trigger-itch; I thought that because fewer wolves meant more deer, that no wolves would mean hunters' paradise. But after seeing the green fire die, I sensed that neither the wolf nor the mountain agreed with such a view.
>
> *(Leopold 2013 [1949], p. 115)*

Why we disagree about conservation

The message so far is that biodiversity conservation is in theory capable of garnering very broad support, across places and cultures. There is scope for a convergence of interests and a basis for a widespread social movement within and beyond the more visible constituency of environmental group members. However, we have to recognise that there is not always agreement amongst different stakeholder groups about what constitutes 'the right thing to do'. There is no consensus about what 'just conservation' looks like and, in practice, the history of biodiversity conservation is notable for its disagreement and conflict. Sometimes disagreements appear as constructive debates over the causes of a problem or the possibilities for its solution; but at other times the consequences for some groups of people are so acute that they become matters of social justice. And as some of the examples in this book will illustrate, we don't need to share exactly the same ethics to be able to agree that some of the impacts of biodiversity conservation have been contrary to any defensible and pragmatic formulation of environmental justice.

One example that will feature in this book is the treatment of the Twa (or Batwa) and other pygmy peoples associated with the montane and lowland rainforests of central Africa. In Uganda, the Twa were evicted from their traditional forest homes to allow for increasing protection of the montane forests of Bwindi, Mgahinga, Echuya and Rwenzori. Many of these evictions took place as early as the 1930s when forests such as Bwindi were first gazetted as forest reserves. However, evictions continued and culminated in the remaining Batwa being forced from Mgahinga in 1991 when it became a National Park. The picture is a bit less clear in nearby Bwindi which became Bwindi Impenetrable National Park in the same year. Whilst the majority of Batwa communities say that they had left the forest much earlier, a few insist that they had to leave the forest at about the time it became a National Park. Regardless of the timing of physical eviction from the forest, it is clear that most Batwa communities suffered from economic displacement, finding themselves cut off from traditional forest-based livelihoods which relied on hunting and gathering, and even denied access to important cultural sites within the forest. The Batwa were undeniably let down by conservation, left to endure lives of hardship marked by economic poverty and social discrimination (Martin et al. 2015). As recently as June 2013, 13 of the 14 Twa households in Ryabitukuru village, on the southern edge of Bwindi, had their homes burned down by local mobs set on driving them away (Forest Peoples Programme 2014).

Whilst the extent and exact nature of such displacement by conservation has not been systematically documented, it has clearly been widespread and much has now been written about it (Chapin 2004; Brockington and Igoe 2006; Agrawal and Redford 2009; Almudi and Berkes 2010). Indeed, much has also been written about how growing concern with the social impacts of conservation led to changing practices in the late 1980s, away from more coercive 'fortress conservation' (or 'fences and fines') approaches and towards more people-friendly approaches such as community-based conservation and integrated conservation and development projects (ICDPs) (Brandon and Wells 1992).

In this book, I am indebted to the work of political ecologists and anthropologists who have worked extensively to support conservation in the tropics by better understanding its social issues. One important lesson from this body of work is that it is not enough to document specific incidences of displacements and the local contexts that surround these. We need to also try to understand bigger pictures that might help to explain why this kind of displacement for conservation has appeared regularly, over a long period of time and across much of the world. In the broadest possible terms, this involves attention to political economy – to the global structuring of power that enables the interests of some groups to regularly subjugate the interests of others. Taking a rather narrower perspective, this will largely be addressed by considering how particular views about 'the right thing to do' come to dominate and to become a driving force of policies that prioritise some interests over others. For example, there are important questions to be asked about whose knowledge is represented by prevailing ideas about protected areas, and about the political-economic contexts in which these ideas gain traction and become the models for conservation on the ground (Brosius and Hitchner 2010; West and Brockington 2006; West et al. 2006).

I will have much more to say about the power of ideas in later chapters. Dominant ideas often serve to frame both the causes of and solutions to declining biodiversity. For those of us who have visited protected areas around the world, and spoken with management from field level to headquarters, it becomes apparent how widespread and engrained some of these ideas are. For example, common narratives about the threats to biodiversity conservation refer to population pressure, to the subsistence needs of local poor people and to the impossibility for humans and highly valued biodiversity to co-exist (Brockington and Igoe 2006; Lélé et al. 2010). The power of such ideas is that they frame the problem in ways which limit the range of possible solutions. They lead inexorably to 'solutions' that involve the displacement of local and indigenous people.

Often, the prevailing ideas that are used to frame conservation problems have the effect of presenting decision-makers with what Martha Nussbaum (2011) describes as 'tragic choices', in which the only possible solutions involve violation of basic social justice. For example John Terborgh argues in *Requiem for Nature* that if you want to save treasured species including top predators it is necessary to completely exclude people from their habitats (Terborgh 1999). This framing of the conservation problem presents us with tragic choices, for it is notoriously difficult to respect the human rights of people being subjected to forced displacement.

What I am getting at here is that if we don't stand back and examine critically the dominant ideas about biodiversity conservation, then it becomes harder to see ways of making conservation more just. But when we do examine these assumptions, we can help to expand the range of possible solutions and perhaps see more pathways that involve decisions that are less tragic, and more options for aligning conservation with social justice. For example, the assumption that nature can only be saved by separating it from people may well hold in some circumstances (it would be naïve to think there will never be tragic choices), but it is not tried and tested everywhere (Agrawal and Redford 2009); furthermore, its blanket application is often to the detriment of local people, and at times also to the detriment of conservation (Lélé et al. 2010). Such ideas can serve to narrow down analysis of the causes of conservation problems and foreclose on analysis of more political causes such as issues of tenure, authority, knowledge hegemony and the expanding sphere of capitalist relations.

Conflicts over conservation are often between groups of people who are relatively affluent and groups who are economically poor, and between local people and more distant stakeholders. Whilst there is widespread sympathy for protecting forests such as Bwindi, the local stakeholders involved also have other interests that they understandably prioritise, such as having a home, food security and rights to self-determination. The presence of competing interests means that doing what some would consider to be 'the right thing' for conservation – even when rooted in some kind of ethical appeal – will not always appear to be 'the right thing' to others. As Thomas Sikor has argued, ecosystem management interventions can simultaneously create claims that both justice and injustice have been done, reflecting the different vantage points from which different groups of stakeholders experience the same processes and outcomes (Sikor 2013).

Conflicts of interest are not confined to locations that suffer high rates of poverty. For example, if more Europeans switched to vegetarian diets there would be very substantial potential gains for addressing climate change and biodiversity conservation (Westhoek et al. 2014). But pushing such a solution on people can lead to negative reactions (de Boer et al. 2013). Indeed, I would speculate that only a minority of professional biodiversity conservationists are willing to give up eating meat, even knowing that this would help to spare land from intensive food production.[1] But whilst such conflicts exist everywhere between the apparent needs of conservation and the rights and freedoms of individuals, they do tend to be more visible and intense in areas with poverty, not least because it is all too often those who are economically poor and politically marginalised who are the ones expected to give things up. Not only are people very often expected to change their diet (e.g. through laws and campaigns against bushmeat consumption), but sometimes they are also expected to reduce their use of a host of other environmental goods such as firewood, construction materials and animal grazing. During one visit to Bwindi, a Twa woman described how they suffered from cold following their displacement from Bwindi, when they were not allowed access to firewood and were not supplied with blankets. There has been relatively little action to overcome this disparity between those who most value the benefits of biodiversity conservation and those who more often bear the costs (Adams et al. 2004).

Whilst the compulsory displacement of people is becoming a less popular strategy amongst states and conservation biologists, new mechanisms for separating people from nature have become possible through recent trends towards market-based environmental conservation. In his *Brief History of Neoliberalism*, David Harvey (2005) explores the dramatic spread of neoliberal ideology since the late 1970s, capturing hearts and minds through its underlying claims to be the ideology of personal freedom. In its heartlands such as Chile, the US and the UK, neoliberal political practices have reversed decades of gradual dispersion of wealth and power, re-concentrating capital back into the hands of a small elite dominated by CEOs and financiers. In the US, the share of economic assets held by the wealthiest 1% was more than 40% in the 1920s, fell to little over 20% in the late 1970s under predominantly Keynesian policies and was then restored to about 35% by 1998 under neoliberal policies (Duménil and Levy, cited in Harvey 2005). The wave of free market economics took a little longer to make its mark on biodiversity conservation but did eventually arrive in the early 2000s as evidenced by the growth of supposedly (but often not actually) market-based

---

1 I should declare that I don't eat meat – but any green kudos I might deserve from this is spoilt by the fact that I have pet cats that do.

mechanisms such as privatisation of parks, carbon trading, payments for ecosystem services and biodiversity offsetting. Green consumerism has a rather longer history, supported by systems of labelling such as Soil Association certification of organic foods (since 1973) and Forest Stewardship Council certification of sustainable timbers (since 1994). Market-based approaches have generated new opportunities for biodiversity conservation, including methods that are more conducive to securing the interests of the new breed of powerful financiers and CEOs. Players like Wal-Mart have entered the offsetting scene, buying land for conservation to 'offset' areas of land they cover with their stores, and these so-called 'markets' for biodiversity offsets were worth at least \$2.4 to 4 billion annually by 2010 according to the *State of Biodiversity Markets* report (Madsen et al. 2011). Western consumers are widely encouraged to participate in new markets for biodiversity; for example in the run-up to Christmas the Rainforest Trust encourages us to 'Give the gift of rainforest acres this holiday season!' (Rainforest Trust 2014).

This book is not an attack on market-based approaches. At the optimistic end of the scale, market-based approaches have the potential to solve age-old conflicts of interest by facilitating voluntary transactions that link those willing to pay to preserve biodiversity with those willing and able to make it happen. For example it allows those living near to valued habitats to be compensated for any constraints on their use, thereby addressing the imbalance of costs and benefits that has plagued conservation in the tropics. But we do need to think critically about markets if we are to understand connections with social justice. As a prelude to this thinking, imagine that those willing to pay for protecting the mountain gorillas of Bwindi could have made ever increasing financial offers until the Twa 'voluntarily' agreed to take the money and leave. This could be viewed as a more just solution, transforming a 'tragic choice' into a voluntary and mutually beneficial transaction. But it could equally be argued that, in the context of cash-poor communities, the use of financial incentives is itself a form of coercion (Schroeder 2008): an alternative method of dispossessing marginal people of their rights and territories.

We might also want to ask what kind of freedom is being granted by allowing 'markets' to determine how land is used and managed. Is it an illusionary freedom, or even what Karl Polanyi (1944) referred to as a 'bad' freedom: the freedom to exploit others or to deny them access to things they need? And as the philosopher Michael Sandel (2012) states, a world in which everything can be bought and sold for money is a world in which money is everything. And in a world where money is everything, being poor is the worst thing that can happen to you. If Michael Sandel is correct, in what sense can the incorporation of the environment into market mechanisms be considered to be favourable to the poor?

So an ideology that makes its appeal to our sense of freedom turns out, under some relatively gentle scrutiny, to require careful examination in terms of the kinds of freedoms it purports to deliver and the links it forges to environmental justice and injustice. For some scholars, neoliberal markets are a new mechanism – a new freedom – for appropriation and displacement. In the same way as markets for large land investments have raised widespread concerns about 'land grabbing', the growth in markets for investing in conservation are now leading to accusations of 'green grabbing' (Fairhead et al. 2012). There is concern that some big global conservation players are too eager to embrace these new sources of funding, despite their embedded inequalities. Such eagerness to embrace new opportunities is largely driven by the desire to do 'the right thing' – to attract new sources of finance for conservation and to use financial resources more cost-effectively. But as I will now highlight, it is vital to keep sight of the means by which we seek to achieve conservation success, even where there may be consensus that the ends are good and proper.

Justice matters

As the title of this book suggests, the focus is more about the social failures of conservation – its injustices – than its biological failures. At first take, that might seem a bit obscure or peripheral – surely we should first and foremost be concerned with whether conservation is achieving its primary goal. In some ways, yes, we should. There is little doubt that loss of biological diversity is central to a complex nexus of environmental changes that humans need to urgently address, including climate change, biogeochemical cycles and ocean acidification. Indeed, so serious is this combined, human-induced global environmental change that it is becoming increasingly popular as a metaphor for our age – the anthropocene – the geological age in which humans are responsible for dangerous changes to planetary processes. It is a metaphor that places humans in the driving seat. We are now the constructors of climates, of biological assemblages, as well as of societies, and we are responsible for taking urgent actions to steer the planet towards a more sustainable future.

And yet in spite of the urgent need to turn the tide on biodiversity loss, I suspect many readers will also share my concern about how conservation affects the lives of different people. Just as we hold different motives for conserving biodiversity, we might also make different arguments for promoting social justice. No doubt we would all prefer that, where possible, conservation should protect habitats like Bwindi without having to harm local cultures and livelihoods in the process. A proportion of us might make an additional claim that safeguarding the wellbeing of local people is not only a preferable outcome but also an important means to achieving long-term conservation success. This introduces an important distinction between two types of reasons for pursuing a more just conservation. The former simply holds that being 'just' to people is the 'right thing to do'. This is a normative or moral argument that pursuing a more just conservation is an intrinsically good thing. The latter suggests that a more just conservation is not only a good in itself but is also a pragmatic means to achieve more effective conservation. This is an instrumental argument in which the goal of conservation is what ultimately matters most. It might seem like an inferior motivation motive for justice but there is a long tradition of employing instrumental rhetoric in favour of social justice, such as Martin Luther King's pleading that if we fail to live together justly now ('as brothers' as he put it), we will 'perish together as fools' in consequence.

I consider the instrumental case for conservation with social justice in some detail in the following chapters. It requires careful examination because, whilst we might dearly want to believe that a more just conservation will be a more successful conservation, there are cases where exactly the opposite appears to hold – where successful conservation results from social injustices, and that such success can be durable (Brockington 2004). One can look, for example, at the eviction of native American people to make way for some of the iconic parks in the USA. Whereas there has been a substantial rethink about whether the extirpation of wolves was bad for the ecosystem (e.g. leading to their re-introduction in Yellowstone in 1995), I am not aware of any similar rethink about whether forceful removal of people has been bad for the ecosystem. This poses some interesting questions for the current inquiry: can enhanced attention to social justice really be instrumental in bringing about improved conservation performance? And if so, under what circumstances and via what pathways of change?

The idea that 'justice matters' is of course central to this book, and central to the many local environmental struggles around the world that choose to frame their cases in justice terms. The sense of justice and injustice comes to most people at an early age, often expressed in terms of whether something is seen to be fair or not. This sensitivity to justice remains a powerful force over human behaviour and can often crowd out baser motives such as financial gain (Fehr and Falk 2002; Deutsch 2011). The importance of understanding how people think about and experience justice is for this reason an important area of concern in areas such as labour relations in which it has long been understood that perceptions of fairness and justice have an important effect on job satisfaction and motivation (Moorman 1991; Colquitt et al. 2001). Indeed, there is now a vast body of research into organisational justice, in contrast to comparatively little on conservation justice.

This is perhaps understandable given the much smaller cadre of academic social scientists who research social aspects of biodiversity conservation. And yet it seems too crucial an aspect of conservation's problem to leave unexamined. Conservation is deeply influenced by and engrained with ideas about justice. These ideas might not always be expressed explicitly but they can easily enough be inferred from the reasons expressed in support of conserving species (e.g. concerns for animal rights, the common heritage of humans or responsibility to future generations), the selection of co-benefits considered rightful goals of conservation interventions (e.g. poverty alleviation, equity or cultural rights), and the detailed design of specific interventions (e.g. compensation, benefit-sharing or payments for ecosystem services schemes).

Given that the science and practice of conservation are deeply connected with ideas about justice, and given the preceding point that humans are predisposed to being sensitive to justice, it is not surprising to find that conservation conflicts are often underpinned by different ideas about what constitutes a just or right conservation intervention (Whiteman 2009; Redpath et al. 2013). Such conflicts are not restricted to competing material interests or disagreement about which solution will best solve a problem. The issues of concern can run deeper, touching on the different ways in which people understand and value nature and its relationship with human society, and the kinds of knowledge that should be valued when it comes to understanding and responding to environmental challenges.

Justice as normative and empirical

Regardless of our reasons for wanting to bring social justice concerns into conservation scholarship and practice – whether our sympathies lie with intrinsic reasons, instrumental ones, or both – we are likely to end up facing broadly similar questions that have become evident in the preceding discussions. We need to ask what is meant by 'justice' and 'injustice' in the context of conservation? And how are meanings of justice constructed and contested? What kinds of injustice appear regularly? And what are the underlying drivers of such regularly unacceptable outcomes? How, if at all, are these justice outcomes linked to conservation effectiveness? And how should we go about making conservation more just?

These kinds of questions require some kind of strategy in terms of how to define and give meaning to the terms 'justice' and 'injustice'. I will develop this strategy in more detail in subsequent chapters but at this point it is helpful to develop one key element of it: the choice of an empirical rather than a purely normative approach to understanding justice. This can be thought of as a choice between the way in which political philosophers have historically sought to think about justice and the ways in which contemporary social scientists think about it. Philosophers have generally taken a normative stance, seeking to use the power of reason to arrive at widely applicable principles by which actions can be judged to be right or wrong. These ethical principles might refer to the motives for an action (defining the duties we should live by), the outcomes of an action (defining the consequences our actions should be judged by) or, as is more popular in ancient philosophies, what actions reveal about the character of the person (defining the characteristics of a virtuous life) (see Box 1.1).

Normative approaches to investigating justice are typically contrasted to approaches that are variously called 'contextual', 'experiential' or, as I will call them, 'empirical'. Empirical approaches are grounded in observation of what people say and do in the real world. They describe and analyse how justice ideas are conceived and used in practice, in the context of dealing with real-world problems (Konow 2001; Miller 2013). Environmental justice scholars such as Bryan Norton (2005), Gordon Walker (2012) and Thomas Sikor (2013) reflect the trend towards more empirical studies of justice, seeking to begin their investigation by exploring and understanding the cases that people make about what is just and unjust, rather than seeking to identify generalised principles that define what is just and unjust.

An empirical approach to studying justice does not preclude an interest in the kinds of normative theories referred to in Box 1.1. Indeed, part and parcel of this approach may be to compare empirical observations of the justice cases that people make with more abstract ethical traditions (Sikor et al. 2014). For example, it might be interesting to know whether the arguments made in real-world conservation struggles resonate with the kinds of principles we find in normative theories. But whilst an empirical study of justice is likely to engage with normative theory in some way, the main purpose of the study will never be to arrive at a grand theory of justice and nor will it be to employ a single theory of justice to judge whether certain acts are right or wrong. This book is primarily based on an empirical, social science strategy and does not seek to develop a normative theory of justice.

BOX 1.1   THREE NORMATIVE TRADITIONS IN ETHICAL INQUIRY: DUTY, CONSEQUENCE AND VIRTUE

1. Duty-based (or deontological) principles of justice

Deontological approaches to moral philosophy determine what is right and wrong by reference to one's duty to conform to generally applicable moral rules of behaviour. The moral status of an action is not determined by its outcome (as these can be unpredictable and arbitrary) but by its intention (its good will). In practice, the only way to demonstrate such good will is to obey absolute moral rules that apply in all circumstances. Thus there is a tradition of moral philosophy that concentrates on trying to establish what these rules should be, either through rational thought or through recourse to divinity: for example, Immanuel Kant's (1785) famous categorical imperative:

> Act only according to that maxim by which you can also will that it would become a universal law.

Deontological thinking supports liberal, rights-based approaches to justice such as the International Bill of Human Rights. In conservation, the most explicit attempt to work from deontological principles is the Conservation Initiative on Human Rights (CIHR 2010). Here, conservation actions are to be guided by internationally agreed conventions on human rights.

2. Utilitarian (consequentialist) principles of justice

In contrast to deontological thinking, utilitarianism prioritises consequences over rules, and societal outcomes over individual ones. The moral status of an action is determined by its outcome, measured by the net impact on happiness or 'utility'. Thus an action could in principle be right, even where it involves

(continued)

(continued)

disregarding the rights of some individuals. In Chapter 1 of his *Introduction to the Principles of Morals and Legislation* (1789) Jeremy Bentham states:

> An action then may be said to be conformable to the principle of utility . . . when the tendency it has to augment the happiness of the community is greater than any it has to diminish it.

The focus on aggregate outcome, or 'the greater good', can be seen as a way of justifying some conservation actions that serve the common heritage of humankind but in doing so bring unhappiness to a few. For some, this is precisely why biodiversity conservation involves hard choices.

3. Virtue ethics

Virtue ethics stems from ancient philosophers such as Plato and Aristotle. Doing the right thing does not flow from systematic adherence to general rules, nor only from attention to the consequences of actions. Instead, moral behaviour is seen to flow from a person's inner character or 'virtues'. If a person is able to develop a virtuous character then it will follow that they will make the right moral choices. In his *Nichomachean Ethics* (1980/c350BC) Aristotle states:

> . . . the good for man is an activity of the soul in accordance with virtue, or if there are more kinds of virtue than one, in accordance with the best and most perfect kind.

One way of thinking about virtue ethics is to propose that caring for nature is a contemporary virtue and that lack of care is a fundamental cause of biodiversity loss. By this thinking, it is wrong-minded to think that we can act morally towards nature whilst not caring for it. E.g. Kant is wrong to suggest we can act morally purely out of duty (rather than care) and Bentham is wrong to suggest we can act morally by attending only to aggregate utility. Instead we need to re-establish our relationship with nature, as a basis for caring.

The attraction of an empirical approach to environmental justice is that conservation involves diverse groups of stakeholders, influenced by different ideas and holding very different positions in the world. Even amongst groups of people facing seemingly quite similar challenges, very different claims to justice might be made. For example, I have been involved with research in the Albertine Rift area of Africa, working with local communities (including the Twa) around parks in western Rwanda, southwest Uganda and, to a lesser extent, eastern Democratic Republic of Congo.

Here, as in many of the world's 'biodiversity hotspots', local people have increasingly found their traditional uses of forests to be outlawed through the designation of progressively more strictly protected areas. Whilst a variety of views certainly exist, the main expressed sense of injustice revolves around the material consequences of this exclusion from park resources: the loss of land and resources, as well as the damage done by wild animals that come out of the park to raid their crops (Martin et al. 2013a). By contrast, a colleague of mine (Iokiñe Rodríguez) has worked for many years with the Pemon people in the Canaipa National Park in Venezuela. Here the main expression of injustice is quite different. Of course, the Pemon are concerned about the material consequences of imposed conservation interventions, but their immediate concern is with what we might describe as a cognitive or discursive injustice. Their people are treated unjustly through the introduction of a pernicious narrative that presents the socio-ecological history of the landscape as one in which a rich forested landscape has been degraded by the Pemon's use of fire. Knowledge is very clearly power in such cases because whoever gets to write the history of this landscape also gets to frame the environmental problem and the moral status of its actors. The Pemon understand this well enough and thus seek to exert their own version of history (Rodríguez et al. 2013; Martin et al. 2016).

This comparison informs us that there are different types or dimensions of environmental justice concern, such as the material and cognitive. But the main purpose of the comparison is to illustrate that environmental justice struggles are deeply contextual and that universal theories about what constitutes justice and injustice are rarely useful for understanding problem-based issues such as the environmental justice struggles of the Batwa or the Pemon. As Bryan Norton recalls from his own experience with collaborative conservation policymaking in the United States, when you are working with non-philosophers such as conservation biologists and planners, and when the group you are working with has been tasked with real-world problem-solving, engaging them in abstract discussions about generic moral rules is often neither welcome nor helpful (Norton 2005).

The fact that different people and communities think and respond differently to apparently similar circumstances comes as no great surprise. There are aspects of human responses to external circumstances that can be generally predicted through an understanding of our psychological predispositions and the ways in which we tend to react to economic and other incentives. Indeed, this is the basis of 'nudge theory', the idea that the general public's behaviour can be predictably manipulated by understanding regular patterns of behavioural responses. But we also know that there is an ideational basis for human behaviour (Parsons 2007), in which responses to external circumstances are strongly mediated by the subjective ideas that we hold. Such ideas are often locally and historically situated and less homogeneous, rational and predictable (Parsons 2007).

A classic example is the huge differences with which people have responded to wilderness across eras and cultures. In the West for example, there has been a long tradition of perceiving forests in highly negative terms, as a source of evil and as having an uncivilising effect on the human character (Short 1991). For example the word 'savage' has roots in the Latin *silvaticus*, meaning 'of the woods'. Ideas about wilderness began to change around two hundred years ago, led by the Romantic movement, in Europe, and by associated transcendental philosophies of nature in North America. For example, Henry David Thoreau directly inverted the view of wilderness as uncivilised, describing the remaining forests in New England as 'little oases of wildness in the desert of our civilisation' (Thoreau 2001, p. 168). The key point here is that the way in which we perceive nature, the way in which we experience it, both intellectually and emotionally, is highly contextual, shaped by our ideas and our position in the world. In a similar way, we would expect individuals and groups to construct different cases about what is right and wrong based on a complex assemblage of ideas and circumstances which shape the way they experience a particular problem or issue.

What seems to matter most – and what interests me considerably as a social scientist – is how different groups and individuals experience justice in particular instances and what their actions and arguments reveal about this. This leads me towards a largely empirical analysis of conservation justice, with a tendency to observe the ways in which various involved actors argue their own justice cases individually and collectively. However, I do complicate this a little in Chapter 3 where I argue that we cannot abandon the need for some generalised normative judgement.

Justice versus equity

As a final introductory point I want to explain why I choose the term 'justice' in preference to the term 'equity'. The term 'justice' is starting to take hold in the public discourse of biodiversity conservation. Take, for example the 'Promise of Sydney Vision', an output of the 2014 World Parks Congress. It includes in its vision the following elements:

> . . . by working in partnership with and recognizing the long traditions and knowledge, collective rights and responsibilities of Indigenous Peoples and local communities to land, water, natural resource and culture, we will seek to redress and remedy past and continuing injustices in accord with international agreements.
>
> . . .
>
> We will collaborate with new partners to promote sustainable and equitable economies that respect planetary boundaries and social justice.
>
> *(IUCN 2014)*

Nevertheless, the history of Convention on Biological Diversity (CBD) discourse on social issues is dominated by the term 'equity' and this remains far more prevalent among conservation practitioners.

I have yet to discover any clearly and systematically defined differences in meaning between justice and equity. However, differences are emerging through usage and my approach is to build on this precedent of usage rather than to refer to dictionary definitions. I believe that recent usage in relation to the environment is making justice the more inclusive, integrated and ultimately stronger term to use. There are four main reasons for this:

1. As applied to environmental issues, justice tends to throw a wider protective embrace that in theory can speak to the beliefs of all stakeholders. Whilst equity tends to be applied to human subjects only, environmental justice theorists prefer framings that can accommodate non-human stakeholders also (Schlosberg 2013). Justice thus provides the potential to combine both social and ecological concerns whereas equity tends to restrict itself to the former.
2. Justice also tends to reach further than equity in terms of spatial scale. Whilst we have noted that equity is in principle applied both between and within generations of humans, its practical applications to conservation have largely been local in scope, concentrating, for example, on the allocation of costs and benefits between stakeholders associated with a particular protected area or national policy process (Sikor et al. 2014). By contrast, environmental justice more often considers global relationships, in terms of how it analyses the drivers of injustice and the scales of responsibilities to address these.
3. Justice analysis also tends towards a broader engagement with different dimensions of justice. The term equity has mainly been used to refer to (a) the distribution of the social-economic impacts of protected areas and (b) the participation of different stakeholders in decision-making. Justice tends to refer to an enlarged set of concerns, including distribution and participation, but also incorporating calls for cultural recognition. These dimensions of environmental justice will be further defined and discussed in Chapter 2.
4. Justice is more often the term chosen by those involved in environmental struggles. The idea of environmental justice has its roots in the social movement that arose in the United States in the 1980s. But it is rapidly becoming a global movement and calls for a more just conservation can be viewed as part of this. Calling upon states and global institutions to act justly is a potentially powerful form of rhetoric, arguably much more so than calling for equity.

This is admittedly a highly generalised synthesis of current usage. These differences are not crystallised in any dictionary definitions and you would not have to look too hard to find exceptions. For example, the term equity clearly is sometimes applied to global-scale issues. Despite these limitations, it does serve to scope out how I am using the term justice in this book.

Justice as distribution, procedure and recognition

Figure 1.1 summarises three commonly observed dimensions of environmental justice: distribution, procedure and recognition. Distributive justice concerns the distribution of 'goods' and 'bads' between different individuals and groups and has dominated environmental justice debates to date (Walker 2012). This is perhaps not surprising given the materiality of environmental goods and bads such as natural resources, pollution and hazards, and the implications of inter- and intra-generational distribution for the wellbeing of current and future people. Procedural justice is concerned with governance, often with an emphasis on participation and decision-making. Procedure is sometimes treated as a separate dimension of justice (e.g. Schlosberg 2004) and other times subsumed under distribution (e.g. Vincent 1998). In the latter case, procedure is seen to be an antecedent of distribution, i.e. good procedures facilitate just distribution, but are not just or unjust in their own right. I prefer to treat procedure as a separate dimension on the basis that participation in decision-making is not only a means to good decisions, but potentially also an end in itself, for example because it is a form of freedom (Outhwaite 2009; Dryzek 2000).

Justice as recognition is rather more difficult to define. Its place in justice thinking became prominent during the 1980s as a result of the study of social movements and the terms upon which they construct justice claims. In this way, the shift to theories of justice as recognition arose from the moral grammar of contemporary social movements that centred on respect for difference and the struggle to avoid domination by others (Bohman 2007). Recognition injustice or 'malrecognition' refers to lack of respect for cultural difference. In the US environmental justice movement, the main social fault line was ethnicity, with malrecognition expressed as a problem of environmental racism (Pulido 2000). Malrecognition is embedded in at least three inter-twined mechanisms. Firstly, discrimination arising from the rights allocated by formal and customary institutions: for example, formal tenure rules that

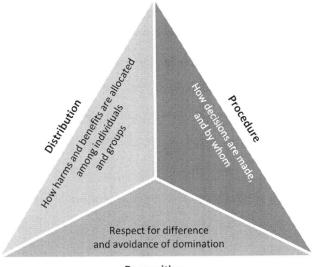

FIGURE 1.1 Dimensions of environmental justice.

privilege male land ownership can discriminate against women's eligibility to benefit from Payments for Ecosystem Services schemes (Corbera et al. 2007). Secondly, discrimination arising from informal cultural norms at large in society: for example, even where land tenure rules do not openly discriminate against women, more pervasive cultural norms can still lead to women receiving less compensation than men for land given up to conservation (Hall et al. 2014). Thirdly, discrimination arising from discourse and language that pushes some problem solutions to the foreground whilst rendering others invisible. For example, an ecosystem services discourse might encode a problem with a male viewpoint, privileging the formal economy over less visible contributions to household wellbeing.

Within literature on environmental justice, recognition has largely been expressed in relation to the claims of indigenous and local peoples to cultural respect and self-determination (e.g. Escobar 1998; Castree 2004; Schlosberg 2004; Vermeylen and Walker 2011). Here I take malrecognition to include all instances in which forms of formal and discursive power discriminate against difference and suppress the right to alternative ways of thinking and doing. This extends to framings of justice itself: malrecognition can occur where conservation organisations uncritically assume that they are the legitimate source of justice norms (Whiteman 2009). Such framing can determine whose knowledge counts and which problems and conflicts are rendered visible or invisible (Escobar 1998). The exercise of such discursive power (McAfee 1999; Schroeder 2008; Sullivan 2009) might be quite subtle, for example where local actors have little choice but to sign up to a revenue-sharing scheme even where this does not align with the real nature of the injustice that they feel. For example, around the Mgahinga Gorilla National Park in Uganda, Batwa communities have entered into tourism partnerships even where these reinforce the very exclusionary approach to conservation that prevents them from visiting important cultural sites. As I will discuss further in Chapter 3, different dimensions of justice are non-tradable – by which I mean that the involvement of the Batwa as a financial beneficiary of the tourism industry might help to resolve an injustice of material distribution. But however much this is resolved, it is hard to conceive of this somehow making up for failures of recognition (Martin et al. 2015).

Overview of this book

Chapter 2 sets up the need for just conservation in more detail, discussing the current crisis of biodiversity loss and explaining why a new approach is needed. In particular, it suggests that inequality and injustice undermine conservation effectiveness. Chapter 3 builds a stronger case that there is an inverse link between injustice and conservation effectiveness, elaborating the ways in which communities become disenchanted with and resist conservation. Chapter 4 develops a conceptual framework for thinking about and moving towards a more just conservation, drawing on thinking about human capabilities to pursue a broadly contextual approach to conservation justice but whilst also exploring possible justice benchmarks: outcomes that we can confidently describe as just or unjust. Chapters 5 to 8 draw on aspects of this conservation justice framework to consider some particular challenges and issues. Chapter 5 considers global distributional injustices and their relationship to biodiversity loss and Chapter 6 considers connections between biodiversity and cultural diversity in terms of the need to consider justice as cultural recognition. In chapters 7 and 8 I critique the main responses of the conservation sector to the need to be fair to local people. Chapter 7 considers the limitations of integrated conservation and development and explains in more detail why a 'just conservation' promises to be a better approach. Chapter 8 looks at the case for market-based conservation and again argues the need for justice. Chapter 9 considers how we can track progress towards more just conservation, firstly by looking at current efforts to develop a framework for assessing equity and justice in protected area governance and secondly by exploring the kind of research agendas needed to support this.

2

EXTINCTION

Can we be fair during a crisis?

Some problems are presented as being so urgent that they require states to operate outside of everyday norms of fairness – to act in the wider interest of a nation, or the planet, even if this rides roughshod over the rights of a few. There is a danger that conservation is thought of in this way: that its need for action is so exceptional that almost any activity to save biodiversity is morally justified. A key argument of this book is that it would be a mistake to allow the urgency of the problem to legitimise a weakening of resolve to uphold social justice. There is little doubt that the current rate of biodiversity loss represents a crisis for humanity. However, it is flawed thinking to conclude that effective responses to this crisis will necessarily run into conflict with norms of social justice.

This chapter considers current concern for biodiversity as a 'crisis' and reflects on how this might justify exceptional measures. In particular, I pose the question of whether it is realistic to – whether we *can* – achieve conservation success whilst at the same time striving for better standards of social justice. For the current chapter, I will confine myself to the concern that conservation should, at a minimum, do no harm to economically poor and vulnerable people. This is only one element of a broader framing of conservation justice that I will develop in the next chapter. However, it is a particularly important element because it is a commitment that has been widely adopted within conservation. For example, it was agreed at the 2003 World Parks Congress that 'Protected areas should strive to contribute to poverty reduction at the local level, and at the very minimum must not contribute to or exacerbate poverty'. It is this aspect of conservation justice that comes under the greatest scrutiny and it is a very helpful starting point for exploring questions about whether conservation and social justice are compatible objectives.

The theoretical synergies between biodiversity conservation and poverty alleviation seem clear enough because the livelihoods of the rural poor are often the most dependent on biodiversity for their sustainability. The poor thus stand to gain the most from biodiversity conservation. Yet despite such apparent convergence between the interests of the rural poor and the interests of a global conservation community, attempts to turn this potential into a reality have often been disappointing. Conservation with poverty alleviation has been pursued through integrated conservation and development projects and community-based conservation, and more recently through market-based approaches such as tourism revenue sharing, fair and ethical trade, and payments for ecosystem services. The optimism that comes with each new approach soon loses its shine as the complexities of field implementation begin to bite and the evidence of disappointing results begins to dampen expectations. On the one hand there is a substantial literature that argues that ICDPs have not been effective (e.g. Wells et al. 1999; Brandon and Wells 1992; Ferraro 2001) and on the other, a literature that highlights the persistence of 'exceptional measures' such as displacement of local people (Lélé et al. 2010) and the militarisation of wildlife protection (Duffy 2014).

Over the years I have visited quite a number of communities living in or adjacent to protected areas in tropical Africa and Asia. During those visits I have frequently spoken to people who have formed a negative opinion of conservation, normally arising from the harm which they feel has been imposed on their family and neighbours, and often involving some implicit or explicit claims regarding a lack of fairness. Along the coast of the Indian state of Odisha, for example, artisanal fisherfolk operating around the Gahirmatha Marine Sanctuary talk of how they are persecuted over turtle conservation despite the fact that it is the larger vessels that cause the real problem. Those living next to the adjacent Bhitarkanika National Park complain that the mangroves that help to protect the wider delta area from cyclone surges also harbour the saltwater crocodiles that take local people from their paddy fields. Around the Nam Et-Phou Louey National Protected Area in northern Laos, villagers have little affinity with tiger conservation (the decline in tiger numbers has made their lives better not worse) and whilst they proclaim respect for the rules, they are concerned that these are applied too strictly and sometimes unfairly. Around the Echuya Forest reserve in Uganda, local people complain that they pay the costs of protecting the reserve. The benefits literally flow downhill to the urban centre of Kisoro in the form of piped water, whilst the locals face health-threatening water shortages. In the southern portion of the Nyungwe National Park, in a narrow strip of land sandwiched between the park and the Burundian border, villagers recall the land taken from them in the run-up to park designation in 2005, and still complain that they received no compensation. In Kilwa district in Tanzania, some villages have benefited from considerable efforts to make conservation yield benefits for them, first through Participatory Forest Management, then through Forest Stewardship Council timber certification, then through a pilot REDD+ project (see Chapter 7). But even in these villages, the majority say that they would not want to see any more of their village forests managed for conservation.

There is nothing new about a state of affairs in which local poor people pay the costs of conservation whilst an economic and political elite are the most obvious beneficiaries. In India, for example, gazettement of elephant forests and hunting preserves began more than two millennia ago, and with it a form of state territorialisation that curtailed resource access for resident tribal peoples (Gadgil and Guha 1992). Many of India's present day National Parks evolved from the private hunting reserves of the Maharajas and biodiversity conservation was in many ways born from inequality and exclusion, serving first and foremost the recreational demands of the privileged. A similar story later unfolded in East Africa where the European colonial 'scramble for Africa' was followed in the early twentieth century by a surge in popularity of hunting safaris for the aristocracy and the privileged. As in South Asia, such unequal beginnings served as the foundations for the modern conservation movement. Similar stories could be told from many times and places, including my own country, the UK, where in 1079 William the Conqueror is reported to have unsympathetically demolished as many as 36 parishes to create the *Nova Forestra* for the royal hunt, eventually becoming the New Forest National Park in 2005.

Does it have to be like this? Dan Brockington (2004) observes that many of the protected areas formed with little or no attention to social justice concerns have fared rather well in their biological objectives, sometimes over long periods of time. He concludes that it would be naïve to claim that conservation has to be just in order to be sustainable. This seems like a sound history lesson – the nature of power is such that winners are not obliged to care about losers. But history cannot always repeat itself and the circumstances in which parks are formed in the twenty-first century are not what they were in the nineteenth century. One might therefore argue that it has become less acceptable and less effective to pursue conservation in ways that are unjust to local people. That is an important point, but even now, and even under the new breed of conservation interventions, it is still not unusual to see claims of injustice going hand in hand with claims of effectiveness. In a recent review of Payments for Ecosystem Services (PES) schemes that pay for tropical forest conservation, we found 24 schemes that researchers described as inequitable in respect to at least one dimension of equity. Of these, 11 were found to be effective, 10 contained no evidence of outcomes and only 3 were found to be ineffective (Calvet-Mir et al. 2015).

So, again, can we have an effective conservation with justice? Will too much attention to social outcomes distract conservation from its primary directive to save species and genetic diversity? And if we agree that this directive is both vital and urgent, can we allow this to happen? If social justice significantly detracts from conservation effectiveness, then there is a case for not mainstreaming justice as a conservation objective. Recently, for example, I have spoken with conservation biologists who lament the recent shift towards people-friendly conservation within big conservation NGOs such as Conservation International. It is seen as a weakening of resolve that will make it harder to respond to the urgent imperative to conserve biodiversity. I will argue to the contrary, that we should and we can do better – that we can have conservation with justice without detriment, and often with benefit for conservation performance. Above all, I will argue that there has been a quiet but profoundly important shift in our knowledge: from an understanding of how inequity and injustice has played such an important role in the history of conservation to an understanding of how equity and justice can and should be a key feature of its future.

This shift in perspective is in part driven by the changing contexts in which conservation is conducted. For example, the history of parks might not be that reliable a guide to the conduct of conservation interventions that go beyond park boundaries: conserving crop genetic diversity in agricultural landscapes may be less easy to sustain through brutish power alone. Such changing geographies and ecologies of the conservation challenge are driven by emerging scientific under-standing of: what measures of biodiversity are important; what biodiversity exists where; how this is threatened; and how significant this is for ecosystem functioning and human welfare. For example, we are becoming more aware of the benefits of genetic diversity for crop yields and stability. But the shift in perspective is also partly resulting from our learning about the possibilities for different ways of doing things – for example the positive results that can arise from more procedurally inclusive ways of doing conservation (Pascual et al. 2014) and an understanding that biodiversity is not always best served by the separation of humans from nature (Lélé et al. 2010). In other words we are not only learning about the new contexts that conservation needs to operate in, but also about the different ways in which we can think about conservation – beyond exclusion.

It is also worth stressing that, despite the concerns of some conservation biologists (see above), there is to some extent an open door to be pushed at. In particular, there is evidence of a growing receptiveness towards conservation which is designed to observe the rights of poor and marginalised people; this represents a shift from utilitarian to rights-based ethics. Utilitarianism is in many ways an enlightened and radical school of thinking, asserting the equal value of all people's welfare regardless of arbitrary individual characteristics such as country of birth, ethnicity, gender, sexuality, occupation or wealth. But utilitarianism also holds that ends can justify means and that actions that bring welfare gains to the many can be considered just even when they bring misery to the few. As a basis for conservation with justice, this is clearly superior to an era in which conservation could harm the many for the enjoyment of a bored aristocracy. And it clearly remains influential to conservationists who think the urgency of the crisis of conservation should keep our focus on the ends more than the means. But it is out of step with the kind of standards being adopted (on paper at least) by a range of conservation stakeholders, including local communities, practitioner organisations, donors and government agencies. For example, the broad consensus that emerged around 'do no harm' (e.g. Scherl and Emerton 2008) is generally felt to apply at the individual level and thus specifically precludes the utilitarian view that individuals might be harmed if this is necessary in pursuit of the greater good. Such a shift from utilitarian to rights-based ethics (see Chapter 1) is exemplified by a move made by eight of the largest non-government conservation organisations to establish the Conservation Initiative on Human Rights (Box 2.1), a commitment to uphold and support the rights of individuals (for example prescribed in the 1948 Universal Declaration of

Human Rights), as well as the rights of communities (for example prescribed in the 1986 Declaration on the Right to Development and in the 2007 Declaration on the Rights of Indigenous Peoples). What we are seeing then is a shift in expressed morality within the conservation industry, away from a utilitarian fix on the biological mission, and towards a rights-based focus on individual welfare.

BOX 2.1 CONSERVATION INITIATIVE ON HUMAN RIGHTS (CIHR)

CIHR is a consortium of international conservation NGOs that came together in 2009 to agree a set of principles and working practices to promote rights-based approaches to biodiversity conservation. The key partners are: International Union for the Conservation of Nature, Birdlife International, Conservation International, Fauna and Flora International, The Nature Conservancy, Wetlands International, Wildlife Conservation Society and WWF.

Founding organisations signed up to the following principles:

1. Respect Human Rights

Respect internationally proclaimed human rights; and make sure that we do not contribute to infringement of human rights while pursuing our mission.

2. Promote Human Rights within Conservation Programmes

Support and promote the protection and realisation of human rights within the scope of our conservation programmes.

3. Protect the Vulnerable

Make special effort to avoid harm to those who are vulnerable to infringements of their rights and to support protection and fulfilment of their rights within the scope of our conservation programmes.

4. Encourage Good Governance

Support the improvement of governance systems that can secure the rights of indigenous peoples and local people in the context of our work on conservation and sustainable natural resource use, including elements such as legal, policy and institutional frameworks, and procedures for equitable participation and accountability.

(*Source*: IUCN, CIHR Factsheet)

And yet the greater good in question – the common heritage of biodiversity for all humanity and for all time – is truly profound. And the resources to secure this vital resource are of course limited. For these reasons, the door to rights-based conservation is hardly wide open and there remains a healthy debate about whether justice and equity are appropriate goals for conservation interventions (Kinzig et al. 2011; Pascual et al. 2014; Martin et al. 2014b). The debate is not about whether social justice is a worthy goal, but whether it is sensible or cost-effective to pursue it in tandem with conservation interventions. In the 1950s, the Dutch Nobel Laureate economist Jan Tinbergen proposed that governments needed a separate policy instrument for each independent policy goal (the Tinbergen rule) – where there are fewer policy instruments than there are goals, one or more goals will not be met (Minang and Noordwijk 2013). In an analogous way, it has been argued that conservation instruments should optimise their primary conservation objective by leaving other objectives such as poverty alleviation or equity for separate instruments to tackle (Ferraro 2001; Kinzig et al. 2011). This is an argument for efficiency – in this case that externalising considerations of equity is the right thing to do because the resulting efficiency gains will maximise overall human welfare gains. We should still pursue social justice, but this is best done separately, through dedicated social welfare instruments, not through conservation.

The remainder of this chapter is devoted to rejecting calls to address conservation and social justice objectives through separate policy instruments. First, I look at the scale of the biodiversity crisis and its significance to humans. In doing so, I am essentially presenting the case for crisis and urgency and supporting the need to be effective. Following this elaboration of why 'biodiversity matters', I proceed to an initial case for why 'justice matters', with a particular emphasis on issues of poverty. In doing so I argue that there is strong interdependence between conservation and social justice outcomes and that calls to deal with them separately may not be realistic. In other words I argue that even when we recognise the depth and significance of the crisis humanity is facing, there is still not a reasonable case for a state of exception, for abandoning the kind of rules of fairness that most of us cherish in more everyday circumstances.

Biodiversity matters

This section makes the point that biodiversity is diminishing at historically unprecedented rates, that human welfare is ultimately connected to the decline of life on earth, and that this connection is often most apparent for the rural poor in the global South. Just as the book as a whole makes the case that we cannot do conservation without justice, so this section makes the important point that we cannot do justice without conservation. The continued failure by global leaders to adequately address the conservation challenge is an injustice to all.

The term 'biodiversity' is a truncation of 'biological diversity'. It was coined in the mid 1980s and provides a unifying concept for understanding the phenomenon of extinction (Wilson 1988). The Convention on Biological Diversity

(CBD) began life at the 1992 United Nations Conference on Environment and Development in Rio de Janeiro (the Earth Summit) and defined biodiversity as:

> the variability among living organisms from all sources including, inter alia, terrestrial, marine and other aquatic ecosystems and the ecological complexes of which they are part; this includes diversity within species, between species and of ecosystems.

BOX 2.2   DIMENSIONS OF BIODIVERSITY

Species diversity: the number and abundance of *species* is the unit most often used for current biodiversity datasets such as the IUCN Red List. Higher taxonomic orders of *genera* and *families* are more often used when dealing with the fossil record.

Genetic diversity: the variability within a population or species, based on the variety of genetic characteristics or traits. Genetic diversity is essential for evolution and for adaptation to environmental change.

Functional diversity: the variety and abundance of functional traits – the range of roles that organisms perform within an ecosystem. This can be as important a predictor of ecosystem functioning as species diversity.

Phylogenetic diversity: a measure of the evolutionary distance between species and other taxa. E.g. diversity between two species is greater where more time has elapsed since evolutionary divergence.

Spatial and temporal diversity: the rates of turnover of species across time or space.

Landscape diversity: the number, relative abundance and distribution of habitats within a landscape.

(*Sources*: Adapted from Naeem et al. 2012, with additional material from Cadotte et al. 2008 and Tilman et al. 1997.)

As Box 2.2 suggests, the unifying power of 'biodiversity' is by no means straightforward. Nevertheless, there is now strong scientific consensus that biodiversity is declining, and that this represents a serious crisis for humanity, requiring urgent action. The first 3 billion years of life on earth was characterised by microscopic organisms alone, with very little diversity or evolutionary dynamic. By contrast the last 540 million years (the Phanerozoic) has been characterised by a flourishing of life on earth, with larger organisms, complex food webs, ecological succession, the emergence of distinct biogeographical regions, greatly increased productivity in ecosystems, and much more dynamic evolution (Butterfield 2007). At the same time, this period has witnessed occasional crashes in species diversity as a result of increased rates of extinctions and/or declined rates of origination of new species (Alroy 2008; Barnosky et al. 2011). There have been five mass extinction events during this time, defined as a decline of at least 75% of estimated species numbers over a geologically short time period of generally less than 2 million years (Barnosky et al. 2011). The causes of these events are not known definitively but rapid climate change seems to be the most common proximate cause, brought about by different geophysical events such as volcanoes and meteor strikes (Wake and Vredenburg 2008).

The current decline in biodiversity is described by some as the earth's sixth mass extinction, this time confidently attributable to anthropogenic causes such as pollution, habitat destruction, extractive industries, infrastructure development and of course climate change. It is not easy to assess current extinction rates, not least because many of the species currently being lost are unknown to us in the first place. What seems clear, however, is that current extinction rates are between 100 and 1000 times more than background rates (Rockstrom et al. 2009). Such rates are higher than those that caused the 'Big Five' extinction events and if causes such as global warming go unchecked, similar levels of depletion could occur within hundreds rather than millions of years (Barnosky et al. 2011; Wake and Vredenburg 2008). For example, current extinction rates for amphibians are estimated to be 211 times higher than background rates, but could be an additional two orders of magnitude higher again if current 'Red List' threatened species were to become extinct (McCallum 2007). Recent estimates of mammal extinctions specify the loss of 80 out of 5570 known species in the last 500 years. This might not sound highly alarming but set against background rates of less than two extinctions per million years, we start to see just how rapid this is, and how dramatic rates will become if even a fraction of Red List mammals become extinct (Barnosky et al. 2011). The overall rate of species loss continues to accelerate and, worryingly, there is no significant deceleration in any of the pressures that are causing this loss (Butchart et al. 2010; CBD 2014).

The current era of mammalian extinction is marked by the loss of large animals and especially of apex consumers across terrestrial, marine and freshwater systems (Estes et al. 2011). As described by Estes et al. (2011), the removal of apex consumers is now understood to have significant consequences for ecosystem functioning, based on three theoretical insights into ecosystem behaviour. First, the idea of 'trophic cascades' describes the way in which changes at the top of the food web reverberate down through the chain. Second, connectivity within ecosystems means that the changes to the status of one species can lead to impacts for many other species. Third, ecosystem dynamics are non-linear and tipping points occur wherein perturbations do not lead to gradual change but to a shift to a new stable state, such as a shift from closed forest to savannah or grassland. Estes et al. (2011)

find that the impacts of trophic cascades occur widely, with negative consequences for species diversity and ecosystem services, and that such changes may only be observable many years after the apex species are removed.

Turning again to Aldo Leopold's classic essay 'Thinking like a mountain', he recalls the learning process that accompanied his transition from the man whose mission was to rid the US of apex predators to the man who understood their vital place in a healthy ecosystem. If we observe nature at appropriately large spatial scales, and across sufficient lengths of time – if we think like a mountain – then we can understand the significance of such apex species:

> I have lived to see state after state extirpate its wolves. I have watched the face of many a newly wolfless mountain, and seen the south-facing slopes wrinkle with a maze of new deer trails. I have seen every edible bush and seedling browsed, first to anaemic desuetude, and then to death.
>
> *(Leopold, 2013 [1949], p. 116)*

Indeed, there is an ecological narrative that wolves and other predators manage the ecosystem from the top down, keeping the population of species such as deer to levels appropriate to ecosystem health. In Yellowstone, for example, the re-introduction of wolves in 1995 is widely reported as having led to the control of ungulate populations, notably elk, the subsequent recovery of willow and aspen woodlands, and the resulting improvements to river catchment and protection, river bank trees providing more insects for fish and amphibians, greater capacity for beaver populations, and so on (Marris 2014). Whilst Marris (2014) shows how this narrative has at times been simplified and exaggerated, for example the impact of wolves on elk is disputed, the general importance of apex predators is widely accepted. Recent work has even found that the loss of apex grazers can contribute to climate change, for example where loss of sea otters results in heavier grazing of kelp forests (Wilmers et al. 2012).

We might expect to see such trophic cascading in areas such as the Congo Basin where rates of deforestation are still classified as low, but where hunting and other forms of human disturbance are rapidly taking out apex consumers. The population of Central Africa's forest elephants declined by 62% between 2002 and 2011, and is becoming concentrated in a fraction of the elephants' former range (Maisels et al. 2013). About half of the remaining 100,000 population live in Gabon, but even here they are threatened, with as many as 11,000 individuals killed in the Minkebe National Park alone between 2004 and 2012, driven by the demand for ivory in China (Maisels et al. 2013). Forest elephants consume a lot of fruit, and in doing so play an important role in dispersing tree seeds. Beaune et al. (2013) study 18 fruiting tree species that are dispersed by megafauna and found that none are able to sustain their populations in the absence of elephants; Beaune finds very similar results for tree species that are dependent on seed dispersal by apes (Beaune 2015). Seeds that remain undispersed at the base of a parent tree suffer higher mortality rates from being destroyed by consumers such as bush pigs, and in some cases are less able to germinate having not passed through the elephant's digestive tract. The extirpation of elephants from such forests is therefore expected to have a cascading effect – reducing the regeneration of elephant-dependent fruiting trees, and subsequently impacting on their many fruit consumers, including primates.

There are now many important forest areas that are in danger of undergoing significant phase shifts as a result of losing apex species. For example, the Nyungwe National Park is a highly biodiverse montane rainforest in Rwanda, sitting on the crest of the Congo-Nile watersheds. In 1974, the last buffalo was killed and in 1999 the last elephant. Leopards are still officially reported as being present but those who know the forest well are sceptical of this, especially as camera traps have failed to spot any. The impacts of such losses remain unknown but we can be increasingly confident that there will be significant trophic cascading, for example via the impact on frugivores such as primate and bird species. Furthermore, such effects are likely to interact with those of climate change in ways that amplify future threats to biodiversity.

We might still ask whether it really matters if there is cascading species loss in places such as the Nyungwe forest, or even a shift to a functionally different ecosystem state. Such a question might be answered in an ecocentric way, through reference to an ethical duty towards non-human species, perhaps emphasising the need to protect the wellbeing of all sentient creatures. Or it may be answered anthropocentrically, as I do here, through reference to the benefits that current and future humans derive from nature. Amidst rising concerns about environmental issues, the discipline of environmental economics emerged in the 1960s, asking questions about the value of ecosystems to humans and, correspondingly, the hidden costs of environmental degradation (Pearce 2002). Walter Westman (1977) was amongst the first to describe ecosystem functions in terms of the free 'services' that they provide for humans, and posed the question of what these social benefits from nature were worth. Twenty years later, Robert Costanza and colleagues took their best shot at answering this: using 1995 data they suggested an average of $33 trillion per year globally (Costanza et al. 1997). In a follow-up study using 2011 data, they estimated a figure of $125 trillion per annum and that ecosystems contribute more to human wellbeing than does global gross domestic product (GDP). They also found that land use change was resulting in a loss of between $4.3 and $20.2 trillion each year (Costanza et al. 2014).

In the early 1990s biological scientists began in earnest the task of understanding the role biodiversity plays in the productivity and stability of ecosystem functions and associated 'services' for humans. This task became more focused on how such ecosystem functions support human wellbeing following the Millennium Ecosystem Assessment framework that popularised the idea that biodiversity underpinned a set of supporting, provisioning, regulating and cultural ecosystem services that are needed for human wellbeing (Figure 2.1).

In the decade since this publication an intense research effort has explored and to a large extent validated the basic logic of this framework. This research has confirmed that biodiversity affects the functioning of ecosystems which in turn

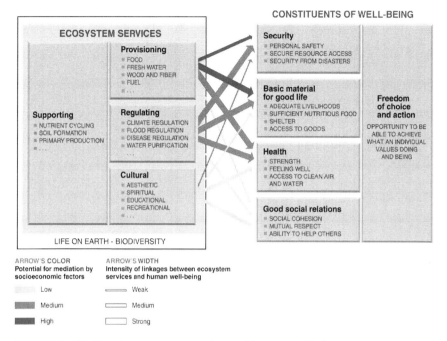

CONSTITUENTS OF WELL-BEING

ECOSYSTEM SERVICES

Provisioning
- FOOD
- FRESH WATER
- WOOD AND FIBER
- FUEL
- ...

Supporting
- NUTRIENT CYCLING
- SOIL FORMATION
- PRIMARY PRODUCTION
- ...

Regulating
- CLIMATE REGULATION
- FLOOD REGULATION
- DISEASE REGULATION
- WATER PURIFICATION
...

Cultural
- AESTHETIC
- SPIRITUAL
- EDUCATIONAL
- RECREATIONAL
- ...

LIFE ON EARTH - BIODIVERSITY

Security
- PERSONAL SAFETY
- SECURE RESOURCE ACCESS
- SECURITY FROM DISASTERS

Basic material for good life
- ADEQUATE LIVELIHOODS
- SUFFICIENT NUTRITIOUS FOOD
- SHELTER
- ACCESS TO GOODS

Health
- STRENGTH
- FEELING WELL
- ACCESS TO CLEAN AIR AND WATER

Good social relations
- SOCIAL COHESION
- MUTUAL RESPECT
- ABILITY TO HELP OTHERS

Freedom of choice and action
OPPORTUNITY TO BE ABLE TO ACHIEVE WHAT AN INDIVIDUAL VALUES DOING AND BEING

ARROW'S COLOR
Potential for mediation by socioeconomic factors
- Low
- Medium
- High

ARROW'S WIDTH
Intensity of linkages between ecosystem services and human well-being
- Weak
- Medium
- Strong

FIGURE 2.1 Biodiversity, ecosystem services and human wellbeing.

Source: Millennium Ecosystem Assessment (2005).

determines the benefits available to humans from ecosystem services (Naeem et al. 2012). There is now scientific consensus that higher biodiversity leads to enhanced ecosystem functioning (Cardinale et al. 2012; Naeem et al. 2012; Thompson et al. 2012). Firstly, diversity results in *complementarity*, wherein resources that constrain ecosystem productivity, such as nutrients and water, are used more efficiently because different species use different resources in different ways, or at different times, i.e. they have different ecological niches. By contrast, where there is little diversity, such as in an agricultural monoculture, all plants compete for the same constraining resources at the same time. Secondly, diversity supports *facilitation,* wherein one species helps to provide the conditions necessary for another species, such as nitrogen fixation or shade. Thirdly, diversity enhances productivity through the *sampling effect*, wherein it becomes more probable that a highly productive species will be present (Thompson et al. 2012).

In addition to increases in the productivity of ecosystems, biodiversity can also improve ecosystem stability. Resistance to environmental change can be enhanced by the different and complementary responses of different species to environmental change, known as an 'averaging' or 'portfolio' effect (Naeem et al. 2012). Such a 'portfolio effect' is analogous to a financial portfolio in which stability is enhanced by holding diverse investments that respond differently to market signals. Furthermore, biodiversity at genetic, species and landscape levels enhances resilience, the capacity of a system to regain its initial functions following major disturbance (Thompson et al. 2012).

There is now considerable evidence that biodiversity enhances some provisioning ecosystem services; examples include: crop genetic diversity increasing yields; fish genetic diversity increasing stability of fishery yields; tree species diversity increasing productivity in forest plantations; and species diversity enhancing productivity and stability in grasslands (Cardinale et al. 2012; Naeem et al. 2012). There is also evidence for the positive effect of biodiversity on some regulating ecosystem services, including: plant diversity reducing invasion of exotic species and prevalence of plant pathogens; plant species diversity enhancing above-ground carbon sequestration and soil nutrient availability (Cardinale et al. 2012). On the other hand, we should be careful to note that the evidence for the benefits of biodiversity is not so strong for all ecosystem services, and that response rates to changes in biodiversity vary greatly with context (Mace et al. 2014). Some monocultures can sustain high productivity of products that benefit humans whilst high biodiversity can enhance the productivity of undesired outcomes, for example where diversity of pathogens may be a threat to human health (Cardinale et al. 2012).

The challenge of conserving biodiversity is connected to the challenge of preventing dangerous climate change. On the one hand, loss of biodiversity is often found to reduce biomass production and can therefore reduce the potential to mitigate climate change through carbon storage in terrestrial and marine environments. On the other hand, climate change is itself a serious threat to biodiversity, reducing the scope for preventing species loss through protected areas and other means. There is wide agreement that these combined threats to ecosystem health will result in widespread social and economic impacts if not addressed. Such impacts will be felt far and wide, via the range of ecosystem services that bring benefits at local to global scales. However, it is also widely agreed that changes in ecosystem services will not be evenly distributed, partly because some people and places are more exposed to rapid change, and partly because some are more vulnerable to this exposure than others. As a generalisation, those living in the tropics are likely to suffer the greater impacts in the next two decades. Global increases in annual mean temperatures are likely to be in the range 0.3°C to 0.7°C for the period 2016–2035 relative to 1986–2005, but with larger temperature rises expected in the tropics and subtropics during this period (IPCC 2014), and greater resulting threat to biodiversity (Sachs et al. 2009). This greater exposure to environmental change in the tropics is matched with greater vulnerability to its effects, resulting from higher rates of poverty.

Justice matters

The preceding section showed that biodiversity is declining at historically high rates and that we now have evidence that this is a real and present danger to human welfare. With the global population set to reach 9 billion by 2050 and global surface temperature warming now considered likely to exceed 2°C by 2100 (IPCC 2014), this nexus of problems, of which biodiversity is part, is widely regarded as urgent. In this section I will develop a bit more the idea that, despite the urgency of the problem, and the high stakes, the biodiversity challenge cannot be separated from objectives to uphold and enhance social justice.

At the same time as the term biodiversity was becoming popularised in the 1980s, so too was the term sustainable development. The Brundtland Report (WCED 1987) played a big role in introducing this concept into the political domain and it is worth recalling that it defined sustainable development in relation to equity:

> Even the narrow notion of physical sustainability implies a concern for social equity between generations, a concern that must be logically extended to equity within each generation.
>
> *(WCED 1987, p. 43)*

This idea that sustainable development was premised on both inter-generational and intra-generational equity led to social equity being considered as one of three pillars of sustainability (along with economy and environment) at the 1992 Earth Summit in Rio de Janeiro. Looking back, the view that equity within the current generation was a pre-requisite for sustainable development was quite a radical framing of the conservation challenge.

Two decades later, the 2012 United Nations Conference on Sustainable Development (Rio+20 conference) failed to deliver any meaningful agreement that would have stiffened global-level commitments towards actions for sustainable development. Agreement could not be reached on what constituted fair outcomes, what mechanism could deliver on this or how responsibilities should be allocated. The resulting declaration entitled *The Future we Want* (UNCED 2012) is a watered-down document tabled by the host nation, Brazil. It contains little beyond what had been previously agreed in earlier meetings and was essentially an attempt to ensure that at least something was signed when in fact there was strong disagreement about the future that was wanted and how to get there (Pattberg and Mert 2013; Bulkeley et al. 2013).

For biodiversity conservation in the global South, one of the key equity questions is about whether conservation initiatives benefit the poor and marginalised. As was proposed earlier in this chapter, in theory at least, it is a relatively simple matter to present conservation as pro-poor because the poorest are often the most vulnerable to the impacts of biodiversity loss, and conversely, stand to gain the most from conservation. For example, the poor are the most dependent on ecosystem services from forests, with estimates of 350 million living in forests, including 60 million indigenous people (Millennium Ecosystem Assessment 2005); a much larger number of rural poor are dependent on forests for significant contributions to their livelihoods (Strassburg et al. 2012). The poor are also the most disproportionately dependent on the productivity of agricultural systems, for example with 62% of the workforce in Sub-Saharan Africa occupied in agriculture and 46% in South Asia (Table 2.1).

But whilst the objectives of conservation and poverty alleviation converge in theory, bringing about such convergence at particular points in time and space has proved something of a holy grail, found occasionally in particular projects but elusive when it comes to scaling up into general practice. The fact remains that the bulk of the benefits from conservation accrue at the global scale and for future generations, whilst some of the principal costs fall locally and now. At the local level, such costs can include the need to live with increasing numbers of wild animals that take crops and livestock, the need to curtail subsistence hunting and gathering activities in protected areas, and sometimes the need for eviction to make way for protected areas. At a national level, there are opportunity costs associated with designating land for conservation rather than alternative land uses such as mining or agribusiness. Such financial trade-offs associated with conservation are part of the reason why negotiators at events such as Rio+20 cannot agree about how to get to a future of lower rates of biodiversity loss. For example, African nations tended to want a strong emphasis on 'green economy' approaches that would bring market-based rewards for environmental protection, whereas Latin American countries were morally opposed to such commodification of nature (Bigg 2012).

Conservation in developing countries has seen consistent claims that it leaves the poor relatively worse off and therefore fails in its commitment to 'do no harm'. If one considers this claim at a large scale, as a question of 'do parks make people poor?' the answer would appear to be 'no'. There is evidence that people living in and around parks are poor compared to national averages, but there is no evidence that they are worse off *because of* the parks (Brandon and Wells 2009; Ferraro and Hanauer 2011). Other factors associated with park locations, notably their remoteness, may be much stronger determinants of persistent poverty (Bird et al. 2002) and the presence of parks might actually help mitigate such locational disadvantages (Beckmann 2014; Brockington and Wilkie 2015). However, if one considers this

TABLE 2.1 Employment in agriculture, by region, as share of total employment

Region	1991 (%)	2013 (%)	Change (%)
World	44.5	31.3	−29.7
Developed Economies & EU	6.9	3.6	−47.8
Central & SE Europe (non-EU) & CIS	28.8	17.7	−38.5
East Asia	56.8	30.3	−46.7
South-East Asia & the Pacific	58.9	39.3	−33.3
South Asia	62.1	46.3	−25.4
Latin America & the Caribbean	24.7	14.8	−40.1
Middle East	24.5	14.3	−41.6
North Africa	34.9	28.0	−19.8
Sub-Saharan Africa	65.9	62.0	−5.9

Source: ILO 2014.

claim in terms of impacts on individuals instead of large-scale average effects, i.e. if the question posed is 'do parks make some people worse off?' then the answer is certainly 'yes' and this is reported in a multitude of cases, especially where there is displacement of homes and livelihoods (Brockington and Igoe 2006).

Another claim is that conservation produces injustices owing to its failure to attune to, respect and protect cultural diversity, an accusation that has been strongly made against some of the biggest international conservation NGOs (see Chapin 2004). This claim will be explored in detail in subsequent chapters but for now it will suffice to make two elementary points. Firstly, the scope for conservation to impact negatively on indigenous and local cultures is high because of the spatial association between biodiversity hotspots and cultural diversity (Gorenflo et al. 2012). WWF commissioned a map that superimposed the locations of indigenous peoples and ethnolinguistic groups onto a base map that shows ecoregions and areas of high biodiversity value, revealing a strong overlap between biological and cultural diversity (WWF 2000). Secondly, it is increasingly understood that respecting and promoting cultural diversity is important in itself but also intimately connected to the goal of conserving biological diversity (Pretty et al. 2009).

Linking justice and conservation

For the remainder of this chapter, I will provide some provisional support for the view that striving to make conservation more socially just is compatible with the need for conservation interventions to be effective. In doing so I will begin by making reference to work that focuses on 'equality' rather than equity or justice. In this book, equality is treated as a descriptive measure of the distribution of access to material assets and choices. It is not in itself a normative term because an unequal distribution is not necessarily a bad thing. Inequality of participation, for example where women are excluded from decision making in a participatory forestry project, will generally be considered a bad thing. However, unequal distribution of revenues from protected areas, for example where distribution of ecotourism receipts favours the poorest, might be considered fair in some circumstances. Whilst the primary focus of this book is on equity and justice rather than equality, these concepts are clearly connected. For John Rawls, for example, a substantial element of his theory of justice was the proposition that inequality is only compatible with justice where it favours the less well off (Rawls 1971).

Interestingly, there is evidence to suggest that inequality is bad for the environment. If we take a simple measure of economic wealth, such as GDP per capita, we do not see any clear association with threats to biodiversity. For example, there is no clear evidence to predict that beyond a certain threshold, increasing wealth would help to protect biodiversity (Mills and Waite 2009). In other words, threats to biodiversity are not known to conform to an Environmental Kuznets Curve. However, if we introduce a measure of the wealth inequality within a country, there is a correlation with threats to biodiversity. Inequality, as measured

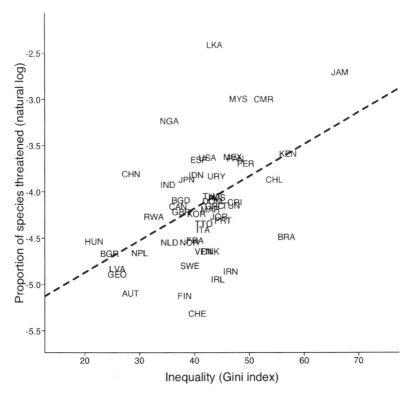

FIGURE 2.2 Correlation between Gini index and the proportion of species threatened.

Source: Holland et al. 2009.

Notes:
1. Countries indicated by three letter ISO codes.
2. A Gini index value of 0 represents perfect equality of distribution, whilst 100 represents perfect inequality.

by a country's Gini index (a measure of the distribution of income among its population), has a detrimental effect on the proportion of threatened species in a country (Holland et al. 2009; Mikkelson et al. 2007).

As noted, inequality does not necessarily result in inequity. However, inequality of environmental consumption is frequently associated with inequity, notably where the more affluent impose their over-extraction or pollution on the less affluent and less powerful. One aspect of this is 'burden-shifting', whereby the costs of consumption by the affluent are made to fall on those less affluent. At sub-national levels, the burden of toxic pollutants has been unfairly imposed on poorer communities and on those with large ethnic minority populations, as widely evidenced in the United States (e.g. Bullard 1990) but also for example in Russia (Vornovytskyy and Boyce 2010). At international level, this shifting of burden from rich to poor is suggested by evidence of the ecological footprints of nations which show that per capita consumption in wealthier countries greatly exceeds the world's biocapacity

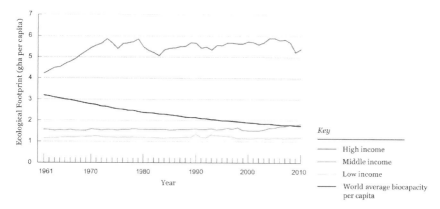

FIGURE 2.3   Ecological footprints in global hectares (gha) in high (1), middle (2) and low (3) income countries (World Bank income classification).

Source: Global Footprint Network and WWF, 2014.

Note: Line (4) shows world average biocapacity per capita.

(Figure 2.3). Consumption by high-income nations is reducing the available world biocapacity and the economic opportunity of those in low-income countries.

It is not only wealth inequalities that appear to be bad for the environment. Political and social equality also seem relevant, with dictatorships performing less well than democracies in matters of environmental protection (Neumeyer 2011) and levels of literacy, political rights and freedoms also having strong impacts on environmental quality (Torras and Boyce 1998; Barrett and Graddy 2000).

Conclusion

The biodiversity crisis is relevant to all, including those in the global South whose livelihoods are most directly vulnerable to changes in ecosystem functioning. The urgency of this crisis has at times been used to justify interventions that do not respect local rights, including hundreds of instances of displacement, sometimes from long-held ancestral territories. Such a conservation imperative can be used in good faith by those driven by utilitarian concerns for the greater good of humanity, or by an ethical compulsion to protect the rights of non-humans. But the power of this imperative is inevitably also used more strategically by those with alternative interests in excluding people from landscapes, for example because of the financial returns to be gained from recreational hunting or tourism, or because of strategic military interests in the area.

A justice analysis points to weaknesses in the view that the conservation crisis warrants exceptional measures that preclude prioritisation of social justice. On the one hand there is a simple, normative weakness in that support and funding for conservation is now strongly premised on its claims to be pro-poor. If biodiversity conservation is to maintain its place as one of the pre-eminent, mass-supported social movements of our time, then it will increasingly need to live up to the standards it sets for itself. On the other hand, the weaknesses I have stressed most in the latter part of this chapter are more instrumental ones: that inequality and injustice may actually undermine the effectiveness of conservation interventions. In the next chapter I make a more substantial case for this and try to identify the mechanisms whereby injustice prevents conservation success.

3
JUSTICE AS MOTIVE

Introduction

I have argued that there is an intrinsic, moral reason for striving to develop more socially just conservation practices. Quite simply, most of us would prefer to live in a world where justice is accorded high priority. I have also argued that there is an instrumental reason – that striving for a more just conservation will help to support more effective conservation. At the end of the last chapter I reviewed some evidence in support of this, suggesting that inequality is bad for the environment in general, and for biodiversity in particular. For example, countries with greater wealth inequality tend to have a greater proportion of threatened species. In this chapter I want to explore such connections in more detail and develop a stronger instrumental case for justice. A key limitation of the evidence linking inequality to environmental degradation is that it merely describes an association, without seeking to understand the underlying reasons. In this chapter I seek to remedy this – initially by exploring the reasons why inequality is bad for the environment, but then extending this analysis to the broader phenomenon of justice. The main argument is that perceptions of justice are powerful motives and that responses to conservation interventions are very much dependent on how fair and legitimate they are seen to be. Where conservation policies and practices are perceived to be unjust, there is more likely to be resistance, acts of resentment, difficulties fostering collective action and higher enforcement costs. Conversely, I finish the chapter with some examples of more positive evidence. When conservation governance attends to those things we know to be critical to perceptions of justice – where it strives to be procedurally inclusive, to distribute costs and benefits fairly and to recognise and respect different stakeholders – it is more likely to be effective.

Inequality revisited

In the previous chapter we saw evidence of an association between inequality and loss of biodiversity, at least at national level. I begin by considering two reasons for this association but conclude that neither are fully convincing. I then switch the focus from inequality to justice which provides a conceptually fuller and more helpful way forward. The first reason why inequality is thought to undermine environmental conservation is simply that large asymmetries in wealth and power provide the conditions that make it both profitable and feasible for the elite to ignore the needs of less powerful groups. Examples might include the exploitation of African fisheries by East Asian and European fishing fleets (Agnew et al. 2009), the ravaging of Indonesia's forests by a corrupt elite (Laurance 2004) or the afore-mentioned dumping of pollution in poor areas of the United States (Bullard 1990). More generally, the wealthy and powerful have historically benefited from lowering environmental quality because they benefit disproportionately from activities that draw down on stocks of resources and which produce pollution. At the same time, the wealthy are better able to insulate themselves from the environmental costs of such accumulation because of their ability to live in safer and less polluted places and to purchase insurance, air conditioning and so on.

Inequality produces an elite but also produces poverty. The second reason why inequality is bad for conservation is the idea that poverty itself is a cause of environmental degradation because poor people are forced to live hand to mouth and unable to manage resources sustainably. This idea was given international attention at the 1972 Stockholm (UN) Conference on the Human Environment and was subsequently popularised through the influential Brundtland Report:

> Those who are poor and hungry will often destroy their immediate environment in order to survive. They will cut down forests; their livestock will overgraze grasslands; they will overuse marginal lands; and in growing numbers they will crowd into congested cities. The cumulative effect of these changes is so far reaching as to make poverty itself a major global scourge.
>
> *(WCED 1987, p. 28)*

This 'poverty and environmental degradation' narrative subsequently featured in reports such as the World Development Report:

> Poor families who have to meet short term needs mine the natural capital by excessive cutting of trees for firewood and failure to replace soil nutrients.
>
> *(World Bank 1992)*

This idea that the poor are the greatest threat (a 'scourge') to biodiversity may be popular but it is clearly unsound. For example, Cavendish (2000) provides a detailed study of rural Zimbabwe that shows that the poorest 20% of households might be more dependent on natural resource use for their livelihoods, but it is the wealthier quintiles of the population who make the heaviest use of resources. To give an example from the Bwindi Impenetrable National Park in Uganda (introduced in Chapter 1), Baker et al. (2012) conducted a study of all incidents of violent conflicts between local people and park staff between 1986 and 2000. They found that these conflicts were not stimulated by the poorest people or from resentment about the loss of household subsistence resources. Rather, conflicts were mainly driven by business people – those who profited from commercial scale extraction of forest resources. At a global scale, it is equally true to say that consumption by the more affluent is the bigger driver of biodiversity loss (I explore this in the next chapter) and furthermore, that the poor often endure enormous immediate hardships in order not to harm their future livelihoods (Moseley 2001; Martínez Alier 2003). Nevertheless, the idea that poverty causes environmental degradation is one that is highly persistent: over the past fifteen years or so I have spoken with many protected area managers in South Asia and Sub-Saharan Africa, and have often heard it said that it is the poorest who are mainly responsible for illicit activities in the forest. This is typical of a powerful narrative: it is hard to break it down, even when there is strong evidence that contradicts it.

From inequality to injustice

The ways in which injustice is linked to environmental outcomes is fundamentally different to the ways in which equality is linked to environmental outcomes. Equality is concerned with a particular form of distribution, whether it be distribution of rights, wealth, decision-making authority, jobs, access to resources, allocation of pollution and so on. Equality and inequality are descriptions of distribution rather than claims about whether this is right or wrong. By contrast, whilst equality and inequality are universal, objective and described, justice and injustice are contextual, subjective and felt. Justice is therefore one step closer to behaviour. This is important because whilst justice is the broader concept, and whilst the experience of injustice can be shaped by complex contextual and subjective factors, I suggest that the mechanisms linking justice to conservation outcomes are clearer than those linking equality to conservation outcomes. If one of my daughters observes that I have a bigger slice of cake than she has, this might barely trouble her conscious thought because she knows I am bigger, eat more and am a bit partial to cake. But if it is a special cake made for her, and I have not even asked if I can have any, it might result in some neurons getting quite heated. In this case, it is not the unequal share per se that explains the behavioural outcome; it is the bundle of contexts in which this is perceived, interpreted and felt.

Here I preview the main mechanisms that make social justice and conservation outcomes interdependent and, in practice, inseparable. This is presented as a set of relationships that connect the principal dimensions of social justice (distribution, procedure and recognition) with the two sets of goals common to most conservation interventions: to achieve defined conservation and human wellbeing outcomes (Figure 3.1).

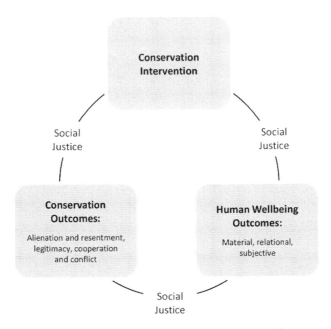

FIGURE 3.1 Connections between social justice, conservation and human wellbeing.

1. *Social justice mediates the impact of conservation interventions on human wellbeing*
   The design and execution of conservation policy and practice will determine changes in access to resources, including restrictions on the use of subsistence goods such as firewood and bushmeat. It can also involve changes to financial benefits, including schemes to compensate for wild animal damage, tourism revenue sharing schemes, payments for ecosystem services, and in-kind benefits such as investments in health centres and agricultural inputs. In addition to immediate changes to rights and resource access, conservation interventions also have longer-term impacts that result from planned or unplanned environmental change. Longer-term costs may include rising numbers of wild animals which can increase the threat to human lives, crops and livestock. The benefits can include enhanced ecosystem services such as improved micro-climate, landscape beauty, insect pollination or greater resistance to invasive species and crop pests.

   As will be explored further in the next chapter, impacts on human wellbeing are not simple material relationships. Changes in access to the material requirements for wellbeing are clearly fundamental. However, wellbeing outcomes are also determined by the social relations that determine what particular people are able to achieve with the resources that they have, and by subjective factors that determine how satisfied groups and individuals are with these resources and achievements. This is the three-dimensional view of human wellbeing as (i) material, (ii) relational and (iii) subjective (e.g. McGregor and Sumner 2010). Subjective feelings of wellbeing are influenced, among other things, by conceptions of social justice, for example whether the distribution of costs and benefits is perceived to be fair, or whether there has been respect for one's cultural identity.

2. *Social justice mediates conservation outcomes*

It is hypothesised that perceptions of justice determine how legitimate an intervention is considered to be and how well supported it is. When the design and governance of conservation does not resonate with local conceptions of justice, its legitimacy will be questioned and it is likely to encounter higher compliance costs and to risk unproductive conflicts (Pascual et al. 2014; Martin et al. 2014b). In short, it will be less effective or efficient at achieving its stated conservation objectives.

For the rest of the chapter I will focus on the left-hand side of Figure 3.1, on the way that social justice mediates conservation outcomes, although this is very much connected with the impacts of conservation on human wellbeing. I begin by focusing on largely negative cases that illustrate the way in which the perceived injustices of conservation undermine its effectiveness. I then consider some evidence of more positive outcomes, where greater attention to social justice issues is leading to improved conservation outcomes.

Alienation and resentment

The idea of 'alienation from nature' originates in Karl Marx's *Economic and Philosophical Manuscripts of 1844* (Marx 2005). Marx considers humans and nature to be inextricably connected because, quite simply 'man is part of nature' (p. 328). However, he proceeds to propose that this connection can be damaged within a political-economic system that enables an elite class to take control of natural resources and to use this control to bolster its domination over a subordinate class. Through such a process, nature does not only become separated from and external to this class, but also becomes the medium for their oppression: it becomes alien to them. Control over nature becomes a way in which powerful groups accumulate wealth and power and nature becomes associated with injustices. I am not fully convinced by Marx's metaphysics of nature and society – I find it hard to imagine the movement of nature from human interior to human exterior. However, I do find the concept of alienation from nature to be useful and, in particular, the idea that control over nature comes to be understood as a means of subordination. This concept foresees a fundamental problem for an enforcement-oriented conservation, namely that if one alienates local people from nature – if they come to perceive environmental management as a form of injustice – they are unlikely to be supportive. I will illustrate this through an historical example from the Western Ghats of southwest India, a range of hills in southwest India that is considered to be a 'biodiversity hotspot' (Myers et al. 2000), with high species diversity, high levels of endemics and, nowadays, the largest remaining single population of tigers.

As elsewhere in the tropics, forest and wildlife in India were predominantly managed as local assets prior to the nineteenth century, before the advent of colonial forest and game reserves. In the Western Ghats of Karnataka, local princes had formally owned the forests but community use and management remained the norm. This soon changed after the 1878 Forest Act that enabled the colonial rulers to appropriate forest as 'reserved' for state use. Within just a few decades from the late nineteenth to early twentieth century, this resulted in almost total loss of rural communities' rights to forest resources. In Uttara Kannada district (Karnataka State), there was 9191 km^2 of forest in 1882, of which 19% had been classified as 'reserved' forest, to be used exclusively by the state. By 1910, the proportion 'reserved' for the state had risen to 96% (Nadkarni et al. 1989).

Henry Baden-Powell, a High Court judge, forester and scholar in the British Raj, argued that extinguishing all local, customary rights to the forests of southwest India was the right thing to do. It was right because it supported the state's duty to manage resources in the interests of all its people, both current and future. In short, because it served the common good.

> The government of India [is] to watch carefully and satisfy itself that [a state official Robinson's] kindly and warm-hearted sympathy for the semi-savage denizens of the Kanara forests does not lead him into a too lavish dissipation of the capital of the State.
>
> *(Baden-Powell, 1876: cited in Gadgil and Guha 1992, p. 130)*

As in many parts of India, the appropriation of forests was a trigger for peasant resistance to colonial rule, including through *Satyagraha*, a Gandhian pursuit of justice through non-violent but firm insistence (*agraha*) on truth (*satya*). In Uttara Kannada district, the forest *satyagraha* involved large-scale cutting down of forests:

> It was started on the 4th of August [1930] . . . As the procession went on, people in hundreds came from the villages and joined in; so that when it reached the forest, there was a multitude which staggered the authorities who had gone to put down the Satyagraha. Sandal trees were cut down, the wood was loaded in carts, and everyone carried branches, the return procession giving the appearance of a moving forest. The wood was brought to Sirsi and auctioned off . . . Every village in the taluks of Sirsi and Siddapur followed this example. . . . The Government . . . began to arrest the Satyagrahis who had come from outside and a few important local leaders. The latter, awakened the women to action. . . . The jungle Satyagraha could not be put down by force, for the people of whole villages would move out in thousands and would vie with one another in getting arrested.
>
> *(Halappa 1964, cited in Nadkarni et al. 1989, p. 61)*

The 'insistence on truth' is an interesting way to consider a struggle for environmental justice. It illustrates the point made in earlier chapters, that real-world environmental justice struggles are often motivated by combinations of values and concerns. Distribution and access to material resources is of course central to many struggles, including those opposing the appropriation of their forests in the Western Ghats of Karnataka. But insistence on truth captures a more complex set of claims which link material concerns to ones of political and cultural oppression.

Following independence in 1947, there was little change in forest policy. The exclusion of local people continued to be justified on the basis of the national good and sustainability. The national good was in this case framed by a modernising paradigm in which rural resources such as forests should be managed and modernised by the state in order to serve the needs of a modern, industrial and urban sector (following a so-called 'dual economy' model of development).

> Use by village community should in no event be permitted at the cost of national interests. The accident of a village being situated close to a forest does not prejudice the right of the country as a whole . . . rights and interests of future generations [should not] be subordinated to the improvidence of the present generation
>
> *(Government of India 1952, Forest Policy, para. 7)*

Just as Baden-Powell portrayed villagers as lavish wasters of forests, incapable of sustainable use, so too does the government of India, referring to villagers as improvident. There is a failure to recognise the rights of local people or the worth of their local knowledge. The latter is the basis for arguing that local people are not fit to manage forests themselves and that the state needs to take control.

Modern scientific management of Karnataka's forests for the so-called 'national interest' often involved the clear-felling of native forests, for replacement with fast-growing exotic tree species such as eucalyptus, and for infrastructure development (Nadkarni et al. 1989). In the 1980s, in the same locations that villagers had cut trees in protest in the 1930s, a new form of resistance emerged. The Save the Western Ghats campaign was a local social movement to save the forests from logging and infrastructure development. Some of the leaders had been involved in the more famous Chipko movement and once again were inspired by Gandhian methods. The 100 day 'Save the Western Ghats March' ran from November 1987 to February 1988 and brought together more than 100 local movements and organisations (Hegde 1988).

I did fieldwork for my PhD in this area in 1995–6. At the time I didn't think much about why two struggles against state appropriation should take on such different forms of protest: the first involved the protestors cutting down trees, the second involving protestors preventing their being cut. Now it seems easier to understand that these are both instances of resistance to threats and injustices which share common features. For the villagers of the Western Ghats, forests are important assets which support local livelihood strategies and cultures. These locally important uses of nature can be – and have been – threatened both by the state's interventions to conserve forests and by its interventions to exploit them. The narrative of sustainable development has been prominent, such as references to villagers' 'lavish dissipation of capital' by Baden-Powell and the need for the state to protect the 'rights and interests of future generations' in the 1952 Forest Policy. Equally prominent has been the narrative of modernisation, with reference to the savagery of local peasants and the contrast between their 'improvidence' and the needs of the modern state and of future people.

Given the way the colonial state framed the forest conservation agenda as the antithesis of local control and practices, it is not surprising that resistance initially took the form of cutting trees. Elsewhere in India it took the form of incendiarism, such as the 1921 fire in the Kumanon foothills that burned 250,000 acres of forest (Guha 1989; Kuhlken 1999). In effect, the language of conservation and sustainable development had been co-opted by the more powerful stakeholders and employed as a means of dispossessing local people of access and authority over local forests. In this case, then, local villagers were not only alienated from physical nature but from the public ideas about its conservation.

I have dwelt at some length on this example because it makes a critical point about the relationship between local communities and conservation. Villagers in the Western Ghats have risked imprisonment and even death to destroy forests in opposition to state policy. They have acted equally bravely to prevent those same forests from being destroyed by the state. This is in some ways consistent behaviour, because in both cases it is about resisting threats to their livelihoods and to their ways of living with and knowing nature. This might be conceived as the 'environmentalism of the poor' (Martínez Alier 2014) and is in effect driven by the imperative to oppose environmental injustices. In saying that, I am suggesting that the pursuit of environmental justice is a motive for environmental behaviour. And in that, I am thinking about justice motives as multi-dimensional, as discussed in Chapter 1. Concerns about the distributional outcomes of policy, and in particular access to forest and wildlife as livelihood assets, are clearly important. But distributional concerns are inter-twined with matters of recognition, including the colonial and neocolonial derogation of local cultures and livelihoods as savage, improvident and, ultimately, as morally inferior.

There is some evidence to suggest that perceptions of injustice are a widespread cause of resistance to protected area conservation and in particular the motives for illicit hunting. A review of the motives for 'wildlife crime' in Uganda finds that 'perceived injustice' is one of the drivers that encourages local people to disobey the park rules and in effect to kill animals as a form of revenge (Harrison et al. 2015). In a study of illicit hunting in the Bamu National Park in Iran, hunters are very explicit about being motivated by resentment (Ashayeri and Newing 2012). Again the authors of the study refer to 'perceived injustices' as a motive for killing wildlife, with grievances dating back to the formation of the park. These grievances follow the pattern identified above: there are concerns about the distributional consequences of the park due to the restriction on access to grazing lands and other resources. But there are also concerns about recognition and part of their claim to injustice is articulated in terms of 'lack of respect' by park authorities. One hunter tells the researchers that if they are successful in their hunting there will be nothing left for leopards to prey on and that the extirpation of leopards will be a good thing as it will remove the rationale for the park and rid them of its authority (Ashayeri and Newing 2012).

Legitimacy and cooperation

Alienation and resentment is one way of conceptualising the connection between (perceived) injustice and the undermining of conservation effectiveness. An alternative but related way in which to present this connection is in terms of legitimacy and cooperation. The degree to which people view an authority as 'legitimate' is thought to be determined by three related factors (Van der Toorn et al. 2011): firstly, the fairness of the procedures used for exercising authority; secondly, how favourable the outcomes of their actions are viewed as being; and thirdly, how much control the authority is considered to have over these outcomes.

Pascual et al. (2014) employ the concept of legitimacy to explain the relationship between fair and inclusive procedures and conservation effectiveness. It proposes that the way in which conservation interventions are designed and governed determines whether local communities (and other stakeholders) consider them to be legitimate. Exclusionary approaches are likely to lead to unfavourable outcomes involving reduced access to resources, elite capture of any benefits, loss of local participation in decision-making and failure to respect local traditions and cultures (Figure 3.2). This combination of exclusionary procedures and unfavourable outcomes leads to feelings that the protected area authority is acting unfairly and its legitimacy is undermined. In turn this reduces the motive to participate in supporting park management and increases the motive for rule-breaking and resistance. The perceived lack of legitimacy has negative consequences for conservation effectiveness in the short and/or long term. Conversely, inclusive approaches to protected area management will involve appropriate access to resources, equitable distribution of costs and benefits, participatory decision-making and respect for local culture and knowledge. This is more likely to support a sense of fairness and legitimacy, leading to stronger support and more effective conservation. This explanatory framework is validated by quite an extensive set of studies, some involving large-sample quantitative studies and others based on more in-depth local case studies which seek to qualitatively understand these social and ecological dynamics (Pascual et al. 2014).

An example of loss of legitimacy leading to resistance can be seen in a study of the Kumbhalgarh Wildlife Sanctuary in Rajasthan (Robbins et al. 2009), where formal rules that forbid use of the sanctuary for grazing livestock were found to be almost universally ignored. This behaviour was certainly motivated by the economic costs which would result from the exclusion of grazing; but it was also because of the imposed rules and norms being in conflict with locally held norms about forest use and governance (Robbins et al. 2009). In this case, the local forest staff were complicit in the resistance to central government authority, conspiring to conceal the scale of forest use from their senior officers. Such quiet and often hidden resistance to conservation interventions is almost certainly widespread and

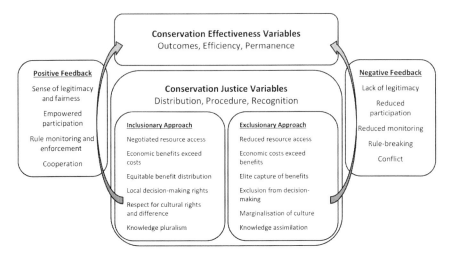

FIGURE 3.2   Emerging understanding about connections between treatment of local communities and conservation effectiveness.

Source: Adapted from Pascual et al. 2014.

the more overt conflicts and confrontations that grab our attention might merely represent the tip of the iceberg in terms of resentment and resistance.

Collective action

I have been focusing on the relationship between local communities and an external protected area authority. However, it is important to remember that protected areas involve a range of governance configurations. According to IUCN classification, governance of protected areas falls into four types: governance by government, shared governance, private governance and governance by indigenous peoples and local communities (Borrini-Feyerabend et al. 2013). In the cases of shared, indigenous and community governance there is typically a need for strong local governance institutions such as local forest or fisheries committees. Here the perception of justice or legitimacy is equally important as it is an important condition for collective action (Ostrom 1990). For example, a sense of fairness helps to foster trust and shared objectives that support successful community forestry institutions in Mexico (Kloosters 2000). Whilst perceptions of justice are important to local-level collective action this connection is also evident at higher levels of collective decision-making, with perceived inequities between countries greatly reducing the prospects for international environmental agreements (Tavoni et al. 2011).

Whilst I am making a general point that perceptions of unfairness are generally unfavourable to collective action, it is important to recognise that this does not always hold. For example, the economic benefits which flow from community forest management in Tanzania are often quite small (Khatun et al. 2015), and the effort exerted on management activities may in some cases exceed the resulting benefits (Meshack et al. 2006), bringing into question why these local collective action institutions continue to operate. One reason appears to be that the elite are able to capture a larger share of the benefits and therefore have an incentive to exercise their power over others to ensure sustained 'collective' action (Meshack et al. 2006; Blomley et al. 2008). In this case then, the injustice of elite capture might be the reason why collective action is sustained. Another example can be seen in David Mosse's (2003) study of collective action for maintaining irrigation systems in South India. Here the ability to sustain collective action to maintain local irrigation ponds is rooted in social structures that include discrimination based on different caste groups. Mosse observes a complex set of historical and ecological contexts that support this status quo in which collective action is sustained amidst discrimination. These examples remind us of the importance of local context and the dangers of over-generalising.

Evidence linking justice and effectiveness

As mentioned above, there is now a considerable body of evidence that suggests that attention to enhancing the justice of conservation has a positive effect on the likely outcomes of conservation interventions. Approximately half of tropical forest protected areas have performed quite well over the past 20–30 years whilst the other half have been losing both species and functional biodiversity (Laurance et al. 2012). According to this study, it is apex predators and large herbivores that have suffered most, primarily due to habitat destruction, hunting and resource extraction, both within and outside of protected area boundaries. As has been mentioned, good performance (in terms of biological objectives) can sometimes be achieved through strong enforcement (Brockington 2002, 2003). Perhaps unsurprisingly, protected area managers believe that effective parks require basic protective functions to be adequately resourced and managed, including boundary demarcations and the staff to enforce these (Bruner et al. 2001). But there is now plenty of evidence that effective demarcation and enforced exclusion by park rangers are not the only factors relevant to successful conservation and that old style 'fortress conservation' is less likely to be effective than more open and inclusive governance regimes. Here is a summary of some of this evidence:

- In a comparison of areas of Amazonia managed as exclusionary, uninhabited parks with those managed as community-based extractive reserves, the reserves perform better at reducing both deforestation and fires (Nepstad et al. 2006).
- In a global study of coral reefs, the places that stand out for better conservation performance are often places where there is strong local engagement. The authors propose that effective conservation will be supported by investment in participatory approaches and local resource rights (Cinner et al. 2016).
- In a comparative study of protected areas in different tropical countries, it is found that there is no systematic performance difference between forests that

are managed by the state, those managed by communities or those that are co-managed by both state and community. What appears to matter more than governance type is the perceived legitimacy and fairness of the governance. Where communities perceive governance to be fair they are more likely to contribute to the monitoring of rules. Such local cooperation with rule enforcement is critical to conservation effectiveness (Ostrom and Nagendra 2006).

- In studies of 46 and 100 forests respectively, researchers again find that governance type is not itself a key determinant of effectiveness and that the critical factor is active monitoring by local people. Furthermore, they find that such monitoring is less likely to occur where people are excluded and more likely to occur where local people are given rights to harvest forest products (Coleman 2009; Coleman and Steed 2009).
- In a study of 84 sites in East Africa and South Asia it was found that forms of participation that include local communities in forest governance are strongly associated with both improved biodiversity conservation outcomes and improved livelihood outcomes (Persha et al. 2011).
- In a comparison between 40 exclusionary protected areas and 33 community-managed forests, the latter perform better at preventing deforestation (Porter-Bolland et al. 2012).
- In studies to examine the potential for forests to be managed locally for both carbon storage and livelihoods, it is found that these twin objectives combine best when local people are given rule-making autonomy (Chhatre and Agrawal 2009; Hayes and Persha 2010).
- In a global assessment of 165 protected areas, based on a meta-analysis of previous studies, it was found that the inclusion of local people in park management, and the generation of benefits for local people, are both factors associated with better biodiversity conservation (Oldekop et al. 2015).

Conclusion

The idea that inequity and injustice can undermine sustainability has been around for decades, as evidenced by the focus on equity in the 1987 Brundtland Report and the 1992 Earth Summit. But these analyses were founded on a limited and flawed understanding that, for example, perpetuated a myth that poor people were unable to manage resources sustainably. This myth has been influential in leading major conservation organisations to embrace equity concerns, but only in a limited way. Equitable conservation has in practice been defined as conservation that is economically favourable to the poorest or, more often, that doesn't do any economic harm to the poor. There is nothing intrinsically wrong with such an agenda – protecting local livelihoods from harm is no bad thing. However, as will be explored more in Chapter 7, it is erroneous to assume that this in itself will be instrumental in achieving better conservation outcomes. A justice analysis adopts a broader set of concerns, incorporating distribution, procedure and recognition;

and correspondingly, a broader set of pathways by which conservation outcomes can be positively and detrimentally affected.

As the example from the Western Ghats illustrated, responses to environmental governance interventions are motivated by the perceived justices and injustices surrounding these interventions. Perceptions of injustice regularly lead to the break-down in local support for conservation, ranging from a simple loss of engagement to far more serious conservation conflicts involving deliberate acts of protest, hunting wildlife as acts of revenge and violence against park staff. All of the examples cited in this chapter (from India, Uganda and Iran) illustrate that these behaviours cannot be well explained by reference to poverty and livelihoods alone, or by economic inequality. Livelihoods and other economic outcomes are clearly important but so too are claims about unfair procedure and about lack of respect. A justice analysis is much better attuned to understanding these conflicts than a livelihoods analysis.

On a more positive note, recent research into protected areas effectiveness is starting to build evidence that more inclusive forms of governance (in terms of participation in decision-making, rights of access and tenure, and sharing of benefits) are associated with better conservation outcomes. These studies do not directly consider 'perceptions of justice' as a motivating factor for how communities engage with conservation, but their findings are nonetheless aligned with this instrumental view of just conservation.

4

THE CONDUCT OF ENVIRONMENTAL JUSTICE INQUIRY

Introduction: pragmatism, pluralism and capabilities

The Chagos Islands are a remote archipelago of coral reefs in the middle of the Indian Ocean. Between 1968 and 1973 the British government evicted the residents of these islands, in a deal that involved providing the US with a new military base in return for discounted Polaris missiles (for the UK's nuclear submarines). Initial tactics involved pretending that all Chagossians were non-permanent visitors to the islands, thus avoiding the kind of responsibility to uphold rights of permanent residents under United Nations' rules. Those visiting Mauritius were then prevented from returning to Chagos, and eventually remaining islanders were evacuated from the main island of Diego Garcia in 1971, and then from the archipelago as a whole in 1973, with a choice to be taken to the Seychelles or Mauritius (Morris 2013). Whilst it is unlikely that many Chagossians would now find it feasible to return to these Islands, they nonetheless demand the right to do so. But the UK and US governments have thus far sought to prevent this, most recently by supporting the creation of a marine protected area. In a consular communication dated 15th May 2009 (leaked by WikiLeaks), the UK's Foreign and Commonwealth Office's director for Overseas Territories, Colin Roberts, bragged to his US counterpart. 'Establishing a marine park,' he argues, will 'put paid to resettlement claims of the archipelago's former residents' because the UK 'environmental lobby is far more powerful than the Chaggossians' advocates' (Embassy, 2009).

The plight of the Chagossians should remind us that conservation is rarely a completely innocent and apolitical exercise, that the stakes are often high, and that claims of justices and injustices frequently result. In Chapter 2 I asked whether the urgency of conservation could morally justify denying the rights of a minority. But how should we inquire into the justness of a conservation intervention? In this example, we could think of it in legal terms, such as whether the case for the marine protected area (which succeeded in 2010) was based on improper motives; or we could disregard the bad behaviour of bureaucrats and make a more fundamental argument about human rights to homelands. In fact there are many ways of looking at a conflict such as this and we must conclude that observing injustices and justices is not a simple matter. It is certainly not a matter of asking whether something is legal, because the laws of nations allow what many of us would consider global injustices, such as the disproportionate harm to low-lying island states which arises from perfectly legal emissions of greenhouse gases. This point suggests that we recognise injustice when we see it, but abstracting generalisable norms of justice from such observations remains elusive and is perhaps even a futile exercise. Whilst the previous chapters have largely addressed questions about whether it is possible for conservation to be more just, this chapter proceeds to ask how we might characterise environmental justice. If our interest is ultimately in how conservation might become more just, how should we conduct such an inquiry?

The title of this chapter pays tribute to Abraham Kaplan's more comprehensive title *The Conduct of Inquiry*. Published in 1964, his book confronts the intellectual dogmas which limit the capacity of scientific research to adapt to the complex worldly circumstances it confronts. One illustration used in the book is the scenario of a child who is given a hammer – every object subsequently encountered appears to the child as something in need of a good pounding. Another of Kaplan's illustrations is the story of the 'drunkard's search'. In its most popular rendering, a man is seen searching for his car keys under a street-light. When asked how he knows they are in that location, he says he doesn't think that they are, but at least there is a light to look under here. An examination of conservation justice should avoid looking at the world from the perspective of a single instrument or dogma, or only where a particular light shines. Realistically, we are not going to find a perfect light to look under, no model for a perfectly just society against which we can measure our earthly predicament, and no discipline or theory which provides perfect vision to guide us. A degree of pragmatism is called for, both in selecting the kind of lights we choose to look under and where we choose to shine them.

This chapter raises and discusses four questions about the conduct of environmental justice inquiry and in doing so outlines what I consider to be the main features of a pragmatic approach to exploring the justices and injustices of biodiversity conservation.

Firstly, I return to the question of whether justice inquiry should be normative or empirical. Should we be looking to identify theories about justice (about how to define right and wrong) which can serve as a moral compass? Or should we reject such a 'normative' grand theoretical approach to justice and instead pursue a more 'empirical' approach? An empirical study of environmental justice would focus our inquiry on the claims about justice and injustice that are made by various stakeholders, without necessarily seeking to draw out more generalisable moral principles.

Secondly, I ask the closely related question of whether justice should be considered as universal or as plural. Can there be definitive statements about the right way to act which transcend particular contexts? Or is 'the right thing to do' always subject to circumstance and perspective? If the latter, then some of the key questions for a pragmatic justice inquiry are about whose ideas of justice are seen to gain traction and how this comes about. For example, how has an exclusionary model of protected areas gained so much traction as the right way to protect biodiversity?

Thirdly, having established my approach as an empirical one which embraces justice pluralism, I nevertheless pose the question of what space remains for a normative dimension to environmental justice. What, if anything, can we build consensus about and use as a guide to our actions? And in particular, what social objectives of conservation are very widely supported? My general approach to this question is to introduce theories of human development and specifically, the capabilities approach developed by Amartya Sen and Martha Nussbaum. I argue that one can be committed to value pluralism whilst also adhering to some generalised ideas about what constitutes essential human needs and rights.

Fourthly, I consider the range of subjects that should be considered by environmental justice inquiry. The range of possible subjects includes current humans, future humans, past humans, non-humans and more. I ask whether an approach to environmental justice based on a theory of human capabilities is necessarily confined to individuals (as opposed to communities) and to humans (as opposed to non-humans) as the subjects of justice inquiry. Whilst I see no particular constraint to applying the idea of capabilities to communities as well as individuals, I find it harder to extend this framework to non-human animals.

I have summarised a basic framework for inquiry about conservation justice with three main interacting elements (Figure 4.1). Firstly, the framework proposes an empirical social science approach that studies what people actually think and communicate about environmental issues, the contexts in which these individual and collective conceptions of justice are formed, and the mechanisms by which some views flourish whilst others are marginalised. This empirical approach is aided by the distinction between the justice dimensions of distribution, procedure and recognition that were described in Chapter 1. Secondly, I propose that this more 'bottom up', empirical study of environmental justice can be usefully complemented by way of conceptualising the ends of justice: in general terms, how would we gauge whether an outcome is good or bad? I propose that the capabilities approach can serve this function. This retains a pluralist vision of what humans value, maintaining that different people choose *to be* different to each other and *to do* different things. What is constant is that all people should have equal capabilities *to do and to be* what they want, implying that what is relevant to justice is the opportunities people have, rather than the outcomes that they achieve. The third element of the framework seeks to introduce a minimal normative content (a minimal universalism) by suggesting that there are some basic human needs for attaining an adequate set of capabilities.

There is an important thread that feeds through these three components, namely that environmental justice inquiry should be concerned with not only the material and objective conditions for human wellbeing, but also the social/relational and subjective ones. Regarding dimensions of justice, distribution is

FIGURE 4.1 A pragmatic, empirical framing of environmental justice inquiry.

largely concerned with material outcomes, whilst recognition deals with the intersubjectivity of human relations. Regarding capabilities, freedom to make choices comes in the form of both material capabilities such as good physical health and subjective ones such as self-esteem and agency. Closely related to this, both material needs, such as adequate nutrition, and social needs, such as autonomy, make up the basic conditions for an adequate set of capabilities. Whilst these are represented as separate domains, they are of course strongly linked, just as the physical and psychological elements of human health can be connected.

Justice for conservation: normative or empirical inquiry?

In the social sciences, being 'normative' is less common than in political philosophy. Indeed, normative is often a derogatory charge, an accusation of poor scholarship that results from mistakenly attributing transcendental qualities to beliefs which are really local and contextual and which are therefore best described in sociological rather than normative terms. This might be one reason why much recent environmental justice scholarship has sought to avoid imposing judgements of what is just and unjust, and sticks to observations of the way in which different claims about environmental justice are constructed and how these play out in real-world contexts. This non-normative or, better to say, empirical approach to environmental justice has much to recommend it (see Walker 2012; Sikor 2013; Sikor et al. 2014). It takes what I think is a sensible and pragmatic view that beliefs about fairness and justice are part of our cognitive state, amenable to empirical social science research in the same way as other beliefs and preferences. As such, it is quite appropriate to undertake research into the origins of normative beliefs (e.g. the social contexts and life histories in which they take shape), their interactions (e.g. how they play out in different public situations) and their consequences (e.g. how they shape conservation behaviour and receptivity to conservation ideas). Whilst the empirical observation of justice cognition is subject to the usual epistemological quandaries, it is probably fair to say that the methods for such observation are developing across the social sciences, from ethnographic approaches in political ecology, to experimental games-playing in psychology and behavioural economics.

Whilst an empirical approach is both rich and pragmatic in itself, I remain sympathetic to the idea that inquiry into environmental justice should be action-guiding; that is, that it should provide a vocabulary and analytical categories which not only help us to observe how stakeholders view the rights and wrongs of the situations they find themselves in, but also provide some basis for comparison between more and less just policy options. If the idea of environmental justice fails to provide yardsticks that help us to observe and articulate social injustices, then it may become divorced from its roots in activist movements and leftist environmental politics. For example, for those activists and intellectuals fighting against the perceived discrimination against ethnic minorities observed in the location of US toxic waste dumps, the bottom line was and is that discrimination based on arbitrary characteristics such as colour, ethnicity, gender or wealth is wrong, not only in specific contexts, but everywhere.

Developing the idea of conservation justice as an action-guiding philosophy requires some careful navigation between two major approaches to justice thinking. The empirical, contextualist approach holds that justice is a social construct, that it means different things to different people, and that claims about justice and injustice can only really be understood through reference to the particular circumstances that surround it. I should also mention that the same applies to many of the salient reference points for conservation justice, meaning that key referent terms such as 'forests', 'biodiversity', 'indigeneity' are themselves social constructs rather than objective givens. As Kenneth Worthy (2013) stresses in *Invisible Nature,* this is not to deny the existence of important distinctions between nature and human artifice (a tree has complex properties that a wristwatch clearly does not), but to be aware that most things fall somewhere along a spectrum that is neither wholly natural nor wholly artificial. If we accept that justice and its referents are at least part artifice (partly socially constructed) then we must accept that the eviction of a people from their island archipelago might be deemed unjust within one setting, but just in another – depending on a potentially wide set of historical and cultural circumstances, and even according to our understanding of basic constructs such as 'permanent resident' or 'indigenous'.

The opposing approach to justice thinking – a more objectivist and universalist one – seeks to establish principles of justice that have a bit more reach. To state the extreme case, it is the search for universal ethical maxims or commandments that hold good across all forms of human relationship (and potentially human–nonhuman ones), and across all times and places. There are many shades along the spectrum between these two ways of thinking but the schism remains quite clear and important as a point of departure between social justice thinkers. There are those who are more disposed to objectifying justice as an assessment tool, identifying justice categories and principles that can be used to judge policy processes and outcomes. And there are those who reject such universalising and objectivist approaches to justice thinking and are suspicious of any attempt to judge people according to principles that are not of their own making.

This important intellectual fault-line also tends to distance academic social scientists from activists and practitioners (Gough 2007). Whilst shades of social constructivism may dominate the intellectual life of social scientists, a comparative comfort with universalism pervades the real world of political intervention and global institutions. There is thus a disconnect between intellectuals who put human self-interpretation at centre stage in the attempt to understand wellbeing and justice, and practitioners who seek more generalised and prescriptive judgements about the components of human wellbeing that are salient to social justice, how to measure progress in relation to these, and how to assess and influence policies. Bridging these camps is really quite challenging. Those advocating far-reaching, action-guiding forms of assessment are criticised for a sort of cultural imperialism – for imposing on and seeking to measure others by *their* ideas of justice or wellbeing. For example, when Allison et al. (2011) proposed the use of human rights as an action-guiding benchmark for fisheries policy, they found themselves criticised by anthropologists who argued that universal human rights frameworks impose Western neoliberal values 'thereby betraying the very people claimed as beneficiaries' (Davis and Ruddle 2012, p. 245).

This is an interesting and important debate. We must avoid assumptions that our own way of making claims about justice resonates with the views of others or speaks for others; and we should not assume that our arguments are somehow superior to the claims made by others (Walker 2012). But at the same time, the motivation of environmental justice movements is to support progressive policies that make a difference to the real lives that people lead. To do this there arguably needs to be some basis for assessment – a normative basis for social justice. As described in Chapter 1, those who seek out a basis for assessment, and for guiding action, fall into different traditions of ethical thought. In particular, there are those who focus on the procedure or means for deciding between claims, a tradition occupied for example by John Rawls and Amartya Sen, and there are those who focus on defining the ends of justice – what justice should help us to have or to be, a position most commonly associated with utilitarianism.

Whose justice? The case for pluralism

What is justice for some is injustice for others. Local people who lose access to a protected area may feel aggrieved, at the same time as those living further afield may consider that the greater good has been served, for example because they believe an endangered species has become better protected, or that the needs of future generations have been respected. Thus conservation justice is not a singular and politically neutral concept and we must always be alert to questions about whose ideas of justice prevail and, conversely, whose do not. Questions about 'whose justice prevails' reminds us that environmental conflicts occur between competing conceptions of justice rather than between just and unjust acts per se (Harvey 1996). For some groups, the very act of being incorporated within the justice framings of others is itself the root of their claims of injustice. Thus, for example the domination of tribal people in India was accelerated by the extension of the constitution into tribal lands following Indian independence in 1947 (Madhu Sarin, pers. com.). Similarly, the incorporation of Inca people within Peru's justice system serves to block their claims to alternative ways of conceiving environmental justice (Alejandro Argumedo, pers. com.). And ecofeminists have argued that women have been disadvantaged by the dominance of male conceptions of virtuous relationships with nature (e.g. Merchant 1980). Not surprisingly, such examples suggest a wider pattern in which the views of more economically and politically powerful stakeholders tend to gain traction and foreclose on the views of more marginalised groups. The Roman goddess of justice, *Iustitia,* is depicted as the blindfolded 'lady justice', reassuring us that we are all equal before the judiciary. But the concern for some of these groups is about who writes the rules that the judiciary upholds, and whose values and interests these represent.

Anthropologists have helped to raise awareness of how sets of ideas, backed by communities of exponents in positions of influence, can serve to undermine the freedoms of people living near to sites identified for biodiversity conservation. West et al. (2006) describe how prevalent conceptions of conservation – notably parks and their IUCN protected area categories – serve to describe right and wrong behaviour in those places that they are applied. Whilst categories of parks may be rather arbitrary and abstract models of how the world might be, these ideas take on material agency as they gain traction and the world becomes transformed in their image. As West and Brockington (2006, p. 609) put it, 'protected areas are coming to form a way of *thinking* about the world, of *viewing* the world, and of *acting* on the world'. Such a connection between thinking and acting is not a simple and linear one, but an unfolding of practice amongst many stakeholders, some with competing interests. As Li (2007) describes, what we see is a coming together in practice of an 'assemblage' of disparate elements of governance, such as scientific models, moral propositions and legal and regulatory institutions. In the field of biodiversity conservation, such assemblages typically involve quite subtle and fragile alignments of interest, for example between conservation organisations (motivated by biodiversity), state agencies (say motivated by foreign exchange earnings from tourism) and local communities (say motivated by formal employment opportunities). Understanding how such assemblages congeal into dominant ways of framing a problem and its solutions, of how an assemblage serves to 'conduct the conduct' (as Foucault puts it) of different stakeholders, is important for understanding the role played by ideas: the discursive form of power that this book will view as a critical mechanism of injustice. In a nutshell, injustice can stem from processes that seize control in the mind in advance of seizing anything on the ground (Li 2014).

The flourishing of a particular way of framing a problem, at the cost of others, can take many forms and is often tied up in particular local or national political contexts as well as the global political economy. This can be illustrated through the case of the Nyungwe National Park in Rwanda. This is among the largest remaining montane tropical forests in Africa and forms part of the Albertine Rift biodiversity 'hotspot', valued for its biodiversity and species endemism (Plumptre et al. 2002). It is also highly valued for ecosystem services. Globally it contributes to climate regulation via carbon storage and it also provides a nature tourism destination, especially for birders. Nationally, it is estimated that 75% of dry season flow in Rwanda's principal river systems arises from headwaters in Nyungwe (Plumptre et al. 2004). Locally, farmers report a micro-climate effect in terms of rainfall and temperature, and associated health benefits such as suppression of malaria. But local people also value Nyungwe and its environs for subsistence cultivation and for extractive, provisioning services such as bushmeat hunting and fuelwood collection (Gross-Camp et al. 2012). As was stated in Chapter 2, the recent extirpation of Nyungwe's apex grazers and carnivores (elephant, buffalo and leopard) can be expected to have a cascade effect down the trophic chain, leading to further biodiversity loss, reduction of ecosystem productivity and loss of service provision at all scales. It is then a classic conservation problem in which some of the current benefits enjoyed by local people are, it seems, at odds with the interests of people further afield spatially and temporally.

The Rwandan government tends to draw on moralities of national-level public good to justify preservationist interventions which align with the interests of international conservation partners. Thus the contribution of the park to Rwanda's hydrology and to foreign exchange earnings from tourism is highlighted. The subsistence agricultural practices that conservation interventions seek to curtail are characterised as directly threatening such national goods (Dawson et al. 2016b). The National Land Policy refers to these practices as 'simple self-subsistence agriculture based on working the land without caring for its conservation or the improvement of its production capacity'. It is written off in its entirety as 'a mediocre agriculture that has no future' and government intervention is justified in order 'to manage the land and use it in an efficient uniform manner' (Republic of Rwanda 2004). Such statements appear to be backed up in global development circles, for example in a World Bank analysis that reports that Rwandan farmers achieve only a quarter of the potential crop yield from their land (Deininger and Byerlee 2011).

There is little or no sentiment for traditional ways of doing things or for alternative ways of thinking about relationships between society and nature. For example the indigenous Batwa people are not officially recognised as being indigenous and the histories of Rwanda currently favoured by the state do not acknowledge ethnic or cultural diversity. This is in large part understandable because Rwanda is committed to eliminating the ethnic distinctions that devastated the country during the war and genocide in the 1990s. Rwanda is thus constructed as culturally homogeneous, without any alternatives to the mainstream way of thinking about and living with nature (Martin et al. 2013b). But by denying that the cultural cost of conservation is a morally salient issue, the state and other conservation actors essentially reduce the costs and benefits of conservation to the single metric of economic returns. Thus, whilst the government does acknowledge that there might be local losers (Republic of Rwanda 2011) it only recognises that they lose material, economic inputs to their livelihoods, not that they lose socially or culturally. As will be discussed later in this book, this is a common characteristic of the way that more powerful actors seek to frame conservation justice: there is a tendency to view justice for local communities in terms of distribution of material benefits (remedied by e.g. revenue-sharing and compensation schemes) whilst rendering invisible claims about cultural freedom and rights to self-determination. In this way, conservation conflicts are presented not as political struggles for recognition, but as matters of local-level distribution.

But these are generalisations and it would be misleading to say that the elite are always able to define and depoliticise justice in their own interests. Indeed the very attraction of 'environmental justice' analysis for scholars and advocates alike is that promoting strong alternative claims to justice can be a powerful tool for democratic deliberation and advocacy. For example, the iconic Chipko movement drew on Gandhian principles in its struggle against state-sanctioned deforestation in the Himalayas, eventually prompting the government to declare a moratorium on felling in 1980. It also had a deeper impact on Indian environmental politics that continues to this day to reverberate in the struggles of tribal people to assert their territories and freedoms.

Whilst it is possible to contest framings of justice promoted by more powerful actors, it is rarely easy to do so. We might say that the transaction costs of seeking discursive power are higher for more marginalised people in terms of the material resources but often also in terms of the risks of persecution. For example, in April 2013 the Supreme Court of India ruled that local tribal councils had the right to self-determination over bauxite mining in the Niyamgiri mountains, and thus the right to assert and uphold their own religious and cultural values in decisions about their environment. But this has been a hard-fought struggle in which people have given their lives in the fight for the justice system to recognise their values and rights (Kumar 2014b). A case like this reminds us of our responsibility to take care in asserting pre-determined framings of the ends and means of justice, however benign they may appear to us. Even framings such as 'rights-based approaches' have histories of contention and require a reflective stance if they are to avoid reinforcing dominant ways of thinking at the expense of valid alternative perspectives (Kashwan 2013).

In *The Idea of Justice*, Amartya Sen (2009) illustrates the plurality of conceptions of justice through the example of a flute that has been found and which is claimed by a number of children. The first child claims the flute based on her expertise; she alone can play the flute. The second child is uniquely poor having no other toys to play with. The third child reveals that she actually made the flute. Our moral persuasion will likely dictate who the 'winner' is and will differ accordingly from individual to individual. Sen (p. 13) suggests a libertarian might favour the property-based claim of child 3, an economic egalitarian might favour the reduction in inequality that would result from selecting child 2, and a utilitarian might be swayed by the greater happiness the flute would bring to child 1. His point is to show that there will always be more than one *rational* argument for resource allocation and it may be impractical for us to think that we can agree: 'There may not indeed exist any identifiable perfectly just social arrangement on which impartial agreement would emerge' (p. 15). As David Miller (2013) states in his book *Justice for Earthlings,* there are many ways in which humans relate to each other, from very intimate ones to distant ones. Any attempt to develop forms of assessment that apply to all of these is unlikely to be useful. We might employ one principle when dealing with a family member face to face, but another whilst considering how to act towards an anonymous person in another country. Deutsch (2000) also suggests that individuals apply different principles depending on the situation they are considering. So, even if I happened to take the utilitarian view of the flute, I might tend towards an egalitarian view of how electoral votes should be distributed, and perhaps a meritocratic stance towards how jobs should be allocated.

Decisions about distribution are part and parcel of the everyday politics of conservation interventions. For example, I was involved in a trial payments for ecosystem services scheme in parts of Nyungwe, in which communities received performance-related payments for efforts to reduce certain threats to the park's flora and fauna (I return to this in Chapter 8). We made decisions about how much people were to be rewarded through calculations of mean household opportunity cost (i.e. what they would have to give up by not hunting bushmeat and cutting trees), how they would be paid (cash rather than public works; at household level rather than community), and of course we also made decisions about the consultation procedures for making these decisions.

At the outset we did not particularly think about these and related questions as carrying conceptions of fairness and justice, but we soon learned that they do. Take, for example, our decision to determine payment levels by average opportunity cost – this was based on a view that differential payments would be less fair and would be perceived as less legitimate by local people. Differential payments would involve paying more to those who had to give up more (e.g. those who were very dependent on bushmeat hunting or on artisanal mining) and less to those who weren't (including some of the least advantaged households whose poverty had been triggered by death or illness, and who have insufficient human labour to benefit from forest-based collection).

Such decisions are justice-carrying in the sense that they entail principles of fairness. And crucially there tends to be more than one reasonable decision that can be made: I can present what I think is a reasonable and rational argument for equal payments, based on egalitarian traditions of fairness, but I also acknowledge that there are equally reasonable arguments for differential payments, based on reward for effort or some other reason for deserving reward. It helps to find out what local people consider fair and just. This takes time and money but if it leads to greater support for the conservation intervention, then this is likely to be well spent. For example, Table 4.1 summarises data from surveys in Nyungwe, and two other protected areas: Bwindi Impenetrable National Park in Uganda and the Nam Et-Phou Louey National Protected Area in Laos. Respondents were asked to rank different principles for distributing park benefits, according to what they thought was best. The four different principles represented distribution according to effort, need, equality and desert.

The table shows the percentage distribution of first preferences – i.e. statements ranked as first choice by respondents. The first thing to note is that there is a diversity of thinking both within and between communities. The differences between the choices made in each case study location are stark, with an 'egalitarian' distributional principle most preferred in Nyungwe, distribution according to 'desert' in Bwindi and according to 'need' in Nam Et-Phou Louey. The second point to make is that the reasons for these differences are not straightforward. These reasons include broader cultural differences based on political and cultural histories. In Rwanda, for example, prevailing cultures of public behaviour have been profoundly affected by the 1994 genocide (Martin et al. 2014a). Receiving the same as others (egalitarian) is seen as fair because it protects everyone against any accusations of prejudice or corruption. The reasons also include more specific contextual conditions including the nature of the benefits to be distributed: the amount of benefits to be distributed is likely to influence conceptions of how it should be distributed, as is the source of the benefit. In Nyungwe, for example, the source of benefits was cash payments from the PES, in Bwindi, it was mainly revenue from gorilla tourism, and in

TABLE 4.1 Percentage of respondents selecting different distributional principles as their first choice.

Principle for distributing benefits from the park	Nyungwe (Rwanda) n = 100	Bwindi (Uganda) n = 101	Nam et Phou Louey (Laos) N = 99
Those households that participate most in conservation should receive more than others (Distribution according to effort)	30	11	4
The poorest households should receive more benefits than others (Distribution according to need)	23	25	60
All households should receive the same amount (Egalitarian distribution)	38	5	35
Those households that bear the greater costs should receive more benefits than others (Distribution according to desert)	9	60	1

Source: Author's data.

Nam Et-Phou Louey it was largely non-cash benefits from natural resources. To be sure, comparison between the three sites is more or less meaningless without attention to understanding context. The third thing to note is that, whether or not we fully understand them, the existence of these differences does matter. For example, PES schemes often use calculations of opportunity cost (represented by 'desert' here) to determine the appropriate level of payments offered. Our findings suggest that this method might be considered fair in some contexts (Bwindi) but not in others (Nyungwe, Nam Et-Phou Louey).

To summarise the arguments so far, even having limited the scope of our interest to relationships involving conservation planners and local communities, we have to be extremely cautious of generalised statements about justice beliefs or principles. Different interests exist between different groups of actors who prioritise different ends. Even where groups of actors have some positional similarity, they can still display quite different conceptions about fairness and justice in practice. For example, amongst conservation practitioners who broadly agree that the greater public good should be pursued, but that this should be accompanied by benefits to local people, we can see quite different conceptions of what is fair and equitable. Likewise, within local communities with relatively homogeneous livelihood strategies and wealth levels, there is considerable difference in thinking about what constitutes just decision-making or distribution; and this can also vary considerably from community to community.

The ends of justice: a view from development studies

The above findings provide support for the view that justice is deeply contextual. Whilst the framing of justice summarised so far stays true to this important observation, it is also my intention to reject moral relativism – the view that ethics and justice are entirely context-dependent. The question that I turn to now is what generalisations can we make about the meaning of environmental justice? I pose this question initially in relation to the 'what' of justice: what is the end of justice? Or to put it another way, what is the good that justice advances? We frequently see calls for justice to be done within conservation policy communities. The Aichi targets call for protected areas to be 'equitably' managed by 2020; the Conservation Initiative on Human Rights calls for a raft of rights to be acknowledged and protected; the 2014 World Parks Congress ended with a promise 'to seek to redress and remedy past and continuing injustices' (CBD 2010b; Springer et al. 2010; IUCN 2014); the UN's Sustainable Development Goal number 15 incorporates the CBD target to 'promote fair and equitable' sharing of benefits' (UN 2015). But is there anything we can agree on that provides us with some guidance to the meaning of 'just', 'equitable' or 'fair'?

This question identifies a primary fault line between utilitarian and rights-based political philosophies of justice. Utilitarianism builds from the premise that defining what is good is a matter of identifying the sum of individuals' utility. According to Jeremy Bentham's famous take on this, justice could then be achieved through pursuit of the greatest satisfaction for the greatest number (Bentham 2009/1789). This is egalitarian to the extent that the satisfaction of each individual is treated equally, regardless of who they are. But this apparent equality of treatment might not be so desirable when starting from a position of major asymmetries in power and in terms of which groups of people are more likely to be winners or losers. In the case of conservation, it is well established that the group most likely to lose out in pursuit of the greater good is the poor (Adams et al. 2004). The first objection to utilitarianism is therefore that defining the end of justice as the greater good allows for the real possibility that poor people will be harmed. This runs against the generally accepted norm introduced in Chapter 2, that conservation should 'first do no harm', and also against broader global targets under the UN Sustainable Development Goals.

The second reason for rejecting utilitarianism is also a problem with aggregation, in this case a problem with conflating the different types of things which humans value (see Nussbaum 2011). Utilitarian aggregation is insensitive to the fact that we value different types of things and that these are often not commensurate. It would have us take material satisfaction and social identity-based satisfactions and somehow reduce these to a single metric of utility. It would not allow an individual to report both justices and injustices (as they so often do in real life) but only to give a net balance. For example, in the case above, a member of the Batwa indigenous ethnic group might have been suitably recompensed materially for eviction, through provision of a new house. But they might yet feel that there has been an injustice arising from failure to respect their cultural attachment to place. Indeed, it may be that no amount of financial compensation will make good the failure to recognise their territorial claims. Similarly, at least some members of the Chagossian community are no longer driven by issues of compensation but by the need to have their rights recognised. I am far from satisfied that we can sensibly seek to merge these different experiences into a single measure such as utility. Utilitarianism is therefore unsuitable, on the basis of two aggregation problems: one that fails to protect minorities from harm, and the other that fails to embrace the irreducible plurality of values.

A key alternative to utilitarianism is a rights-based or deontological approach, often linked to liberal political philosophies. Liberalism tends to uphold a plurality of conceptions of the good, and a liberal justice focuses on how to provide individuals with the rights required to pursue their own valued ends (Sandel 1998). In contrast to utilitarianism, this approach tends to assert the equality and sanctity of certain individual rights, regardless of the greater good. In *A Theory of Justice,* John Rawls (1971) does not seek to directly define 'the ends' to which justice pertains, but rather seeks to elaborate the principles by which people get fair opportunity to pursue their own desired ends. He thinks about this problem by designing a thought experiment in which we imagine ourselves behind a 'veil of ignorance' that conceals to us what position we will hold in society. We might imagine that we are taking decisions about how a landscape's biodiversity is managed, not knowing if we will find ourselves to be a subsistence Batwa peasant, or the Rwandan president; or as a Chagos refugee or foreign secretary of the UK government. Rawls challenges us to consider the following: not knowing the position from which we will get to experience the resource-management decision, what principles of just decision-making could we likely develop a consensus around? Rawls suggests two: the first is that decisions must defend equal liberties; the second is that there should be equality of opportunity and that inequality is only acceptable in circumstances where it favours the least advantaged. The latter clause is known as the 'difference principle', which proposes that is right to allow inequalities that reduce the difference between the better-off and worse-off. In summary then, utilitarian liberalism potentially allows inequalities which will widen the gap between rich and poor whilst a Rawlsian, rights-based liberalism will only allow inequality that closes the gap between rich and poor.

Capabilities as ends of justice?

Conservation practitioners deal on an everyday basis with real people facing real risks and hardships. A pragmatic, action-guiding framing of conservation justice therefore needs to take account of the lives that people actually live – what people achieve, what they want to achieve and what they have freedom to achieve. So whilst I find Rawls' 'difference principle' to be brilliant and helpful, I also want to engage more with the actual goods which these principles serve. Indeed, part of Rawls' brilliance was the way his veil of ignorance side-stepped the need to define the good, thus allowing a clearer sight of general principles of distribution. So what can we agree about in terms of the ends of justice and, in particular, what might be the observable indicators of a more just, equitable or fair conservation? As stated earlier in the chapter, my stance on this question is very much influenced by development studies scholars working on the connected ideas of human capabilities and wellbeing.

Those working on human capabilities and wellbeing represent a spectrum of thinking rather than a singular view. However, most have in common a dissatisfaction with Rawls' focus on getting the principles right and an inclination towards what Amartya Sen (2009) terms a more 'accomplishment based' understanding of justice, one that is not indifferent to the lives that people actually live. Another commonality is the belief that a useful conception of justice should be able to facilitate assessment and comparison. Sen, Nussbaum and others reject perfectionist approaches to moral philosophy which seek to describe a perfectly just society and then compare and assess progress towards this utopia. But they nonetheless find it necessary to identify forms of comparison and assessment against which we can collectively observe, deliberate and protest injustice and strive for situations that are more just.

The desire to assess and compare justice performances – let alone measure them – is of course fraught with controversy. If the aim is to add content to justice – to relate it to the lives that people actually live and to compare the choices that they have and what they accomplish – we risk seeking to examine the lives of others through metrics that are not of their own making. For some, this amounts to another form of Western imperialism although such a complaint is strongly rejected by others (Brock 2009; Nussbaum 2011). In my mind, an acceptable justice framework has to steer between an overly constructivist perspective of justice that views any attempt to identify core content as intellectually unsafe, and those that err on the other side by seeking to describe the ends of justice (the good) in too much detail.

The capabilities approach provides a way of steering between these poles – to remain committed to cultural and ethical pluralism whilst at the same time taking a stance against the moral abyss of relativism. It deals with the paradox that what people value is resolutely plural, but that we can't effectively examine real lives unless we have a decent hunch about what we will perceive to be injustice (Nussbaum 2011). So whilst utilitarians choose utility as their yardstick, and Rawls chooses rights, capability theorists choose human capabilities as the essential information that we need if we are to observe, debate and fight against injustice. Capabilities are those personal qualities that enable us to achieve things: education, clean water, nutrition, liberty, security, community, and so on.

> A person's advantage in terms of opportunities is judged to be lower than that of another if she has less capability – less real opportunity – to achieve those things that she has reason to value.
>
> *(Sen 2009, p. 231)*

What people have reason to value is of course plural – it is what *they* have reason to value – and cannot be distilled down to single measures such as income. The critical question is 'what is each person able to do and to be?' and definitively not 'what is average income?' (Nussbaum 2011). Justice is, then, about activities which constrain, protect and enhance the set of opportunities that people have to do and to be what *they* value. In the language of Sen, capabilities are opportunities to achieve functionings, which are outcomes such as good bodily and spiritual health – what people actually manage to do and be. Choice is therefore integral to the idea of capabilities – everyone will benefit from certain choices, but not everyone will use those choices to achieve the same functionings or accomplishments.

This leaves the question of whether some capabilities are so special – are so essential to the wellbeing of all humans – that they can be treated as more concrete benchmarks for a justice analysis – the core informational content. Indeed, without such concrete indicators, the capabilities approach is notoriously difficult to operationalise for assessment and comparison in a manner that its key protagonists would wish (Alkire 2007). It asks:

> among the many things that human beings might develop the capacity to do, which ones are the really valuable ones, which are the ones that a minimally just society will endeavour to nurture and support?
>
> *(Nussbaum 2011, p. 28)*

It is on this question that Sen and Nussbaum part company. For Sen, it is important for the answers about the specific content of essential capabilities to remain open – the detailed content of justice is always a matter for public reasoning. For Nussbaum, on the other hand, the imperative to know what we are looking at – to have a yardstick and basis for a progressive politics of the left – justifies directly tackling this question of which capabilities are so central to human wellbeing that their curtailment denies human dignity and can be described as an injustice.

BOX 4.1   MARTHA NUSSBAUM'S TEN CENTRAL CAPABILITIES

1   Life
2   Bodily health
3   Bodily integrity
4   Senses, imagination, and thought
5   Emotions
6   Practical reason
7   Affiliation
8   Other species (concern for)
9   Play
10   Control over one's environment

Source: Nussbaum, 2006, pp. 76–77.

Nussbaum identifies a list of 10 essential or 'central capabilities' which correspond with a social justice agenda (Box 4.1). Like Rawls, she partly supports her case by appeal to a thought experiment, asking us to imagine a life without one or more of these capabilities and to consider whether such a life would be worthy of human dignity. She contends that this thought experiment would garner broad consensus (Nussbaum 2006), although there are clearly those who think otherwise (Gough et al. 2007). The issue at hand, then, is that a pragmatic, operable framing of justice requires content regarding the thresholds for a life worth living, but it is not clear how 'thickly' we can describe those thresholds. An ultra-thin description (a minimal universalism) might only include things such as water or oxygen (Gough 2004) – things we can easily agree are universally needed. But, as we go much beyond this, as Nussbaum clearly does, we run the risk that we take our personal view of basic needs for a dignified life, and then assert these as essential and universal truths about the human condition.

Doyal and Gough's (1984, 1991) *Theory of Human Needs* identifies two fundamental needs – physical health and autonomy – which are beyond reasonable contention, for reasons that have been partly explored above. Whilst they also consider a set of 'intermediary needs' required to service these two fundamental needs, I stick with the more minimal defining of the ends of justice, articulated as material and social needs in Figure 4.1. Whilst 'thin', such generalised conceptions of the good can nonetheless be action-guiding within particular contexts, particularly in terms of identifying thresholds which cannot be justly crossed. For example, contextually relevant poverty lines are widely used as thresholds below which harms to health are likely.

Subjects of justice: expanding the circle

Any useful framing of environmental justice should be minimally capable of considering the kinds of justice claims prevalent in real-world struggles for environmental justice. In very general terms, this is not a problem for an empirical approach to justice, which is inherently receptive to a plurality of kinds of claims. Nevertheless, having determined that a capabilities approach to justice is well suited, there are important questions about the constraints this places on who or what should fall under the protective sphere of justice. As David Schlosberg (2009) has pointed out, the most common uses of capabilities thinking seem out of sync with existing environmental justice struggles on at least two counts, firstly by considering harms to individuals but not communities and secondly, by considering harms to humans but not non-humans.

Owing to its roots in liberal political philosophies, capabilities thinking identifies individuals as the primary subjects of justice, because the individual is the locus of pleasure and suffering. Capabilities therefore refer to *individual* capacities to achieve desired ends. Social goods such as the survival of cultural practices may be important, but only inasmuch as they shape the capability sets of individuals. The case for treating communities as subjects of justice seems a strong one to me and one which is easily accommodated within a capabilities framework. There are now many studies of environmental justice struggles which find that indigenous and other minority peoples express moral concern regarding the impacts of conservation on communal culture and identity. Indigenous visions of environmental justice tend to emphasise relational concerns over distributional ones (Whiteman 2009). For example, the African philosophical traditions of *Botho* and *Ubuntu* are concerned with achieving the right relationship between self and others, and emphasise community as the foundation for right living (LenkaBula 2008). Such relational and communitarian views of conservation justice have been illustrated in many case studies including the Navajo of the United States (Schlosberg and Carruthers 2010), the Pemon of Venezuela (Rodríguez 2016), and the San of Southern Africa (Vermeylen and Walker 2011).

In my view, the extension of justice considerations to non-humans is equally justified as extension to communities of humans. Again, one source of justification is the kind of claims that are made in actual justice struggles, and in particular the animal rights movement which has long argued that the denial of moral status to other sentient beings is an indefensible form of discrimination based on speciesism (e.g. Singer 1975). Indeed the struggle to promote rights to justice for animals has yielded some initial successes, such as the 2008 Spanish ruling which granted rights of life and freedom to the great apes. But such isolated progress leaves out much of the animal kingdom, including the estimated 17 billion animals raised and killed for human food each year in Europe and the US alone (Matheny 2005).

Nussbaum (2006) argues that a capabilities approach can be extended to include non-human animals as subjects of justice, with a similar set of essential rights as humans. This is a tempting proposition because there is currently somewhat of a chasm between systems of thinking about social justice and systems of thinking about environmental ethics. The latter is primarily concerned with discovering what is intrinsically valuable in nature and worthy of moral respect whilst the former confines itself to what is valuable for humans (Norton 2005). If capabilities were to provide a bridge across this divide – a unitary system of social and ecological values and justice – that would indeed be an enormously important contribution to justice scholarship. It is even tempting to think in practical terms about the potential for human and non-human interests to be aligned in ways which enable the capabilities of both to be the simultaneous pursuit of human politics. I am thinking of interventions which have the potential to be good for current and future humans as well as animals. Increasing vegetarianism for example, is a promising way to reduce suffering to animals, reduce harm done to future people via climate change and biodiversity loss, and perhaps even be a basis to promote health for current people.

Not surprisingly, extending capabilities to non-humans brings some major difficulties. In her attempt to attribute moral status to the essential needs of animals, Nussbaum finds herself in the frankly strange position of advocating for 'an intelligently respectful paternalism' towards them (2006, p. 380). This includes a desire to protect prey such as gazelle from predators such as tigers and with it a view that a wild nature is different from and inferior to a morally just nature (Cripps 2010). For Schlosberg (2004) and Armstrong (2014) it is liberal individualism that leads to this untenable line of thinking. Just as Aldo Leopold had to raise the scale of his thinking to understand the good of predators – by 'thinking like a mountain' – so too the predator–prey problem dissolves if one values the flourishing of species and ecosystems rather than individual animals. Just as the wolf is ultimately good for the flourishing of deer, so are tigers and other predators ultimately good for the flourishing of other ungulate species, and in turn, the functioning of ecosystems for all species including humans. Again, this is a tempting line of thought that one would rather hope to hold true – it certainly sounds more appealing than the view that humans should somehow police the morals of nature. But again it seems deeply problematic. On the whole, extending capabilities from individuals to communities of humans does not require denial of individual capabilities (although Nussbaum raises concerns about this and see also Stephen Marglin's (2010) illuminating discussion of such community–individual tensions in Amish society). But with gazelles, to say that being devoured by a tiger is consistent with the capabilities of the species would seem to absolutely deny moral worth to the capabilities of individuals. This fits well enough with Aldo Leopold's (2013 [1949]) land ethic: 'A thing is right when it tends to preserve the integrity, stability, and beauty of the biotic community. It is wrong when it tends otherwise.' But such a systemic view of the good does not sit well with capabilities thinking and in fact seems more aligned with the greater good of utilitarianism.

Whilst I agree that there is some promise in thinking through the application of capabilities thinking beyond humans and beyond individual subjects of justice, I am also aware that such an effort sucks us back into ethical perfectionism and the search for a universal system of morality. I am in full agreement with Schlosberg that we should pay attention to and be receptive to the claims which people actually make in their struggles for environmental justice, including where these claims make moral subjects of communities or ecosystems. Famously, for example, Mahatma Gandhi claimed that the moral progress of a nation could be judged by how it treated its animals. But I am less convinced of the need to try to fit all such cases into a single theory of justice. I remain comfortable with the idea of (and the need for) a thin conception of what constitutes the good for humans. A capabilities approach to justice holds that all humans have a need for, and a right to, certain thresholds of capabilities necessary for human flourishing. I am comfortable that we can attain a broad-based agreement to some basic social and material needs to thinly define these capabilities – in a similar manner to defining universal human rights. I also accept the need to be receptive to justice cases with a more expansive range of justice subjects; but in doing so I am not convinced that we can simply extend the scope of capabilities thinking.

A minimal universalism

The *distribution* of environmental goods and bads is considered a matter of justice because it contributes to the material conditions for an acceptable set of capabilities and the opportunity to live a life worth living. Such material requirements are of course context-dependent and may vary from country to country and person to person. Adam Smith famously made this point through the example of a linen shirt:

> A linen shirt . . . is, strictly speaking, not a necessary of life. The Greeks and Romans lived, I suppose, very comfortably though they had no linen. But in the present times, through the greater part of Europe, a creditable day-labourer would be ashamed to appear in public without a linen shirt, the want of which would be supposed to denote that disgraceful degree of poverty which, it is presumed, nobody can well fall into without extreme bad conduct.
>
> *(Smith 2008 [1776])*

This reminds us that material and social needs are very much linked, such as in this case where the necessity of a linen shirt stems from the very real social harm which would arise from its absence. This also reminds us of the importance of context. For example, it might seem that the ability to serve meat to eat during a festival is a want rather than a need; but within a particular culture, such expenditure on celebration may be vital to living a life considered dignified (not to feel disgraced by one's own poverty), and to subjective wellbeing. Material and social aspects of wellbeing are inter-twined requirements for human agency, an essential capability that enables people 'to do and to be' what they conceive as necessary for a good life (Nussbaum 2011).

Whilst we have to be open to what is locally conceived as material necessity, I suggest that, in the absence of a real richness of local insight, it can still be useful to think in terms of some cruder thresholds. For our present context, the distribution of goods and bads is largely about the flow of conservation costs and benefits and especially how these affect the already poor. To refer back to the Mgahinga Gorilla National Park, Uganda is a low-income country with 37.8% of the population living below an income poverty line of $1.25 per day, 33.8% suffering from 'severe multidimensional poverty' and an overall ranking of 163 out of 188 countries for its 2014 Human Development Index (UNDP 2015). Even without detailed field-level assessment, the conservation sector can quite safely assume that the poorest within remote rural communities are already close to or below widely used (if crude) material thresholds for wellbeing. In the absence of a better informational base, we could then agree that justice requires that, at a minimum, no material harm is done to these poorest people i.e. it is wrong to make somebody materially poorer when they are already struggling with the material requirements for a decent life. Such a threshold approach to conservation justice would also require that benefits are distributed in ways that strive to assist those for whom essential thresholds are not met. In practice, the idea that a just conservation should make a special effort not to harm the already poor, and that it should also make an effort to assist those living below poverty thresholds (whatever are the best standards to hand, even if not perfect) is not likely to be very controversial: many conservation practices already aspire towards some kind of pro-poor outcomes.

Summary

There is a tension between academic social science thinking about environmental justice, and the expected function of this thinking in advancing a progressive and emancipatory politics of the environment. The former is rightly moving towards empirical approaches to justice analysis which acknowledge that justice is contextual and plural. An empirical approach can serve justice struggles and social movements by employing analytical categories which help to explore a range of claims about just and unjust institutions and outcomes. As described, common categories which help to observe and analyse this range of claims are distribution, procedure and recognition.

For many philosophers of justice, the task at hand is not only to describe claims about rights and wrongs but also to establish the validity of these claims through reference to moral principles. Such principles can derive from divine sources or from human reason and provide systems of inquiry for determining right and wrong actions, such as utilitarianism or Rawlsian fairness principles. But there are many traditions of ethical thought and, correspondingly, an array of different principles by which right and wrong could be determined – it is hard to agree that any of these would be universally applicable, across all contexts. For example, the idea of being guided by the 'greater good' resonates with the widely accepted goal of conservation to protect biodiversity for the good of all current and future humans, and to prevent the few from degrading this common heritage. But context clearly complicates such a system in practice. Firstly, our knowledge of what will lead to degradation is contested: separating people from protected areas may not always be the best way to protect the common heritage. Secondly, even if those seeking to justify harm to the few were acting on secure knowledge of socio-environmental systems, it would still matter who the 'few' were. The prevailing view within biodiversity conservation circles is that local and indigenous communities, especially when poor and marginalised, deserve special protection.

A pluralist stance on conservation justice accepts that context matters and that no single system of principles is likely to generate ethical consensus to resolve questions about just distribution, procedure and recognition. Justice inquiry will always be a process involving deliberation across different stakeholders who may have different views about the ends of justice (what is the good for humans and non-humans), about who are the relevant subjects of justice (e.g. individuals, communities, future people, ancestors and spirits, animals) and about the principles to be applied in particular situational contexts. But is there a core of justice content that can guide such deliberation? Is there a form of guidance which starts from the diversity of the lives that people live and asks us to contemplate injustice in terms of the actions which deprive people of the conditions needed for living lives of dignity? I think there is still work to do to provide a satisfactory response to these questions, but for now I find the capabilities approach to be the most promising framework for pursuing an empirical and pluralist approach to environmental justice analysis whilst also allowing for a 'minimal universalism' – a thin conception of what is 'right' that can be action-guiding across different contexts.

5

TAKING DISTRIBUTION SERIOUSLY

Introduction

> In 2008–9, the world's governments rapidly mobilised hundreds of billions of dollars to prevent collapse of a financial system whose flimsy foundations took the market by surprise. Now we have clear warnings of the potential breaking points towards which we are pushing the ecosystems that have shaped our civilisations. For a fraction of the money summoned up instantly to avoid economic meltdown, we can avoid a much more serious and fundamental breakdown in the Earth's life support systems.
>
> *(Convention on Biological Diversity, 2010.*
> *Global Biodiversity Outlook 3, p. 87)*

The difference of course is that saving banks is comparatively easy. Firstly, the political will is easy to drum up because propping up banks serves the immediate and tangible interests of those with bank accounts – roughly speaking the wealthiest and most powerful half of the world's population. Secondly, efforts to avoid a deepening bank-led recession serve to prop up the popular fantasy of perpetual economic growth. It is argued in this chapter that biodiversity conservation is comparatively hard to sell because it requires the political will to challenge such prevailing fantasies and to address fundamental issues of how we measure social progress and how we tackle distributional problems in the world economy. Following work on ecological economics, environmental sociology and earth systems science, I highlight the increasing global demand for energy, resources and pollution sinks, pointing to consumption as a critical driver of biodiversity loss. At the same time, this growth in the material throughput of the world economy is characterised by inequitable forms of exchange. This gives rise to environmental injustices through continuous cost and risk-shifting, and through ever more extraction and dispossession at commodity frontiers (Martínez Alier 2009a; Muradian et al. 2012). The message is admittedly a hard one to swallow. If our basic concern is with the lack of progress in stemming the loss of biodiversity, then surely making such progress dependent on deep reforms to our economic systems will make it harder to achieve? My approach to this dilemma is to try to show that we don't really have a choice. Neoliberal responses to environmental crisis are not working. This can be shown empirically and it can also be explained more conceptually, in terms of the inter-linkage of social injustice with the drivers of environmental problems.

Concerns about global consumption do make passing appearances in influential documents such as the *Millennium Ecosystem Assessment*, the Convention on Biological Diversity's (CBD's) series of *Global Biodiversity Outlook* reports and the Rio+20 report on *The Future We Want*. But the committees who write these reports are mindful of the need to present a palatable analysis that they judge will not disengage those they seek to influence. The end products therefore tend to describe a set of responses that employ prevailing market-based economics, with a view to bringing about a 'green economy' in which market transactions – corrected to internalise environmental costs – provide a basis for both justice and sustainability. There is a large ready-made political constituency which supports the market promise of efficiency, fairness and personal freedom. Market-based approaches fit with the prevailing political ideology in many countries and can thereby be packaged as largely apolitical: a framework for technical solutions that can slot into prevailing systems of priorities and governance. For its critics however, the 'anti-politics' of the green economy agenda is a smokescreen that conceals the mounting evidence that prevailing economic priorities are incompatible with biodiversity conservation and social justice (Spash 2010; McAfee 2012; Klein 2015).

There is much to agree with in the green economy leanings of global policy statements. It seems fair and pragmatic to try to ensure that market prices reflect the environmental costs of production, to eliminate perverse incentives which subsidise activities that we don't value, to make polluters pay for the costs they impose on others, to subsidise and pay for ecological services that are not suitably rewarded through markets, to strive for more efficient use of resources, and to strive for higher political and budgetary prioritisation for conservation. The argument of this book is not that market-based approaches are inherently the wrong thing to do (a point I will discuss further in Chapter 8) but rather that they are not a sufficient response and that over-selling them can be a dangerous diversion from addressing more fundamental drivers of environmental degradation.

In this chapter I focus primarily on distributive justice – the concern with how material costs and benefits are distributed across different groups of people, both within the current generation and across generations. There is already widespread acceptance that the outcomes of biodiversity loss are likely to hit the poor disproportionately, making them the biggest losers from global failure to meaningfully address the conservation crisis. This is acknowledged in a series of global reports:

- The livelihoods of the poor are more often directly affected by changes to ecosystem functioning (Global Forest Expert Panel 2012).
- Unique ecosystems and cultures are already at risk and we can be highly confident that the gravity of these risks will significantly increase (IPCC 2014).
- Exposure to hazards such as invasive species, fires and floods will increase due to biodiversity loss, more so for the poor (*Millennium Ecosystem Assessment* 2005; CBD 2006).
- The poor also stand to suffer more from catastrophic changes to ecosystems as tipping points are breached (CBD 2010a).
- Future generations may inherit ecosystems that are unable to meet basic needs (CBD 2010a).

This chapter also stresses the way in which social injustices play an instrumental role as a driver of biodiversity loss. As proposed in Chapter 3, perceptions of justice and injustice have an effect on the success of conservation efforts at different scales, from global negotiations to community-level project interventions. The main finding of the chapter is that the challenge of conservation cannot continue to be framed as an apolitical problem that can be solved through improved functioning of markets. Underlying issues of global and local injustice are not only *outcomes* of environmental degradation; they are also *drivers* of environmental degradation. The actions required to reduce environmental degradation therefore need to address the underlying injustices that drive them.

The injustice-extinction nexus

In 2002 world leaders signed up to a goal to reduce the rate of biodiversity loss by 2010. Failure was inevitable. The lag time required for extinction rates to equilibrate with anthropogenic environmental change is much longer than such a short-term target allows. We saw an example of this in Chapter 2, in which the elimination of apex grazers and predators can trigger trophic cascades of extirpation that take tens to hundreds of years to play out. Such delayed and typically non-linear responses can be expected to result from a number of drivers of biodiversity loss such as climate change, reactive nitrogen loads and ocean acidity. A more realistic (though clearly weaker) target would have been to reduce the drivers of extinction: to reduce carbon emissions, nitrogen-loading and so on. But even this weaker goal would have failed: these drivers have become more intense rather than less intense. In a nutshell, two decades of global effort since the 1992 Convention on Biological Diversity, and more than a century of work by various non-government conservation organisations, show no serious indications of reversing biodiversity loss (Box 5.1). In October 2014, the CBD published its 4th *Global Biodiversity Outlook* report. Whilst it found progress on some intermediary indicators, the news at the sharp end was less positive. Of 7 indicators of *pressures* on biodiversity, 6 were found to be worsening. Of 16 indicators of the *state* of biodiversity, 13 were showing significant deterioration. This all sounds dismal and demotivating but below I will suggest that if we can accept the deeply political nature of conservation, including its relationship with social injustice, we can begin a more sensible exploration of what needs to be done.

BOX 5.1 THE FAILED 2010 BIODIVERSITY TARGET

The target agreed by the world's governments in 2002 'to achieve by 2010 a significant reduction of the current rate of biodiversity loss at the global, regional and national level as a contribution to poverty alleviation and to the benefit of all life on Earth, has not been met.

There are multiple indications of continuing decline in biodiversity in all three of its main components – genes, species and ecosystems – including:

- Species which have been assessed for extinction risk are on average moving closer to extinction. Amphibians face the greatest risk and coral species are deteriorating most rapidly in status. Nearly a quarter of plant species are estimated to be threatened with extinction.
- The abundance of vertebrate species, based on assessed populations, fell by nearly a third on average between 1970 and 2006, and continues to fall globally, with especially severe declines in the tropics and among freshwater species.
- Natural habitats in most parts of the world continue to decline in extent and integrity, although there has been significant progress in slowing the rate of loss for tropical forests and mangroves, in some regions. Freshwater wetlands, sea ice habitats, salt marshes, coral reefs, seagrass beds and shellfish reefs are all showing serious decline.
- Extensive fragmentation and degradation of forests, rivers and other eco-systems has also led to loss of biodiversity and ecosystem services.
- Crop and livestock genetic diversity continues to decline in agricultural systems.
- The five principal pressures directly driving biodiversity loss (habitat change, overexploitation, pollution, invasive alien species and climate change) are either constant or increasing in intensity.
- The ecological footprint of humanity exceeds the biological capacity of the earth by a wider margin than at the time that the 2010 target was agreed.

Source: CBD (2010) *Global Biodiversity Outlook 3*, p. 9.

Failure to meet 2010 targets has been attributed to three main weaknesses: firstly, the insufficient scale of actions; secondly, limited 'mainstreaming' of biodiversity conservation into cognate policy sectors such as farming and energy; and thirdly, insufficient attention to 'indirect' or 'underlying' drivers of biodiversity loss (Figure 5.1).

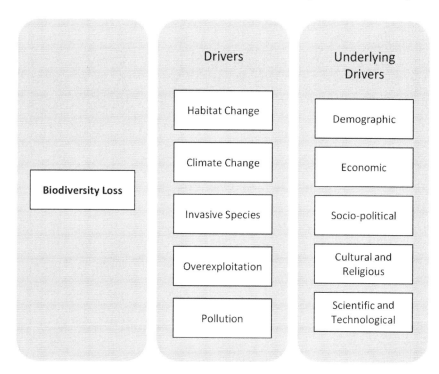

FIGURE 5.1 Underlying drivers of biodiversity loss.

Sources: Millennium Ecosystem Assessment 2005; CBD 2010a; CBD 2014.

Discussions regarding these underlying drivers have at least started to raise some important questions about the sustainability of global consumption levels. Questions about limits to growth became unfashionable in academia in the 1980s. Such ideas were associated with the Malthusian theory which links population growth to unsustainable use of resources that fails to properly account for the transformational power of technological advance. Instead of being framed in terms of limits to consumption, sustainable development became defined as sustainable economic growth – a world in which technological efficiency could perpetuate our cornucopian dreams (O'Riordan 1981). Growth in gross domestic product (GDP) remained largely unchallenged as the measure of a state's performance, and it was assumed that the green economy could serve this goal. More recently, the assumption that GDP growth is an appropriate metric of progress has seen renewed criticism. For example, in 2008, the then French president, Sarkozy, established the Commission on the Measurement of Economic Performance and Social Progress. In their report, this team of Nobel-winning economists (Stiglitz et al. 2009) analogised global and national economic management to a pilot 'flying blind' – guided by a measure of progress and wellbeing (GDP) that was basically not up to the task. And yet economic growth – measured by GDP – remains the everyday measure of whether our economies are doing well or not.

The CBD has largely resisted joining the critique of mainstream economic analysis. As a result, attention to underlying drivers of biodiversity loss, in particular the growth and distribution of consumption, remains tokenistic. *Global Biodiversity Outlook 3* (CBD 2010) ultimately back-tracks into the safety of green economy discourse, under the frankly curious assertion that underlying drivers can be addressed by 'decoupling' them from direct drivers, which can be achieved 'primarily by using resources much more efficiently' (p. 67). In other words we can continue to grow consumption and pursue GDP growth because we will find ever more efficient and renewable ways to produce the things we consume. GBO 4 (CBD 2014) maintains this emphasis on increasing resource use efficiency but also hints at the need to also reduce global demand for resources, suggesting that we will need to 'rethink our consumption habits' (p. 10). Ultimately, however, the report remains vague and weak on the more politically difficult matters of consumption and its distributional dimensions. The overall impression is still that we can use efficiency gains to decouple our growing demand for resource consumption from harmful impacts on the environment.

Questions about the decoupling of the economy from demand for environmental resources and pollution sinks can be answered empirically (Martínez Alier 2009b). The question to be answered might go something like this: after thirty years of attempting to decouple economic growth from environmental degradation, what empirical evidence is there that this is working? I begin by considering this evidence more generally, finding little to support claims that the global economy has been dematerialising in this way. I will then introduce a distributional dimension to the question, asking whether 'over-consumption' by some places is part and parcel of constrained consumption in others – or in other words, that the economic structuring of the world which allows affluence to grow in some parts is unjust because it simultaneously produces poverty in other parts. I suggest that this nexus of material growth and distributional injustice is a fundamental underlying driver of biodiversity loss.

Under-consumption, over-consumption

Notions of under- and over-consumption are partly cultural constructions but also connect with biophysical thresholds of human bodies and of the earth system itself. The assertion that some people don't have access to sufficient materials or energy is hardly controversial – the facts are sadly familiar. 870 million people (about 1 in 8 of the global population) are chronically undernourished (FAO 2012); 780 million have no access to clean water sources (UNICEF/WHO 2012); 2.5 billion have no basic sanitation, leading to an estimated 1.5 million preventable deaths each year (WWAP 2012); 1.8 billion have no access to electricity (World Bank 2013). As argued in Chapter 4, resources such as clean water can be considered as human needs rather than wants, because their absence is likely to lead to serious harm (Doyal and Gough 1991). Such requirements for adequate physical health can be considered as underpinning a decent set of capabilities and associated life choices. Indeed, to deny such capabilities (when there is enough to go around) is considered by cosmopolitan thinkers to be an injustice for which the world at large is responsible: for ethical cosmopolitans, our moral responsibilities do not end at national borders (see e.g. Pogge 2002; Brock 2009).

Proclamations that some nations or individuals over-consume are difficult to support objectively. 'Over-consumption' is obviously a subjective assessment that depends amongst other things on how optimistic protagonists are about 'decoupling'. The term 'social metabolism' is helpful to this discussion. It refers to the biophysical flows between human societies and ecological systems, in terms of the materials and energy dissipated by the economy. Rockström and colleagues (2009) argue the need to limit global material throughputs in ways that keep us within a 'safe operating space for humanity'. They accept that any such 'planetary boundaries' are hard to define and are in essence normative judgments about risk tolerance. But they also maintain that it is better to have imperfect measures of what is safe than to have no measures at all. Like it or not, humans have put themselves in the position of planetary managers – for example we are now constructors of climates rather than passive receivers of climates – and some indicators of where to steer are crucial. Earth systems science has taught us that most environmental change occurs as a non-linear rather than smooth response to changing pressures, and also that shifts to undesirable states typically follow tipping points or thresholds.

Rockström et al. (2009) identify three boundaries that have already been exceeded. Firstly, we have exceeded the atmospheric concentrations of greenhouse gases that would restrict global warming to 2°C above pre-industrial global means. 1.5 to 2°C is currently accepted by the United Nations Framework Convention on Climate Change as the target threshold to avoid dangerous and runaway climate change (Schellnhuber et al. 2016). Secondly, we have exceeded safe levels of nutrient loadings for reactive nitrogen and phosphorous and thirdly, we have exceeded safe levels of extinction rates (as discussed in Chapter 2). Indeed, of all planetary limits, biodiversity loss is the one that has been overshot by the furthest. Defining boundaries for biodiversity loss is clearly not an exact science and their threshold is undeniably a bit arbitrary – Rockström and colleagues suggest we should stick within an extinction rate of 10 per million species per annum (current rates are more than ten times that). These and other boundaries are connected; for example, we know that nutrient loading and climate change are themselves drivers of species loss.

The purpose of this book is not only to support a safe operating space for humanity, but a safe *and just* operating space (Raworth 2012 ; Steffen and Smith 2013). Can this be achieved whilst maintaining current levels of consumption enjoyed by the more affluent groups? The answer is surely only if this allows (in principle at least) scope for some to consume more whilst still remaining within boundaries that protect future people. This would require a strong degree of decoupling of economic growth from social metabolism. I will briefly review a selection of measures by which decoupling can be explored empirically. Not one of these provides any global-level evidence of absolute decoupling and indeed all point to a growing metabolism in spite of half a century of environmental economics as a discipline and more than a quarter of a century since these ideas became the cornerstone of global environmental policy regimes (WCED 1987; Pearce et al. 1989).

At the planetary scale, metabolism continues to rise, with increasing demand for materials, energy and waste sinks being driven by rising per capita consumption, rising population and, in some cases, decreasing efficiency of resource use. Global carbon dioxide emissions continue to grow year on year (Friedlingstein et al. 2014). A 1.8% reduction in 2009, associated with the economic crisis, was quickly followed by 4.9% growth in 2010. Whilst the switch to non-fossil fuels has reduced the amount of CO_2 emission per unit of primary energy supply, it has only reduced this ratio by 6% over 39 years (OECD 2013). Whilst further switching to new energy sources is widely hailed as a strategy for mitigating climate change (IEA 2008; Chum et al. 2011), there is growing evidence to suggest that this might simply intensify other threats to biodiversity and human wellbeing. For example, the race for alternatives to fossil fuels involves the extension of uranium mining into the fragile, ancient and endemic-rich Namib desert and the planned extraction of lithium in Bolivia's Salar de Uyuni basin (Friedman-Rudovsky 2011). The switch to bioethanol and biodiesel are similarly creating new frontiers for land use and extraction, as well as further pressures for deforestation, and also forms of land-grabbing. These new land acquisitions are concentrated in some of the world's poorest places (see Table 5.1) creating new sources of dispossession and food insecurity for marginalised people. These resource frontiers are increasingly the locations of environmental justice struggles in the South (Borras et al. 2011; Muradian et al. 2012).

The measure of human appropriation of net primary production (HANPP) provides a useful indicator of social metabolism, combining the amount of biomass harvested by humans as well as the amount of change to net primary

TABLE 5.1 Top ten target countries for large-scale land acquisitions

Country	Area of transnational land acquisitions
Papua New Guinea	3,792,653 ha
Russian Federation	3,363,012 ha
Indonesia	3,235,335 ha
DRC	3,155,258 ha
Brazil	2,745,758 ha
South Sudan	2,691,453 ha
Mozambique	2,448,695 ha
Ukraine	2,404,407 ha
Congo	2,148,000 ha
Argentina	1,582,516 ha

Source: Land Matrix 2016.

Note: Data includes contracts signed since 2000, for deals over 200 hectares, involving conversion of land from community or ecosystem protection use to commercial use.

productivity as a result of human land use (Krausmann et al. 2013). Globally, HANPP has almost doubled in the last century, from 13% of the potential NPP under native vegetation in the early 20th century to 25% in 2005 (Krausmann et al. 2013). This represents a relative decoupling of HANPP pressure from population growth and GDP (which have grown much faster), but not an absolute decoupling. HANPP per capita continues to correlate with income and consumption and the big picture shows rising metabolism despite considerable efficiency gains (Krausmann et al. 2013).

Talk of 'efficiency gains' is cause for a word of caution. HANPP efficiency has been largely achieved through the intensification of agriculture, including switches from animal draught energy to fossil fuels. Such efficiencies are therefore only gained at the expense of other critical drivers of biodiversity loss: climate change and nutrient loading. The inter-related nature of the drivers of biodiversity loss (and environmental tipping points more generally) appears to be closing down the opportunities for solutions. For example, whilst bioenergy has been advocated as a solution to climate change, if this went ahead at rates envisaged by the IPCC, it would increase HANPP by 78% over its current value by 2050, leading to a 'transformative effect on the planet' (Krausmann et al. 2013, p. 5). These connections – wherein so-called 'efficiency gains' for one form of ecological appropriation might lead to enhanced pressures for another – is one reason why aggregate concepts such as metabolism are useful. A similar point might be made about geographical patterns of consumption. For example, there are considerable regional differences in the level of decoupling of economic growth from resource and energy consumption.

Figure 5.2 shows indicators for both absolute and relative decoupling. The metabolic rate of the economy is a measure of how many tonnes of material are extracted per person and show the metabolic rate of the global economy. This grew from 7.9 tonnes to 10.1 tonnes per person between 2000 and 2010. The material intensity (or material efficiency) of the global economy has historically been reducing – meaning that there has been some decoupling of GDP growth from material extraction. However, this historical trend has been reversed in the early twenty-first century. In 2000, it took 1.2 kg of materials to produce $1 of GDP; in 2010 this had risen to 1.4kg per $1 (UNEP 2016).

So the global picture is that despite a quarter of a century of placing decoupling as the cornerstone of global environmental policy, this trend has been reversed rather than strengthened. This is the result of the relocation of production to locations with comparatively low material efficiency and includes rising material intensity of the Chinese economy which, matched with rapid economic growth, is greatly enhancing extractive pressures both domestically and through imports (UNEP 2016).

Ecological footprints provide another measure of human consumption that presents use of natural resources and energy in relation to the capacity of global ecological supply. Consumption is expressed in terms of 'global hectares' required to supply particular resources, with overall global consumption expressed as the

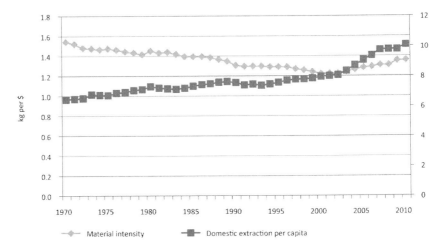

FIGURE 5.2 Global material intensity (kg domestic extraction per $ GDP) and metabolic rate (domestic extraction per capita).

Source: UNEP 2016: 41.

number of planets required to meet total social metabolism. In 2007 the global ecological footprint was calculated at about 1.5 planet earths, meaning that current consumption overshoots the capacity of the earth's ecosystems (Ewing et al. 2010). The global ecological footprint has been growing and again shows no absolute decoupling from economic growth. High-income countries have the highest per capita footprints, with per capita footprints rising from an average 3.8 global hectares in 1961 to 6.1 hectares in 2007. Low-income countries have seen per capita footprints falling to around 1.2 global hectares. Furthermore, countries with the smallest ecological footprints are likely to be those with the highest levels of poverty, as measured for example by the Human Development Index. The conclusion by the Global Footprint Network is that 'relying on a growing level of consumption to attain sustainable well-being for all is unrealistic' (Ewing et al. 2010, p. 21).

Ecological imperialism and unequal ecological exchange

I turn now to the uneven distribution of consumption and the suggestion that consumption by some goes hand in hand with injustice for others. In doing so, I seek to make connections between issues of ecological distribution and social distribution, including how these relate to continued growth in metabolism and associated environmental pressures.

The term 'ecological imperialism' was originally used by Alfred Crosby (1986) to explain how European empire-building up until 1900 went hand in hand with biological expansion, including the export of domesticated species and human pathogens to the tropics. Crosby noted two structural forms of ecological imperialism; firstly, colonialism that involved occupation and an imposed system of social organisation and, secondly, the penetration of the capitalist mode of organisation through incorporation into the world economy. In the twenty-first century, ecological imperialism takes on a slightly different face, but still involves the expansion of more and more territories and commodities into global trade, involving both biological impositions and plunders. Whilst Crosby focused largely on the material aspects of imperialism and the use of political and, where necessary, military power to enforce this, recent years have also seen more attention afforded to the discursive powers which underpin imperialist structuring of the world economy. This involves the incorporation of people and places into dominant ideologies that determine the values, languages and metrics that structure global management of the environment.

My own thinking about ecological imperialism derives from the discipline of ecological economics which has intellectual foundations in the laws of thermodynamics that govern social metabolism. The overlapping systems that form the context for conservation (ecosystems, cultural systems, political and economic systems) do not behave in uniform and linear ways – their behaviour is complex. They are made up of many constituent elements that are related to each other through processes of interaction and exchange. At the same time, understanding system behaviours cannot be reduced to the sum of such relationships. Systems exhibit self-organisational behaviours which transcend isolated relationships and which can often only be observed as emergent properties of whole systems. Living systems such as plants appear to defy the second law of thermodynamics by creating order instead of entropy (Kay and Schneider 1995). Genes in a developing embryo create order from the disorder of atmospheric gases and ingested nutrients to form organs such as skin, and ultimately to form an animal life form. Plants and animals interact with each other and with atmospheric gases, soils and so on to form complex ecosystem structures. People acting independently and socially organise themselves into economies and cultures and societies. In short, elements seeking mutual accommodation somehow transcend themselves to create emergent forms of order (Huckle and Martin 2001). Such systems are described as being 'far from equilibrium', because emergent order is always at the expense of the larger global entropy budget. It is a sort of temporary aberration of thermodynamic equilibrium – a deferral of maximised entropy. Systems far from equilibrium need to rearrange themselves in ways that respond to changes in their environments – changes in resource and energy inputs – and such emergent behaviours are neither linear nor easily predictable. This is the domain of thresholds, tipping points, state-changes and runaway environmental change.

Socio-ecological systems, such as cities, states and regions, are likewise sometimes thought of as dissipative systems that maintain their internal structures whilst far from equilibrium, drawing from their environments and exporting disorder. Understanding how these social units go about maintaining their integrity has been an area of research for those working on social metabolism and unequal ecological exchange, such as Joan Martínez Alier in Barcelona and Alf Hornborg in Lund.

Hornborg states that 'The question we must address is: if organisms draw order into their systems by eating, and export disorder by discharging waste materials, heat, etc., how do cities go about doing it? How do world system centres do it?' (Hornborg 1998, p. 131).

World systems analysis (Wallerstein 1984) proposes that since most places and resources have been progressively incorporated into a global economy, we need to examine the workings of this world system in order to understand uneven economic development. Drawing on Marxist theory of economic structuring, it proposes that places in historically advantageous positions (the 'core') are able to drive the structure of the world economy. They do this via market institutions but also by force where necessary; and they do it in ways that perpetuate their own advantage, incorporating other places, peoples and resources (the 'periphery') into the economy on unequal terms. The resultant structuring of the world economy meets the needs of historically dominant states, initially in Europe but more recently also in Japan, the United States and China. The theory of unequal ecological exchange (Hornborg 1998; Rice 2007; Jorgensen 2009; Martínez Alier 2009a) connects this vision of global economic imperialism with the concept of social metabolism to propose a theory of environmental exploitation. The basic proposition is that inequity, growing metabolism and environmental problems are deeply intertwined. A derivative proposition is that the green economy basically serves to reproduce, deepen and widen these underlying drivers of the biodiversity crisis.

The theory of unequal ecological exchange points to a historical structuring of the global economic system which in effect means that those parts of the world which were early to industrialise and accumulate wealth have been able to fix the terms of ecological exchange, notably through terms of trade. They have been able to do so in ways which favour their own continued accumulation but which have contributed to continued impoverishment and environmental degradation in other parts of the world. For Martínez Alier (2009a, 2012), such unequal exchange is the mechanism that guarantees the metabolic processes that maintain order in (far from equilibrium) world centres. This inequitable structuring is sometimes maintained by brute force and at other times by controlling decision-making institutions and procedures, including international biodiversity negotiations. For many, capitalism is itself a driver of current environmental crisis, owing to its ultimately self-destructive requirement for continual economic growth (O'Connor 1993) and through the mechanisms of commodification and pricing that enfold ever more places and materials into the expanding frontiers of the world economy (Muradian et al. 2012; Sullivan 2013).

Rice (2007) similarly argues that it is the structuring of international trade which shapes the metabolism of different places at different positions in a hierarchy within the global economy, with unfair and disadvantageous terms of trade being the driver that allows two main undesirable outcomes: firstly, environmental cost-shifting (places enjoying the benefits of resource dissipation whilst exporting associated costs to others) and secondly, disproportionate and uncompensated use of resources and sinks that limit opportunities for others.

Protecting biodiversity and alleviating poverty is not a cost issue so much as a structuring issue – this is a key point that is missing in much mainstream analysis including the global conservation policy documents cited at the start of this chapter. For Hornborg, the continued transfer of energy and materials to maintain world cities is 'organised' by (or structured by) market institutions and in particular by price. Rising metabolism, and continued inequities, can be explained by the fact that the market is structured so that manufacturers must always be paid more money for their products than they paid for the inputs. Thus, the more materials and energy that they dissipate today, the more money they will have to buy more resources tomorrow. It is this accumulative tendency inherent in market exchange that drives industrial development, new technologies and more generally the social appropriation of nature.

> We can observe that the resources imported to industrial centres are transformed into quantities of products vastly greater than the fraction which is returned to their peripheries. And we must ask by what ideological means this unequal exchange is represented as reciprocal exchange.
>
> *(Hornborg 1998, p. 133)*

The answer for Hornborg is the notion of market price, the underlying logic of unequal exchange. Thus, whilst neoclassical economics rules out the very notion of a market transaction being unjust, a world systems approach to ecological economics identifies it as fundamental.

We can all think of cases that seem to support this vision of a nexus between Western consumption, threats to biodiversity and threats to the wellbeing of the poor: oil extraction destroying agriculture and fisheries in the Niger Delta; indigenous peoples losing their land to palm oil production in Amazonia; the loss of coastal paddy fields in Asia to supply Europeans with prawns. But the theory of unequal ecological exchange needs to go beyond anecdotal evidence. What is the evidence that the global economic system, in conjunction with its associated ideologies, institutions and measures of progress (GDP), really organises the world in ways that allow high-consuming industrial economies to externalise their real environmental costs, shift the burden geographically and, in the process, constrain the quality of life for those who are already poor? Jorgenson (2009, p. 42) talks of 'mounting evidence of more affluent societies treating less affluent societies as natural resource taps and waste sinks'. But how strong is the evidence?

Economists have long described a 'resource curse' phenomenon (Rice 2010) whereby countries and regions that are rich in tradable natural resources tend to achieve lower human welfare than others. Furthermore, Jorgenson (2009) confirms that the low-income countries that export most to higher-income countries have the lowest ecological footprints (lowest domestic consumption) and the highest rates of malnutrition, infant mortality and other measures of material deprivation. Indeed, his analysis of 25 years of ecological footprint data shows that low-income countries suffered a 10.5% reduction in per capita consumption from 1975 to 2000 whilst high-income countries saw a growth of 16.8%. Given that material exports from low-income countries grew significantly during that period, this is highly suggestive of structural disadvantage suppressing consumption in low-income countries. Bruckner et al.'s (2012) study of materials embodied in international trade adds weight to this finding. During 1995 to 2005 he finds around a 50% growth in materials embodied in international trade, from 10.1 to 14.9 billion tonnes per annum. During that period, high-income (OECD) countries were, on average, net importers of material (rising from 4.3 to 7 billion tonnes of annual net import) whilst the rest of the world exported corresponding amounts.

A further clue to unequal ecological exchange is the observed paradox that those who consume the least of a resource can be the ones who suffer the most from its exploitation. Forests are the most cited example for this, with many higher-income countries being major consumers of both hardwood and soft-wood timbers, and achieve this whilst protecting and increasing their domestic woodlands. Low-income countries consume much less timber but currently experience more deforestation (Rice 2010). This is 'burden-shifting'. It is important to note that it does not hold across all resources and that high-income countries such as Canada, Norway and Australia are themselves net exporters of raw material (Bruckner et al. 2012; Moran et al. 2013). However, Lenzen and colleagues (2012) provide evidence that burden-shifting does occur for loss of biodiversity – meaning that those countries who place most pressure on biodiversity suffer the fewest threats to domestic biodiversity, and vice versa. They connect 25,000 IUCN Red List threatened species to 15,000 commodities, incorporating any associations between product and threat. For example, the threat to the spider monkey in Mexico and Central America is associated with coffee and cocoa plantations. They then trace the trade in these products to final consumption and calculate imports and exports of biodiversity threats at a national level. The result is striking, with the USA, Japan and Europe being the main importers of biodiversity-threatening products whilst low- and middle-income countries such as Indonesia, Madagascar and Papua New Guinea bear the burden (Figure 5.3). Whilst our main interest here is biodiversity, it is worth noting that Bruckner et al. (2012) find a similar result for their broader study of materials embodied in international trade. Although exceptions exist, there has been a 25% increase in material extraction globally, a growth which has occurred at an order of magnitude higher in non-OECD countries than OECD ones; additionally, trade serves to structure this so that the consumption gap is widening. In other words, they find strong evidence for unequal ecological exchange.

International trade is generally considered to be the engine of unequal ecological exchange, evidenced by deteriorating terms of trade for commodities vis-à-vis manufactured goods. Over the very long term – meaning four centuries – there has been a deterioration in the market exchange value for most primary commodities (Harvey et al. 2010). Over the past century, the picture has been a bit more complicated and there has been roughly a halving in the real prices of commodities. This has been concentrated in periods during which the global economy was re-ordering following

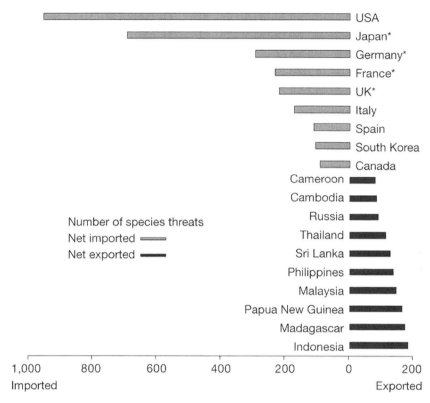

FIGURE 5.3   Top net importers and exporters of biodiversity threats.

Source: Lenzen et al. 2012: 109.

significant shocks – after the 1920s recession and after the oil crisis of 1979 (Ocampo and Parra-Lancourt 2010). However, there was some improvement in the terms of trade for commodities in the early 2000s, stimulated by a rising demand for materials from China, and a corresponding rise in the supply of manufactured goods (Muradian et al. 2012).

Taking stock of the evidence summarised here, it is fair to say that there has been a growth in the export of resource-intensive materials from low-income to high-income countries. The long-run trend has been for the terms of this trade to deteriorate such that exporters receive less revenue for their product whilst paying more for their imports, but there is some more recent evidence that such a trend can be reversed, as seen in the early twenty-first century, driven by the Chinese economic boom. Low-income countries with high exports of raw materials often suffer from a resource curse and this is particularly true for those who deal most with high-income countries. For biodiversity loss, deforestation and climate change, there is pretty strong evidence that burden-shifting occurs: consumption in high-income countries is the principal driver of these problems, but the greater costs fall to low-income countries. However, it is important to note that such burden-shifting cannot be generalised to all industrial pollutants because high-income countries still dominate production. There is clearly still room for interpretation of the evidence but it is hard not to conclude that the economic system is indeed structured in ways that: (a) guarantee the social metabolism in its centres; (b) perpetuate inequitable consumption; and (c) perpetuate continued environmental degradation. The current phase of the world economy is marked by the increasing reliance of Europe and Japan on resource imports and cost-shifting, with China now joining this club and India also facing increasing pressures to cost-shift as a result of growing resistance amongst its people to domestic extraction (Muradian et al. 2012). Such patterns of material exchange are a crucial part of the explanation for why targets for biodiversity conservation and poverty alleviation have been missed.

Studies of international trade are only one part of the evidence for unequal ecological exchange. The other evidence is the rise in conflicts at the new commodity frontiers (Peluso and Lund 2011; Muradian et al. 2012; Temper et al. 2015; Martínez Alier et al. 2016). Environmental justice struggles are sprouting up across these multiple frontiers, opposing land grabs for biofuels, lithium mining and fracking, campaigning against loss of local fisheries and a host of other frontiers that are so hard to fight against because, to do so, is to fight against the metabolism of world centres. Thus, the theory of unequal ecological exchange and social metabolism is ultimately a theory of environmental conflict. To oppose resource extraction and dispossession in the periphery is not only to oppose the specific environmental threat of individual cases but also to oppose the bigger assemblage of ideas and powers that structure the economy and enfold people in systems of unequal exchange. This is one reason why we now see growing opposition to the green economy from those nations and peoples whose wellbeing is increasingly threatened by market expansion. Both non-green and green economies currently present openings at the new resource frontiers, through opportunities to sell resources at relatively high prices (non-green), and through opportunities to be rewarded for not exploiting those resources (green). But even the 'green' opportunities may carry a burden for peripheries, because the expansion of market relations to incorporate more and more of nature's goods and services is a process that reinforces the very structures that perpetuate unequal ecological exchange in the first place.

Seen from the periphery, the ability to reconfigure this status quo appears limited. In 2009 the government of Ecuador requested $3.6 billion of international funding as payment to offset half of the income that would be foregone by not exploiting oil reserves in an important block of the Yasuni National Park. It is an interesting case because it tested, amongst other things, whether guardians of biological and cultural treasures could take advantage of global concern for biodiversity and turn this into effective demands for a non-extractive model of economic development. In this case, the answer seems to be no. By late 2013, having secured only a small fraction of the required payment, president Rafael Correa abandoned the idea and drilling for oil began in early 2016. The area is home to two previously uncontacted tribes (Guardian 2013, 2016).

Conclusions: consequences and solutions

What I have tried to argue in this chapter is that market-based, green economy responses seem unlikely to offer a timely solution to the biodiversity crisis. We undoubtedly need more efficient use of natural resources and this will be supported by more functional markets in which the values of ecosystem services are better represented. Given the prevailing political economy that we live in, the reality is that markets are an important way in which social preferences gain traction, and it is generally a good thing to make it feasible to express environmental preferences through market mechanisms.

However, I have opted to take a largely empirical view on whether a quarter of a century or more of global commitment to a green economy – to economic growth made sustainable by technological gains in efficiency – has really shown the way. The evidence says no. Indicators of the state of biodiversity show decline across most domains. Worse still, indicators of the drivers of these states are mostly also moving in the wrong direction. This is despite increases in the amount of effort being put into specific interventions such as expansion of protected areas networks. As far as it is possible to explain this in a simple equation, the consumptive pressures of social metabolism continue to increase at a faster rate than do the gains in efficiency that come from investments in technology. There will almost certainly be a future 'turning point' where efficiency gains outstrip rising demand, and we start to see actual reductions in biodiversity loss, and actual climate change mitigation. But it would be foolish to proceed with a blind hope that this will occur soon enough to steer us towards planetary safety.

The metabolism that drives us further beyond planetary safety is intimately connected to historical drivers of social and environmental injustice. I have described these as forms of ecological imperialism and unequal ecological exchange. The evidence for hard and unchanging mechanisms of unequal ecological exchange is admittedly not watertight. For example, new urban centres of consumption are able to rise up in places like China and India, whilst some of the older centres in Europe show signs of reducing the ecological burdens they place on peripheries. And since the turn of the millennium we have seen some reversal in the terms of trade between raw materials and manufactured goods, driven by demand from the Chinese economy. But whilst unequal ecological exchange might not offer a complete theory to predict environmental injustice and uneven development, it nonetheless provides a helpful lens through which to grasp the general relationship between dominant political-economic goals (GDP growth in world centres), the material flows that are necessary to support these far-from-equilibrium metropolises, and the ways in which these ultimately drive biodiversity loss in distant places. Even demand for superficially benign consumptions such as non-fossil fuels frequently creates pressures on both biodiversity and human capabilities at the resource frontiers where the environmentalism of the poor often plays out as justice struggles. Hundreds of examples of these frontiers can be seen on the database and map produced by the Environmental Justice Organisations, Liabilities and Trade project based in Barcelona (Temper et al. 2015; www.ejolt.org).

Neoliberalism cannot be the answer to these underlying drivers of consumption and injustice. Indeed, what are hailed as green economy 'solutions' by some stakeholders are already being cast as environmental justice 'problems' by others. Markets are not altruistic. They do not favour those with the least economic power and have been seen, even over periods of centuries, to largely serve to secure the advantages of those already well situated (Piketty 2014). As such, markets are an unlikely mechanism for redistributing current global consumption, or for striving to meet the capability thresholds that I proposed as a basic benchmark of social justice in Chapter 4. Increasingly we understand that some kind of redistribution can be a win-win outcome. The wealthiest 85 people in the world are said to have as much wealth as the poorest 3.5 billion (Oxfam 2014). As for the poorest, we know that in most cases, being deprived of certain basic capabilities is detrimental to happiness. The case for neoliberal approaches to market environmentalism is very thin indeed. Even at national level, there is mounting evidence that rising wealth inequality is not only bad for the environment but bad for welfare. It seems that, domestically at least, we take no pleasure in viewing the disadvantage of others. Reassuringly, we feel quite the opposite (Wilkinson and Pickett 2010).

As I said at the start of this chapter, linking solutions to the biodiversity crisis with the need for global wealth redistribution might seem a bit daunting. Must conservationists really take on neoliberalism and capitalism? How can we ever make progress on such a vastly ambitious endeavour? I think the pragmatic solution is not to give up on many of the things that are already being done and that are achieving some positive outcomes. The point is to additionally bring politics back into conservation – to be honest about the fact that the environment is political.

The economy requires forms of management that markets alone cannot achieve if we are to steer towards more safe and just environmental futures. I am not going to try to map out the guidelines for such management, but it will likely involve some form of negotiated 'contraction and convergence' – progress towards more equal and just levels of consumption that will necessarily require managed contraction of consumption for some. What does this mean in practice for global conservation platforms, biodiversity conservation NGOs, and the large constituencies of environmental social movements? Should they support individual policies that commodify nature for exchange on markets, such as payments for ecosystem services (PES) and biodiversity offsetting? Should they work more closely with private sector partners such as RioTinto, Walmart or Barclays? For my part, I see no fundamental reason not to engage in approaches such as PES. I will justify that position more in later chapters, but for now let me just mention that most operational PES schemes have far less to do with markets than is typically assumed – and in some cases rather more to do with governments and other agencies seeking positive action to redistribute costs and benefits. But at the same time we as conservationists need to be on the serious side of arguments about the economy and sustainability more generally. Being on the side of inappropriate metrics of social progress, of rising inequality and its underlying structures, is not being on the right side.

6

JUSTICE AS RECOGNITION

Reconciling social justice with environmental sustainability

Introduction[1]

Since the 1980s, public intellectuals have observed a shift in the basis for social struggles. In decline are the old, socialist struggles that call for the redistribution of economic goods. On the rise are new social movements which articulate claims for social justice based on the right to be culturally different and to be respected. It is a shift from the politics of the economy to the politics of identity and a shift from justice claims based on the ill-distribution of wealth to justice claims based on lack of recognition.

Recognition is relational, indivisible and multi-layered. It is inherently relational, because a person's freedom is dependent on the respect they receive from others towards their own culture and identity. To live a dignified life I not only need the right to pursue my own cultural preferences, but I also need that these choices are not stigmatised in the eyes of others. Recognition is indivisible because respect cannot be apportioned in the way that say forest tenure or park revenues can be. Nor does it need to be: to respect one person or people does not draw down on a global stock of respect in a way that reduces what is available for others. The conduct of recognition is multi-layered because it is produced and reproduced through the everyday cultural practices of the population at large, but also through formal institutional channels which include laws and policies. Thus gender discrimination can be perpetuated by dominant cultural dispositions which devalue particular functions such as caring and domestic work, and by formal

---

1 This chapter owes a lot of debts to those I have worked with as co-authors and as participants in workshops at UEA and elsewhere. In particular I have learned a lot from co-writing a paper on conservation and justice with Sian Sullivan and Shawn McGuire (Martin et al. 2013b) and a paper on conservation and recognition with Brendan Coolsaet, Esteve Corbera, Neil Dawson, James Fraser, Ina Lehmann and Iokiñe Rodríguez (Martin et al. 2016).

and customary ways of inscribing such discrimination, such as national systems of accounts that render these types of productive activities invisible.

Frances Fukuyama recalls a story about the origins of the Arab Spring. In early 2011, a Tunisian vegetable seller had his stall confiscated by police who insulted and hit him. He was then repeatedly ignored by authorities when he tried to complain. The grim response was to set himself on fire, triggering such widespread empathy and anger that governments started to fall.

> What was it about this act that provoked such a response? The basic issue was one of *dignity*, or the lack thereof, the feeling of worth or self-esteem that all of us seek. But dignity is not felt unless it is *recognised* by other people; it is an inherently social and, indeed, political phenomenon. The Tunisian police were treating Bouazizi as a nonperson, someone not worthy of the basic courtesy of a reply or explanation when the government took away his modest means of livelihood. It was what Ralph Ellison described as the situation of a black man in early 20th-century America, an Invisible Man not seen as a full human being by white people.
>
> *(Fukuyama 2012 n.p.)*

Recognition injustice is concerned with discrimination against particular groups of people based on their economic and cultural difference from more dominant groups. It is especially pertinent to contemporary conservation for three main reasons. Firstly, those areas of the earth's terrestrial surface that are most valued for conservation often overlap with areas of high social diversity including societies with diverse ways of knowing and living with nature (Stepp et al. 2004; Gorenflo et al. 2012). Secondly, the groups of people who live in these areas are often politically and economically marginalised, making them more vulnerable to discriminatory practices (Escobar 1998; Brosius and Hitchner 2010). Histories of the Amazonian Indians, southern African bushpeople and Central African forest cultures invariably record a litany of shameful atrocities including enslavement and genocide. Thirdly, there is a danger that biodiversity conservation will become the new motivation and process for reproducing discrimination, for example by undermining efforts of indigenous peoples to retain or regain ancestral territories, or by continuing to commodify nature within a 'green economy' and thereby imposing values that are not shared locally. A host of studies have now documented cases where the imposed morality of conservation has led to displacement of people, loss of access and associated threats to cultural survival (Chapin 2004; Neumann 2004; West 2006; Whiteman 2009).

In the last chapter I took a global view of distributional injustices related to conservation. This chapter complements that by focusing on recognition. However, one of the main points of the current chapter is that distribution and recognition should not be treated as isolated categories of justice, but as inter-twined and having connected roots. My intention is that this bridge between distribution and recognition will also help to build a bridge between social and environmental justice. As Fukuyama's example is intended to illustrate, social justice has taken a cultural turn, embracing concerns for respect and identity. During the same decades that this change has taken place, the environmental justice movement has emerged and has been dominated by concerns about the distribution of costs and benefits – who benefits most from resource use and who suffers most from the resulting pollution (Vincent 1998; Warren 1999; Dobson 2003; Walker 2012). These distinct trajectories would seem to suggest that social and environmental justice operate in parallel and are unconnected to each other. But that is unsatisfactory and this chapter develops a more integrative approach that owes much to feminist philosophies of justice.

Conceptualising recognition injustice

There is considerable debate about the nature of the harm that results from recognition injustice, and the extent to which such harm is distinct from that arising from inequitable distribution. The German philosopher Hegel is considered a seminal thinker about recognition and for him the harm arising from failures of recognition is subjective and psychological. The potential for harm lies in the fact that we can only be free and feel positive self-worth if others recognise our freedom and worth. Injustice occurs where the opposite happens – where people consistently experience the derogating gaze of those in dominant cultural groups, resulting in negative self-esteem and loss of freedom to pursue one's own cultural preferences. To treat somebody's knowledge as inferior – to force upon them a sense of inferiority – is to remove their freedom and enslave them. It is to deny them their identity in a way that causes actual psychological suffering and ill health (Ohenjo et al. 2006; Coulthard 2007). Malrecognition is also exercised through representation. For example, popular artists from the 'grand masters' of oil painting to contemporary photographers have tended to represent women as subjects of male sexual desire rather than seeking to represent their own identities (Berger 2008 [1972]). Feminists have long argued that suppressing a group's identity – by whatever means – causes harm and is an injustice.

Hegel's subjective and psychological framing of recognition is highly informative, but for Nancy Fraser it is a mistake to allow this to lead us into an identity-based politics of recognition:

> Without doubt, this identity model contains some genuine insights into the psychological effects of racism, sexism, colonization and cultural imperialism. Yet it is theoretically and politically problematic. By equating the politics of recognition with identity politics, it encourages both the reification of group identities and the displacement of redistribution.
>
> *(Fraser 2000, p. 110)*

To reify group identities such as ethnicity or religion – to treat someone primarily as 'a Muslim' or as 'a San bushperson' – is to treat these as concrete social and political categories that can be used to analyse problems and shape actions. This is theoretically problematic both because individuals are not only defined in terms of cultural identity groups and because identities are at any rate hybridised and evolving. To think about or to treat people as off-the-peg clones of a community or cultural group is what Amartya Sen calls an act of 'appalling miniaturisation' based on the mistaken perception that human identities are formed through membership of a single group (Sen 2007).

Various ethnographic studies of conservation stakeholders confirm Sen's view that identities are far more complex and multiple than such a reified conceptualisation would hold. Three examples will suffice. Firstly, Sian Sullivan's work on Namibian conservancies finds a 'communalising discourse' among conservation practitioners in which ethnicity and community are wrongly perceived as unchanging and homogeneous social categories that can be used to understand and anticipate what individuals want (Sullivan 2002). Secondly, Elizabeth Povinelli's (2002) study of Australian aborigines observes the 'moral panic' that individuals can face when deciding whether to oppose or welcome a mining development on ancestral lands. This arises precisely because cultures do not provide unambiguous and unchanging moral guidance about what is the right thing to do. Instead, individual identities combine traditional and new ideas in complex and personal ways, resulting in inevitable dissonances and quandaries. Thirdly, Paige West's (2006a) study of views of conservation among the Gimi-speaking peoples of Papua New Guinea confirms how such evolving and complex identities vary dramatically from person to person, in some cases influenced by age, gender and other social positions. She found that some people retain a cultural preference for forest-based ways of life and have started to perceive conservation as an activity that is aligned with this. For others, however, the idea of conservation is thoroughly meaningless. It conflicts with their ontology of nature, according to which all matter exists forever and organisms such as plants and animals are never lost but merely change form. Others have acquired a more Westernised worldview, wanting 'capitalism and modernity writ large', and preferring to replace forest-based livelihoods with businesses, cars and hotels. In all three examples, affirmative efforts to promote the recognition of a singular identity are observed to be problematic. In addition to the problem of 'miniaturisation', the reification of identity can be politically problematic. Identity politics can provide the power of social mobilisation against abusive states, but it can also lead to separatism and intolerance, seeking in-group advantages rather than universal justice (Fraser 2000; Sen 2007; Fukuyama 2012).

Fraser's alternative to a psychological characterisation of recognition is to focus on the *institutions* that lead to the withholding of recognition in the first place. This means identifying and addressing the institutionalised cultures of discrimination which lead to low social status for some, and dictate their inability to participate as equals in society.

> To be misrecognised, accordingly, is not simply to be thought ill of, looked down upon or devalued in others' attitudes, beliefs or representations. It

is rather to be denied the status of a full partner in social interaction, as a consequence of institutionalized patterns of cultural value that constitute one as comparatively unworthy of respect or esteem.

(Fraser 2000, p. 113–114)

To place that in the context of this book, we would ask what are the underlying, institutionalised values within the conservation sector that systematically lead to failure to recognise the values and identities of local stakeholders. There is, for example, considerable scrutiny of the working of global conservation institutions, based on concerns that certain values and agendas dominate to the exclusion of others. More specifically, a number of commentators have pointed to the way in which predominantly anthropocentric, Western scientific and neoclassical economic views of nature have dominated key global bodies such as the Convention on Biological Diversity (CBD) and the Intergovernmental Platform on Biodiversity and Ecosystem Services (IPBES), for example, promoting the financial valorisation and commodification of nature as the way to save it (McAfee 1999; Borie and Hulme 2015). During negotiations for the formation of IPBES in 2011, the Bolivian government led a critique of the framing being employed and in particular the emphasis on 'ecosystem services', arguing that the conception of nature as a service provider to humans conflicted with views about mother earth that are written into the Bolivian constitution (Brand and Vadrot 2013). In effect, they argued that IPBES was becoming a global science–policy interface body that only recognises some forms of knowledge and thereby reduces the status of some stakeholders. The CBD is in principle protected against such epistemic selectivity, for example through its commitment to 'respect, preserve and maintain knowledge, innovations and practices of indigenous and local communities' (Article 8(j)). But there remains considerable debate about whether it is indeed a space for knowledge pluralism or, to the contrary, whether dominant ideas about the green economy are allowed to flourish even where these conflict with indigenous ways of knowing nature (Escobar 1998).

The special place of knowledge

This question has to do with the co-existence of many knowledges in the world and the relation between the abstract hierarchies which constitute them and the unequal economic and political power relations which produce and reproduce increasingly more severe social injustice.

(Toulmin 2007)

The subjugation of alternative knowledge of nature – sometimes referred to as 'cognitive injustice' (Visvanathan 2007) – is particularly relevant to the analysis of recognition failures within the conservation sector. The stakeholders who dominate what goes for knowledge about nature are those who are already in positions of economic and political power, allowing them to successfully frame both the analysis of problems and the solutions to them. Put another way, those who dominate knowledge production are also often able to promote dominant claims about 'the right thing to do'. In biodiversity conservation, this has involved the construction of moral hierarchies which position local resource users, such as hunters, as wrongdoers (Duffy 2000; Neumann 2004).

For some ecofeminist scholars, a predominantly masculine, Western, Enlightenment scientific worldview has dominated knowledge hierarchies at the expense of alternative ways of knowing nature. This cognitive domination is seen as a root of contemporary environmental problems and their associated social and ecological injustices. In *The Death of Nature*, Carolyn Merchant (1980) charts the impact of the scientific revolution in Europe and the rise of a reductionist, secular and dualistic view of nature. In the seventeenth century, nature became viewed as an assemblage of separate parts related mechanically to each other. Human beings became viewed as separate to nature and the sole repository for the realms of culture and spirit. Nature was thus stripped of both its organic and sacred qualities – hence the 'death' of nature. This anthropocentric view of a 'dead' nature fitted a moral order in which nature could be exploited as a service provider to humans, an order that is arguably reproduced in dominant contemporary framings of nature as ecosystem services. It is an ideological construction of nature which is historically situated in the advent of modernity and the ensuing spread of capitalist relations of production.

The cognitive injustice associated with such a dominant epistemology is not so much that it is a demonstrably false account of the world; rather, the injustice is to insist that it is the *only* valid account of the world. For contemporary critics, there has been a failure to acknowledge that Western science is a situated worldview – a product of a time and place, rather than a universal truth that was simply out there waiting to be discovered.

> Modern epistemology . . . created the figure of the detached observer, a neutral seeker of truth and objectivity who at the same time controls the disciplinary rules and puts himself or herself in a privileged position to evaluate and dictate
>
> *(Mignolo 2009, p. 4)*

Walter Mignolo (2007, 2009) explores how this misplaced epistemological certainty has been at the heart of imperial worldviews and practices, both during and since colonial times. For him, 500 years of imperialist conquest has taken place as much in the mind as in the political and economic spheres; this discursive domination is at the root of contemporary social injustices. The institutionalisation of cognitive forces of injustice involves a process of presenting an ideal, rational worldview and then positioning non-Western worldviews and people as inferior.

Institutions are created that accomplish two functions: training of new (epistemic obedient) members and control of who enters and what knowledge-making is allowed, disavowed, devalued or celebrated. (Mignolo, 2009, p. 18)

I think this broad characterisation of the underlying causes of status inequalities is a central issue for conservation. As a process then, it is like the imperialist constructions of race that Edward Said (1978) described in his classic work, *Orientalism*. For Mignolo, the challenge is not merely to change the *content* of the conversation but also the *terms* of the conversation. With that in mind, it is helpful to return to examples of 'terms' that are important for conservation knowledge-making. In particular I want to provide some more concrete instances of the language and concepts that reflect the underlying dominant ontology and epistemology, and of the institutions which put these concepts to work, recruit and train new members, and control what knowledge-making is allowed to enter.

Biodiversity conservation has its very own organising concept – biodiversity – as well as important shared referents such as wilderness and ecosystem services. As was noted in Chapter 2, biodiversity is a term that was coined in the 1980s (Wilson 1989; Escobar 1998) to describe the variety of life on earth and to provide a unifying scientific construct to serve conservation decision-making. Biodiversity can be seen as a product of modernist reductionist science because it acts to delineate the biological realm from other parts of the environment and from humanity. In that sense it may be viewed as 'unecological' (Martin et al. 2013b) and as incompatible with alternative conservation worldviews such as those which have 'mother earth' as their organising concept. As also discussed in Chapter 2, the concept of 'ecosystem services' was largely developed in the 1990s, constructing and limiting the ways in which we know biodiversity and nature (Norgaard 2010; Lélé et al. 2013). As with biodiversity, it has been heralded as a 'unifying language' for evidence-based conservation, although its usage in practice tends to prioritise particular ways of knowing nature and the associated views of what counts as valid knowledge about nature (Sullivan 2009). Whilst the rapid uptake of this term demonstrates its power of unification among many key conservation stakeholders, it has also proved divisive for those who perceive it as an instrument to serve green economy ideologies. The Kari-Oka II declaration, for example, was a direct riposte to the green economy agenda that had come to dominate the United Nations Conference on Sustainable Development. Using language that resonates with the views of Mignolo (2009) described above, participants described the Rio+20 narratives as the 'institutionalisation of colonialism' and declared:

We see the goals of UNCSD Rio+20, the 'Green Economy' and its premise that the world can only 'save' nature by commodifying its life giving and life sustaining capacities as a continuation of the colonialism that Indigenous Peoples and our Mother Earth have faced and resisted for 520 years. The 'Green Economy' promises to eradicate poverty but in fact will only favor and respond to multinational enterprises and capitalism. It is a continuation of a global economy based upon fossil fuels, the destruction of the environment by exploiting nature through extractive industries such as mining, oil exploration and production, intensive mono-culture agriculture, and other capitalist investments. All of these efforts are directed toward profit and the accumulation of capital by the few.

(Kari-Oka 2 Declaration, 2012)

The emphasis on 'ecosystem services' has become a key target for those who want to 'decolonise' or 'de-westernise' conservation knowledge. Just months after the Rio+20 conference, the Conference of the Parties to the CBD met in Hyderabad and disappointed those opposing the green economy worldview by 'encouraging' an ecosystem services framing of the value of biodiversity:

> *[The Conference of the Parties]* Notes existing efforts by a number of Parties to prepare national studies on the economics of ecosystems and biodiversity, and encourages other Parties and Governments to also consider, as appropriate, the preparation of such studies, making use of the findings of the international study on The Economics of Ecosystems and Biodiversity (TEEB) and of similar work at the national or regional levels, involving all relevant stakeholders, and to identify mechanisms and measures to integrate the values of biodiversity into relevant national and local policies, programmes and planning processes, as well as reporting systems, in a manner adapted to national circumstances.
>
> *(Decision XI/30, CBD COP-11, Hyderabad, 2012)*

Finally, it is worth remembering the much older concept of 'wilderness', a concept that is filled with meanings that reflect the worldviews of particular people, times and places (Short 1991; Cronon 1996). To mention a few examples, wilderness has morphed from the ungodly and fearful places of seventeenth-century fairy tales, to the godly and idyllic places of the nineteenth-century Romantic poets, to the perfectly dehumanised places sought out by twenty-first-century nature tourists. The idea that a perfect nature is one without humans makes little sense in animist cultures where there is seamless continuity between humans and nature. Ideas such as wilderness, when promoted to being a model for conservation, therefore promote the worldview of some over that of others: ideas do not remain as ideas, the world begins to be modelled in their image (West and Brockington 2006). Ideas about how the world should be become institutionalised in disciplinary curricula but also in practical guidelines that govern conservation practice. Parks, for example, are given a hierarchical grading by IUCN from Category 1a, 'Strict Nature Reserve' to Category 6, 'Protected Area with sustainable use of natural resources'. In this way, a dominant conceptualisation of conservation is first a discursive conquest but second an institutionalised form of territorial governance currently applied to 17% of the earth's terrestrial surface.

Whilst our conservation policies and practices are full of calls for the full participation of indigenous and local peoples, we should be aware that institutions such as the CBD appear to take a much harder and exclusionary line when it comes to who gets to frame the basic terms of what conservation aspires to and the approaches it should take. For example, the CBD encourages the 'green economy' *in spite of* opposition from indigenous peoples (Martin et al. 2016). It is important to be aware of these critical views of the global institutionalisation of a dominant conservation science. However, it is equally important to acknowledge that terms such as 'biodiversity' have opened up spaces for debate that can give strength to marginalised groups of resource users. Biodiversity is a powerful global referent that can be used to challenge the monocultures produced by dominant economic and political practices. For example, contemporary agrobiodiversity movements in Europe are becoming more focused on the institutionalised discrimination against farmer science, knowledge and culture; this goes hand in hand with their political and economic marginalisation. AgroBio Perigord (ABP) is an association for organic farming in southwest France which promotes *in situ* conservation of locally adapted food crop varieties (landraces). One of the aims of ABP is to enhance the cultural recognition of small-scale, farmer-driven agriculture (Coolsaet 2016; Martin et al. 2016). ABP are ostensibly seeking fairer distribution of resources to make their farming choices financially feasible, but they are aware that there are discriminatory outlooks and institutions that underpin the problems they face. Central to the success of local landraces is knowledge about their use. But this is obstructed by formal institutions of the state which serve the corporate sector: local landraces are not legitimate food crop varieties under French law and their seeds cannot be traded – they can only be exchanged for purposes of trials. The legal system therefore protects the interests of the corporations that dominate the seed market and marginalises those who want to use alternative seed (Coolsaet 2016).

Linking recognition and distribution

So far I have been emphasising problems of recognition in isolation, considering knowledge hierarchies as one important way in which status inequalities are produced and persist. But the example of AgroBio Perigord shows us that in practice, i.e. in real-world environmental justice struggles, concerns for recognition are not easily separated out from concerns about distribution. That is a key point I want to expand on in this chapter, and indeed in the rest of the book. As the examples such as the Kari-Oka II declaration illustrate, indigenous and local territorial claims combine concerns for physical territories with concerns for knowledge and culture. Struggles over conservation have increasingly incorporated claims for cultural recognition, mirroring the wider shift in social movements (Honneth 2004), but these have not displaced claims about access to resources, loss of crops and livestock to wild animals, and the fair sharing of revenues from mining, tourism, hunting and timber industries. For example, in interviews which I conducted with people living near to the Nam Et-Phou Louey National Protected Area in northern Laos, it became clear that concern for land as a basis for livelihoods was the priority for most. Access to land is ostensibly a distributional concern and is valued for its economic opportunities, in particular maize and rice production, but also for the potential collection of wild foods and other forest products. But these economic activities are connected to self-identity and are a basis for expressing and reproducing important aspects of local knowledge, social relations and cultures. I could say much the same about farmers in my home country, the UK. Their identities are tied to the land, as food producers, as stewards of the landscape for the next generation, as knowledge carriers. More widely, food justice and small farmer agrobiodiversity movements such as Via Campesina involve struggles for sustainable livelihoods based on distributional concerns but increasingly these claims are tied to claims about autonomy, the right to choose lifestyles, and the subordination of local knowledge and cultures.

The idea that the cultural and material bases of environmental justice are linked is also supported by observations of the 'environmentalism of the poor' which tends to be grounded in everyday material struggles for livelihood security but at the same time linked to struggles against status inequalities. Similarly, it is widely observed that discrimination against women has interconnected roots in both the economic arrangements of society and the institutionalised cultures that shape intersubjective relations and define occupational status (Robeyns 2003; Young 2011). In some situations, cultural and economic motives can mix and shift in ways that may appear contradictory. For example, the philosopher Michael Sandel (2012) discusses the case of Canadian Inuit people who were granted quotas for hunting walrus on grounds of cultural significance. Some communities found they no longer needed their full hunting quota and have begun selling on these rights. For $10,000 a wealthy big-game hunter can be paddled to within spitting distance of these stationary creatures and kill them with a powerful rifle. Sandel is clearly unimpressed, and I share his unease. However, the shifting views of the Inuit communities in question should not be that surprising. Identities and the moral compass they provide are not fixed, and the material and cultural components of those identities are themselves connected. As empirical studies of environmental justice become more numerous I am sure we will see many instances of changing views about conservation, the fragmenting of 'communal' discourses of environmental justice and of individual 'moral panic' trying to resolve multiple identities. Whilst concerns with recognition may often be presented as if they were independent of distributional concerns, the emerging empirical approach to studying justice claims is revealing that people often see links between these justice dimensions. Responding to concerns of communities at the frontline of biodiversity conservation therefore requires us to think of 'the ways in which economic disadvantage and cultural disrespect are currently entwined with and support one another' (Fraser 1995, p. 67).

To an extent, the environmental justice movement has always sought to reveal the co-existence and connections between distribution and recognition. The analytical approach employed in a distributive model of justice has itself helped to

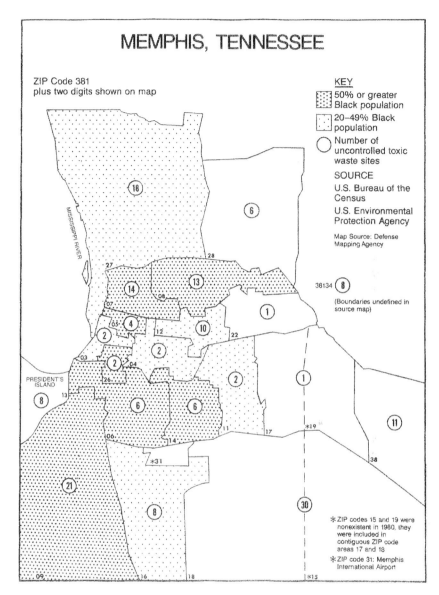

FIGURE 6.1 Uncontrolled toxic waste sites and black populations in Memphis, Tennessee.

reveal important injustices which arise from discrimination based on divisions such as gender, ethnicity, class and species. The key example here is the exposure of institutionalised environmental racism through studies of the distribution of toxic waste in the United States. Maps that superimpose points of industrial pollution with demographic factors such as wealth or ethnicity (for example Figure 6.1) have been used to assert that the distribution of polluting activities has been unjust but also to argue that this unjust distribution is caused by racism or other forms of discrimination (Hamilton 1995).

An important example from the biodiversity conservation sector is the pattern of winners and losers revealed by analysis of the distribution of costs and benefits from protected areas. The poor tend to be burdened with a higher proportion of costs than the rich (Adams et al. 2004). But the distributional model is inadequate for understanding the distribution-recognition nexus for at least two main reasons. Firstly, a distributional approach fails to explicitly analyse the institutionalised cultures and status hierarchies that give rise to distributional injustices. Thus, whilst, for example, the distributional model has helped to reveal the presence of institutional racism, it is the distribution of toxic pollutants that is posited as the injustice. Secondly, as Karen Warren (1999) discusses, a distributive model of justice does not deal with values associated with culture, including deep-seated connections with particular places, traditions and lifestyles. It does not have categories of analysis that seek to reveal the range of ways in which landscapes are valued by farmers and hunters in the Canadian Arctic, the hills of northern Laos, or the East of England.

Cultural attachment to places and practices are often revealed where conservation involves proposals for 'offsetting' environmental losses through replacement assets and services or through offering 'alternative livelihoods' to those whose rights of access are to be curtailed. Offsetting the loss of a local park by creating a replacement park nearby can appear distributionally neutral providing it is replaced with an area of similar size, with the same number (and eventually size) of trees, and so on. But there may well still be loss that is not quantifiable – say the attachment to the park that comes from memories of playing there as a child, of walking a fondly remembered pet dog, or even a sense of the pathways taken by ancestors. Absence of attention to cultural concerns leads to erroneous assumptions of equivalence. A similar issue arises over rights to hunt and harvest in protected forests. For some people, alternative livelihoods are acceptable. For example, the majority of people I have spoken to around protected areas in Rwanda say they are, or would in principle be, content to substitute domesticated meats for bushmeat. They say it mainly tastes just as good, or better, and they would actually prefer it if their children did not have to hunt for food in the forest. After decades of modernising agendas promoted by the state, the church and NGOs, they no longer see their culture and identity as forest-based (see Martin et al. 2014a). Around Nam Et-Phou Louey, by contrast, traditions remain alive; there are sacred forest groves where ancestors are honoured and where there are ceremonial uses for different forest species. For example, a young man seeking permission to marry will take a quantity of rat meat and bamboo to the family of the bride-to-be. Yet even here, identities are changing remarkably quickly and most now consider substitutes as acceptable. For example, shrines to ancestors are now seen with offerings of children's sweets from the local store in place of forest goods. But of course there are other places still where traditional uses of forest resources remain comparatively unchanged and where the ability to continue such practices is critical to individual and communal wellbeing.

Recognition without cultural concerns?

To summarise the above, a distributional model fails to capture cultural values and, perhaps more fundamentally, does not provide a window into the structural and institutional causes of discrimination and related distributional inequities. Following some connected lines of thinking from ecofeminism, critical anthropology and decolonial theory, I have made a special case of Western scientific 'knowledge-making'. The enormous and positive achievements of Western scientific methods are reasonably well known – but that should not prevent us from looking at its history of domination through an environmental justice lens, and posing the question of how we can better create spaces for other forms of knowledge.

I now want to consider those cases where culture, identity and knowledge seem not to be articulated as part of environmental justice claims. Around the forests and marshlands of Central Africa, it is indigenous, pygmy peoples such as the Twa or Baka who tend to express much stronger cultural attachment to forests than their neighbours. This has been seen around the Nyungwe and Giswati forests in Rwanda (Dawson and Martin 2015), the Mgahinga and Bwindi forests in Uganda (Martin et al. 2015) and Trinational Sangha park in Cameroon (Gross-Camp et al. 2015a). But correspondingly, those not from pygmy tribes are less likely to express cultural concerns and this would seem to be representative of a more widespread environmentalism of the poor which is primarily articulated in terms of land and livelihood security. In situations such as these, is recognition a relevant dimension of environmental justice? I explore this question through the example of local people around the montane rainforest enclosed by the Nyungwe National Park in Rwanda. Whilst concerns about cultural heritage seem to be hardly expressed at all here, I suggest that recognition is still a relevant category of justice, providing we define it in terms of status inequalities rather than culture per se, and providing we consider recognition as inter-twined with, rather than separate from, concerns about distribution.

For the people living around the forest of Nyungwe, there is considerable variation in how they have been affected by conservation interventions and how they now view the park and its authorities. Uwumusubeya cell, a cluster of villages near to the border with Burundi, is one of the poorer parts owing to its relative isolation and poor soils. Dependence on forest resources has been higher here than in some other parts of the park, partly because of poverty but also because of the proximity to Nyungwe's small area of bamboo forest which has provided a resource for housing, fencing and crafts. During interviews with households living near to the current park boundary, it became clear that there is considerable resentment. They claimed that their farmland had been taken at the time of park gazettement and that promised compensation had never materialised. One family had considerable stocks of bamboo that had been harvested from the nearby park, and felt justified in continuing this now illegal activity. They can just about get away with openly holding this stock by claiming that it is purchased across the border in Burundi, where forest protection has been less enforced (and where the bamboo forest has been decimated). Bamboos are also grown on village lands but forest bamboos are recognisable, and more desirable, because of their longer intermodal lengths.

In the same village, others complained about the way park rules were enforced, and in particular about a stiffening of rule enforcement in the mainly pine plantations of the buffer zone. One woman complained to me: 'Now when we are caught in the forest we are asked for money and beaten. One month ago I was caught in the buffer zone collecting grass and was beaten and asked for 5000 Rwandan Francs.' Whilst resentment against the park continues to simmer, there exists in parallel a strong narrative of support for its rules. One view that is becoming dominant (expressed in public meetings and in private interviews) is that some forest-based activities which used to be perfectly respectable are now wrong, and that their perpetrators should be punished. Those who continued to hunt

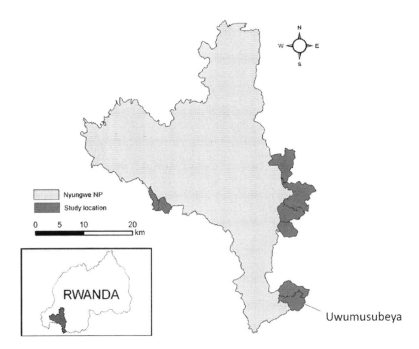

FIGURE 6.2 Nyungwe National Park, Rwanda, showing research locations including Uwumusubeya cell.

with snares were frequently described in negative terms, as thieves and saboteurs. Capturing this widely expressed sentiment, another woman stated: 'I wish it was up to us to punish poachers, we'd give them a heavier punishment than those few months that they spend in prison.' A male interviewee was similarly critical of such 'saboteurs' despite being able to sympathise with their motives. He described forest users as being 'desperate, because they run the risk of being shot in the park by rangers'. However, he clearly did not consider being economically 'desperate' as a sufficient justification for breaking park rules.

What we see is multiple and conflicting views about forest conservation, with widely articulated alignment with the morality represented by park rules, but simultaneous concerns that these rules are unfair, especially in response to personal experience of ill-treatment. Those who do criticise the park and its authorities do so on economic rather than cultural grounds. Of those we interviewed (n = 101) 77% agreed that the rules of the park prevented them from passing on traditions to their children. However, this was viewed as a positive rather than negative social impact of conservation (Martin et al. 2014a). In this area there is little spiritual attachment to forests expressed so the kind of traditions referred to here are material practices connected to collection and use of non-timber forest products. This includes collection of wild foods, collection of materials for making mats and baskets and collection of herbal medicines. When we discussed why people were content to lose these traditional forest-based practices and knowledge, four broad reasons emerged. Firstly, these practices are viewed as primarily economic rather than cultural, and substitutes are therefore broadly equivalent (or often better). For example, modern medicines provided in health centres were considered superior to herbal medicines, and plastic utensils were considered superior to, for example, plates made from wood or leaves. Secondly, the economics of forest-based livelihood activities were unattractive to many. Hunting was viewed as a low-return activity as well as a risky one, and it was observed that few young people took up activities such as basket-weaving in preference to waged labouring opportunities in tea plantations. Thirdly, forest-based livelihoods have not held a central place in cultural identities for a long time. There is a long history of exclusion from the forest that began with the Belgian colonists in the 1930s. Whilst rules only became strictly enforced following National Park status in 2004, local control over the forest was lost long ago. Land for farming retains far greater significance and contemporary conservation narratives align well with this because forest conservation is seen to support agriculture – local residents believe that the forest brings rainfall and is therefore good for their farms. Fourthly, historical events have led to ambivalent feelings about preserving what is 'traditional'. Starting in the 1930s, colonial authorities and the Christian missions that supported them used existing, traditional institutions to attain power. Colonial administrators co-opted local kings and princes who could assert control over land and livestock, thereby equating 'traditional' with oppression in the politics of Rwanda. More recently, attachments to clan and ethnic groups has been associated with war and genocide, this time equating 'traditional' cultural identities with acts of violence that it is imperative to avoid in future. At the national level, such negative attachments to tradition have underpinned strongly modernising political agendas which have undoubtedly filtered down to local levels. Many of those we interviewed connected the substitutes for forest-based livelihoods with 'development', 'new technology', 'improvement', 'moving forward' and 'modern life' and they see this as a long-term trend rather than merely a result of recent national park designation.

There remain a significant minority of people who continue to break the rules of the park by hunting with snares, clearing plots of forest for marijuana cultivation, gold mining, cutting trees and bamboos and so on. This is well recorded by patrols undertaken by park wardens and in additional forest transect surveys undertaken by our research team between 2010 and 2012 (Martin et al. 2014b). These people are not typically members of the very poorest households in the vicinity – the poorest tend to be those which lack the younger, stronger men who are often the ones who undertake such forest-based work. But they are sufficiently poor to choose to undertake work that brings risks of imprisonment and even death, as well as disapproval from their own communities. Recent conservation-oriented policies have made life increasingly difficult for this group, marginalising them within their own communities. But on the other hand, these policies have also created a new group of illicit forest users. Since 2013 the park's buffer zone has been allocated to a private forestry business, the New Forest Company, which has led to the aforementioned tightening of buffer zone rules (Gross-Camp et al. 2015b). Interviewing local residents just prior to this privatisation revealed that this clamping down was seen as effectively criminalising a further tranche of villagers – those, mainly women and children, who collect fuelwood and grasses for livestock from the buffer zone. During 2010 we asked 78 randomly selected households to keep diaries for two weeks recording their household consumption of wood, grasses and other products available in the park and its buffer zone (Gross-Camp et al. 2015b). Of these households 14.1% recorded collection of fuelwood from the park itself but a much larger proportion, 39.7%, recorded collection from the buffer zone, an activity that was already technically illegal, but was generally considered more acceptable than collecting from the natural forest. In addition, 25.6% of households recorded collection of grasses for livestock, an activity that was mainly taking place in the buffer zone. These grass collectors were now finding that they were being stopped, fined and, as in the case mentioned previously, beaten.

If our ambition is to attain more just conservation practices, what, if anything, should we consider to be the injustices present in this example? In Chapter 4 I discussed how a purely empirical approach to conservation justice can be supplemented by some appeal to universal benchmarks. I proposed that a capabilities approach was useful here, partly as it connects well to common social objectives of conservation. In particular, conservation typically seeks to be pro-poor which even in its weakest interpretation would mean not making the poor poorer.

Following an 'essential capabilities' approach proposed by Martha Nussbaum, I suggested that where a person is already struggling to attain essential capabilities such as adequate nutrition, allowing further reduction in such capabilities would normally be considered an injustice. To apply that to the current case I refer to measures of household income that are made by calculating monetary values of total household consumption, including forest-based collections, food consumed, and money spent on education, festivities and durable goods. This showed that 69% of our sample households were living on less than $1 per capita per day. Whilst income does not itself define capabilities, it is one important determinant. For the woman quoted above as being fined 5000 francs (about $9), this was undoubtedly considerable hardship – she was only able to pay the fine by borrowing from neighbours and relatives.

In some ways this is a rather straightforward matter of distributional justice involving financial gains for the government of Rwanda (via leasehold arrangements with the New Forest Company) and losses for those local people who are most dependent on park and buffer zone resources. Under a utilitarian conception of conservation justice there might or might not be an injustice committed, depending on whether the greater good has been served. But according to the more liberal individualism of the capability approach, there is injustice because conservation practice has made some people fall (further) below capability thresholds essential for a dignified life. In this case, the indignity for some includes loss of capacity to eat well, the appearance of being 'desperate' or even criminal in the eyes of others in the community, being forced to borrow money from neighbours, and exposure to physical harm through abuse by forest guards.

If we were to adopt an identity-based understanding of recognition, that is about as far as this discussion would go. An empirical exploration of what local people think about conservation certainly reveals some ill-feelings within communities, but this is not really expressed in terms of failures to recognise particular local identities. If however we employ Nancy Fraser's model of recognition injustice as being linked to status inequality, then there is a case for considering a lack of recognition as a cause of the distributional injustice. In my view, this is warranted. As Warren (1999) argues, distribution does not appear from nowhere but reflects underlying power structures and ideologies which give rise to and normalise ill-distribution. Thus when communities campaign against the harmful siting or inappropriate rules of a protected area, or indeed when they campaign for better enforcement of protected area rules, they are not only making claims about that local instance of what they see as a wrong, but also about the institutionalised discrimination that generated it. I have undertaken a similar study around the Bwindi Impenetrable National Park in Uganda, where it again became apparent that conservation efforts have lacked due diligence towards the essential capabilities of some local people (Martin et al. 2015). Here, the research team asked local people about the nature of interactions with park staff. It confirmed that there is widespread feeling that park staff do not treat them equally, as is clear to them by the asymmetrical nature of communications: 'They want me to listen to them but they won't listen to me'; 'They don't agree with whatever the villagers say'; 'Uganda Wildlife Authority just think about its policies without considering ours'. It is a common theme among respondents who mention that staff never write down anything they say, don't remember what they have said, and essentially act in ways that suggest they are not treating them as equals. It is these institutionalised status inequalities that are very much seen as going hand in hand with particular instances of economic harm.

Who is not being recognised? This is not so simple. It is more clear-cut when there is evidence of discrimination against a particular group such as women, an indigenous people or the poor. In cases I have observed, however, the basic social fault-line along which status inequalities fall is between urban-based professionals and rural peasants. It is something like the culture gap between the urban elite and the peasantry which was described by Robert Chambers (1983) as being a barrier to government agencies and development experts really hearing the voices of the poor. Rural livelihoods continue to suffer from low status in many places. In Sub-Saharan Africa, young people try to avoid following their parents into farming, not only because of the low economic returns but also because farming is considered a low status, 'dirty' occupation (Leavy and Smith 2010). The low social status of farmers has long gone hand in hand with failures to recognise the validity of farmer knowledge and to recognise the rationality and sustainability of smallholder farming practices (Richards 1985). In some cases it continues to lead to stigmatisation of small farmers as part of the problem – as poor managers of resources and as threats to biodiversity conservation (Dawson et al. 2016b).

Conclusion: conservation, recognition and responsibility

Concerns about recognition appear in conservation conflicts in both the global North and South. Small farmers in France have suffered from too little protection of agrobiodiversity, as the state institutionalises systems that support a few dominant varieties of farmed plant and animal species. Small farmers in Rwanda have suffered from the way in which protection of biodiversity has been designed and implemented. They have been made vulnerable to impoverishment by progressive loss of access to forest resources. In other places, conflicts arising from biodiversity conservation will be different again, for example arising from states' failures to protect people's land against industries such as oil and rubber.

In terms of causes, we can observe specific instances of individual behaviour, such as the park guard who beats someone or extorts fines in a corrupt manner. We can also observe specific policies and interventions that increase vulnerability to loss of essential capabilities for groups and individuals. But this chapter has mainly been about exploring institutionalised structures that cause failures of recognition which place some people routinely at a disadvantage by framing the terms on which they are able to participate in social life. Small farmers in France and Rwanda have very different struggles, but at root, they share this problem of lack of recognition owing to status inequalities.

> Structural injustice, then, exists when social processes put large groups of persons under systematic threat of domination or deprivation of the means to develop and exercise their capacities . . . . Structural injustice is a kind of moral wrong distinct from the wrongful action of an individual agent or the repressive policies of a state. Structural injustice occurs as a consequence of many individuals and institutions acting to pursue their particular goals and interests, for the most part within the limits of accepted rules and norms.
>
> *(Young 2011, p. 52)*

Indeed, this quite well describes the everyday injustices that accompany bio-diversity conservation in the tropics. In the Nyungwe example, the Rwanda Development Board, the US-based Wildlife Conservation Society, the UK-based New Forest Company, along with local authorities and civil society, pursue goals that are broadly supported by the development and conservation agendas of that country. These goals receive strong moral justifications on a number of counts, including the need to continue Rwanda's post-conflict economic development, the need to protect globally valued biodiversity for future humans, and the need to show responsibility towards non-human species. But this chapter has nonethe-less suggested that the sum result of these multiple interests and actions is injustice for some. With particular attention to feminist social justice thinkers (Martha Nussbaum, Nancy Fraser, Karen Warren, Iris Marion Young), I suggest a basic disadvantage for local peasant communities linked to their social position and status. This devalues their particular interests and values relative to other stakehold-ers, even where those other stakeholders operate with good intentions. This is not to say that all those who are disadvantaged suffer equally bad outcomes. Some will make better or luckier choices than others and will prosper, some will have better resourced and more people-friendly conservation organisations operating in their territories, and so on. But such structural disadvantage does make large numbers more vulnerable to domination and deprivation.

I have followed Nancy Fraser in thinking about this disadvantage in terms of status and, in turn, considering the example of a basic status chasm in many developing countries between urban professionals and the rural peasantry. Such problems of recognition lead to problems that are often economic rather than purely cultural or subjective in nature, as is the case in the Rwanda example here. But I have also argued that the economic and the cultural are not independent of each other, and nor are justice categories of distribution and recognition. As Arturo Escobar (1998) has argued, conservation conflicts do have a strong cultural dimension, especially relating to alternative ways of knowing nature. The domination of Western scientific constructions of nature ensures that the terms of reference for conservation policymaking and practice are pre-defined and well beyond the reach of the peasantry. It is of course more than coincidence that these framing epistemologies and conceptions tend to be more aligned with the interests of the urban professionals. Indeed the culture–nature dualism at the heart of the modern Western worldview is itself arguably associated with the low status of those who work more closely with nature (Warren 1999). Writing about the history of atrocities against indigenous peoples in the Upper Amazon, Hvalkof (2000) concludes that a nature-culture dichotomy and the association of Amazonian Indians with nature have persistently defined their status. It has 'profound and far reaching effects, and is probably one of the constituting prerequisites for the outrageous situations I have depicted here' (p. 108). For Hvalkof, biodiversity conservation will inevitably prove equally as exploitative as the rubber and oil businesses that preceded it, unless conservationists support a change in the terms of the conversation, for example by supporting local control through granting of territories.

I want to end with a comment about responsibility and some assurance that the identification of structural origins of injustice does not leave conservation practice powerless to act. Nor does it absolve conservation from responsibility. I summarise Iris Marion Young (2011) who points out that it is obvious that different actors will have different kinds and degrees of responsibility for future justice, depending on their position and capacity. She provides some guidance for how we might think about these differentiated responsibilities based on four 'parameters of reasoning' about action to redress injustice. Firstly, the *power* to act is critical, with greater responsibility held by those organisations and individuals with the capacity to effect change. According to this parameter, we might say that a conservation NGO or a state conservation agency may have limited capacity to redress underlying structural causes of injustice (such as gender inequality) but does have the capacity to mitigate the way such structures operate within their own area of practice. Supporting local and indigenous territorial control is an example. Instituting more deliberative and democratic decision-making procedures would be another. Secondly, there are those that existing structures give *privilege* to, at least relative to those who are losers. In the conservation context this will overlap with those who also hold power. But it would also include those global beneficiaries of biodiversity conservation who are not directly powerful in the conservation policymaking arena – those who benefit from visiting 'wilderness' as nature tourists, or by seeing that their contributions to a conservation NGO are spent in ways that they think are good. The privileged also includes those who benefit from cheap consumption goods without immediately suffering the associated costs. For example the billions who benefit as consumers of cheap rubber or palm oil at the cost of habitat destruction. Such privileged beneficiaries have particular responsibilities to act. Thirdly, those with a particular *interest* in undermining an injustice have a special responsibility to do so. This includes the victims of the injustice who need to be involved in confronting and addressing the structures that disadvantage them, in part so that others with responsibility have a clearer sense of the right way to act. Fourthly, *collective action* is essential for a coordinated response to structural injustices. For example, conservation NGOs are in a strong position because of their large memberships and organisational capacities for collective direction achieved through forums such as the IUCN, CBD and IPBES. Likewise, consumer-based responsibility can be exercised much more effectively if collectivised, for example through agreement and monitoring of environmental and ethical product standards.

Finally it is worth remembering the body of work summarised at the end of the previous chapter: a growing number of high-calibre studies find that the adoption of more inclusive approaches to conservation, including greater respect for local rights and knowledge, is conducive to more effective conservation.

7

FROM 'CONSERVATION AND DEVELOPMENT' TO 'CONSERVATION AND JUSTICE'

Introduction

In the mid 1980s Michael Soulé (1985) proposed that the field of conservation biology is shaped by two evolving sets of ideas: firstly, a set of fundamental scientific beliefs about the workings of nature and secondly, a set of normative beliefs about human responsibilities to care for nature. If we agree with this view, then we should expect the goals and approaches of conservation to change over time. Science and norms will evolve as new discoveries come to light, as social preferences shift and as political ideologies are transformed. In recent decades, for example, our ideas about the relationship between nature and society have taken on board sustainable development narratives, integrated social-ecological systems thinking, and the ecosystem services framing (Kareiva and Marvier 2012). Equally important shifts have occurred in the social norms and priorities linked to conservation, including international commitment to strive for global poverty alleviation and to recognise and respect local and indigenous rights.

This chapter considers the recent history of the changing contexts of conservation and the resulting shifts in dominant conservation narratives and models. This recent history includes a shift from the 'fortress conservation' model to more people-friendly approaches that emerged in the late 1980s. It also includes a subsequent shift towards market-oriented approaches and the related 'new conservation' paradigm. I use this chapter to argue for a new direction. Instead of seeking to integrate conservation with calls for 'more development' (the late 1980s shift) or 'more market value' (the 2000s shift), I suggest that integrating conservation with 'more justice' is the better option and in some ways an obvious response to our new understanding of what works and doesn't work in conservation, and of changing normative commitments. I begin the chapter with a generalised history of changing conservation narratives, focusing on what I consider to be the most significant and revealing trend: the shift towards integrated conservation and development and subsequent struggles to try to make this effective. I then zoom in on a case study from Tanzania, which serves two important purposes. Firstly, it shows that, in practice, different approaches to conservation do not operate one after the other, but layer on top of each other such that elements of fortress conservation, integrated conservation and development and market-based approaches contribute to hybrid forms of conservation. Secondly, and more importantly, the case demonstrates the limitations of prevailing narratives of integrated conservation and development and highlights the case for moving towards a justice-centred conservation narrative.

The rise of fortress conservation

Prior to the nineteenth century the vast majority of terrestrial and marine resources in the tropics were available for local management and managed as common property resources for activities such as farming, pastoralism, hunting and gathering. This began to change rapidly following European colonisation, as forests and wildlife became reserved for the colonial state, administered by new imperial forest and game services, in a process that imposed ideas about conservation that were shaped by colonial science and norms. Colonial forestry combined scientific principles of maximum sustainable yields with utilitarian normative principles of 'wise use'. As discussed in Chapter 3, colonial foresters in India made the moral case for dispossessing villages of their forests based on the need to protect the common good – to ensure that the 'semi-savages' (as Baden-Powell described them) living in and around these forests did not waste them at the expense of the nation and future generations. Dietrich Brandis, the German forester appointed to manage the forest estates in India and Burma in the late nineteenth century, epitomised this set of scientific and normative ideas – he was clear that there was no role in forest management for local people because they did not have the necessary scientific training to manage resources productively and sustainably (Saldanha 1996).

From the mid twentieth century, the objective of 'development' entered into the set of dominant normative ideas, especially in newly independent states. In his 1949 inaugural speech to Congress, President Truman claimed that the US and its allies must act to improve 'underdeveloped areas'. Then, in the 1950s and 1960s development was largely defined as 'modernisation', with an emphasis on building a modern, scientific industrial sector served by a scientifically transformed rural sector. The 'dual economy' approach to development positioned rural economies as subservient to the urban and industrial. The function of rural land and labour was to provide low-cost resources which would accelerate the growth of industry and accelerate a nation's progress towards a modern economy (Ellis and Biggs 2001).

In Africa, the governance of wildlife followed a similar transition to that of forests, from common property to colonial preserve. Following the European 'scramble for Africa' in the 1880s, wildlife was progressively reserved for the 'great white hunters', to meet the Victorian fascination with 'natural history', and later for camera tourism (safaris). In Kenya, the North and South Game Reserves were established following the declaration of the British East Africa Protectorate in 1896. The first national park in Africa was the Parc National Albert in the Belgian Congo (now the Virunga National Park), formed in 1925 after King Albert visited Yellowstone National Park. Following the Second World War, the establishment of parks accelerated greatly (Hutton et al. 2005). As with colonial and post-colonial forestry, national parks and other protected areas were created through the exclusion of local people, a model which has come to be known as 'fortress conservation' (Brockington 2002). Morally, this was justified by the utilitarian positions highlighted above, preserving nature for the benefit of the many and for future generations. Scientifically, the case for exclusion was built on a culturally constructed vision that parks should preserve pristine wilderness. 'Pristine' was defined in terms of the ideal community of plants and animals for a particular set of environmental conditions. In the early twentieth century a theory of ecological succession became influential, in which landscapes evolved to an ideal 'climax' flora and fauna, but only in the absence of human interference (see e.g. Hagen 1992).

From fortress conservation to integrated conservation and development

Whilst widely criticised from a social justice perspective, there is little doubt that the case for fortress conservation remains widespread and the majority of parks continue to be dominated by this 'fences and fines' approach to protected area management. However, a variety of factors converged in the 1980s that challenged the fortress conservation model and established the popularity of more people-friendly alternative approaches to conservation (Hutton et al. 2005).

1. The social impacts of protected areas were increasingly made visible, with broadening awareness of the harms done to communities who were evicted to make way for conservation or whose access to resources was curtailed. This led to the relationship between parks and people becoming a focal issue at the third and fourth World Parks Congress meetings in 1982 and 1992 (Roe 2008).

2. There was a shift in the framing of environmental problems brought about by the popularisation of 'sustainable development' thinking via the 1987 Brundtland Report (WCED 1987) and the 1992 United Nations Conference on Environment and Development. The sustainable development narrative supported a critique of the idea that fortress conservation was the only way to save biodiversity. It did this through a shift away from the idea that economic growth and environmental conservation were mutually exclusive objectives and by instead proposing that economic development and conservation are compatible bedfellows.

3. 'Development studies' had itself evolved. Modernisation theory had lost credibility, and the idea that the state should be the sole or primary driver of social

and economic development was losing ground on both the political left and right. On the left there were calls for citizen participation and empowerment; on the right there were agendas to reduce the size and reach of state bureaucracies. This latter agenda was advanced aggressively through International Monetary Fund lending conditions which compelled a rolling back of the state in debt-afflicted countries in the global South. This overarching shift to neoliberal ideology created the political space for a greater role for civil society and the private sector in forestry and conservation.

4. Environmental problems began to be conceptualised in ways that saw greater integration of human and environmental systems (i.e. social-ecological systems thinking), promoting more integrated thinking about the complexity of society and nature relationships.

5. Academic disciplines associated with both development studies and environmental studies saw a shift towards viewing local communities as rational managers within those social-ecological systems. For example, the Nobel prize-winning work of Elinor Ostrom and colleagues challenged prevailing views that common property governance arrangements invariably led to the 'tragedy of the commons' and demonstrated the enduring effectiveness of many local resource management systems (Ostrom 1990, contra Hardin 1968).

6. A preservationist model of parks had largely been supported by a utilitarian ethic of serving the greater good (Miller et al. 2011). However the rise of liberal and conservative individualism could be argued to sit more comfortably with compassion for individuals, the prioritisation of basic needs and with the rise of poverty alleviation as a primary concern of the conservation sector. This shift to rights-based normative frameworks can be seen, for example, in the 2006 Forest Rights Act in India, the 2007 United Nations Declaration on the Rights of Indigenous Peoples, and the 2009 signing of the Conservation Initiative on Human Rights.

This list of drivers could no doubt be expanded but the key point is that a wide network of ideas, about both the scientific and normative basis for conservation, were challenging the fortress model. I think it is also important that the political interests behind these ideas came from across the political spectrum, with both left and right aligned behind ideas for a less top-down approach to conservation. Tania Murray Li (2007) provides a nice illustration and analysis of how such an assemblage of actors (villagers, politicians, entrepreneurs, conservationists, donors etc.) became bound together in promoting community forestry in Indonesia despite the fact that they all had very different interests in doing so (access to resources, livelihoods, political popularity, biodiversity, profit, etc.). In this case then, the conservation model acted like a 'boundary object', a sociological term to denote objects that have different meanings to different groups, but nonetheless have sufficient overlapping interest to support a networked community of support.

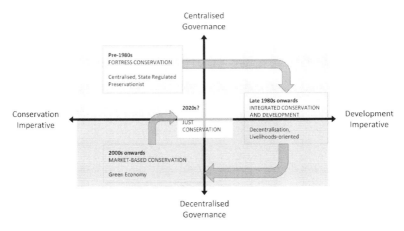

FIGURE 7.1 Changing conservation narratives.

As a result of this confluence of interests, integrated conservation and development projects (ICDPs) came to dominate international biodiversity conservation efforts during the 1990s (Wells et al. 1999). ICDPs were driven by a narrative about conservation effectiveness (that eliminating poverty was a pre-requisite for successful protected areas), strengthening international norms about responsibility for poverty alleviation and a trend towards more decentralised forms of governance which included civil society participation. This shift away from state-dominated, centralised governance appealed to the political left because of the emphasis on bottom-up and participatory approaches, but it also appealed on the political right because of the emphasis on a leaner state and deregulation.

Figure 7.1 illustrates the shift from 'fortress conservation' to 'integrated conservation and development' in relation to two main axes of change. The horizontal axis represents the priority outcomes for conservation, with the imperative to achieve effective conservation at one end and the imperative to achieve human development at the other. The vertical axis represents the kind of governance employed, with centralised regulation by governments at one end of the scale and more decentralised forms of multi-stakeholder governance at the other. The shift from fortress conservation to integrated conservation and development is thus portrayed not only as a widening of objectives to incorporate a strong emphasis on development objectives, but also as a shift in governance approach towards greater participation of non-state actors including communities, non-government organisations and, to a lesser extent, the private sector.

From ICDPs to market-based conservation

By the late 1990s there were concerns that ICDPs were not effective (Wells et al. 1999). With hindsight, this is not that surprising because there was never a clear logic as to why they should work. ICDPs were based on an assumption that if agriculture and other forms of livelihoods became more productive, people would become wealthier through non-park activities and would have less incentive to use park resources. As several scholars have argued, this was a flawed logic. Typically, the income derived from agriculture was not linked or dependent upon successful biodiversity conservation (Brandon and Wells 1992; Salafsky and Wollenberg 2000). So at best such interventions would provide no motive for conservation and at worst they would incentivise conversion of biodiverse landscapes by making agriculture a more profitable land use relative to forests or wetlands (Ferraro 2001; Wunder 2001; Ferraro and Simpson 2005). In other words, ICDPs incentivised the very activity (farming) that was often most directly in competition with more conservation-oriented land uses.

Another flaw in the ICDP logic is that they reproduced a simplistic narrative (introduced in Chapter 3) that poverty was the cause of environmental degradation. According to this narrative, if you succeeded in making people less poor, they would make fewer demands on local natural resources. But this assumption never stood up to empirical observation. In practice, research shows us that on average poorer households in the global South are more dependent on natural resources, i.e. it makes up a larger proportion of their total income, but they still use fewer resources than their less poor neighbours (Cavendish 2000). The upshot is that promoting livelihood development by making agriculture more productive might be a highly desirable intervention in terms of development objectives, but it is often not clear how this integrates with a conservation objective.

In the Nam Et-Phou Louey National Protected Area in Laos, we have found that agricultural modernisation policies have mixed impacts on demand for park resources. In particular, government policy has encouraged farmers to move away from shifting cultivation of traditional rice varieties and to cultivate maize as a cash crop, for export to Vietnam as livestock fodder. In terms of raising average incomes, this transition in farming has been extremely successful. It has also reduced demand for some forest resources within the park. For example, rats have been a major source of bushmeat in this area but we found that demand for this resource reduces as income rises and it becomes more possible to purchase meat from domestic livestock. Similarly, the demand for plant-based medicines reduces as households gain the income to purchase 'Western' medicines instead (Rasmussen et al. 2016). But whilst rising income has reduced demand for these 'inferior' forest products, demand for land is intensifying due to the profitability of maize, resulting in serious pressures on the park. In 2013 alone we found that 1 in 6 households in Phon Song village had been fined for land encroachment (Dawson et al. 2016a) and by early 2015 the authority was forced into degazetting some of the park for use as agricultural land. Again, this is not to say that improving the returns from agriculture is necessarily the wrong thing to do; but it is naïve to think that it is, in itself, a mechanism for integrating conservation and development objectives.

A similar argument can be made about non-timber forest products (NTFPs), another mainstay of ICDPs. Whilst there has been considerable optimism that markets for NTFPs can provide conservation-oriented pathways out of poverty for remote forest communities, the reality is that NTFP collection is mainly a very low-return activity; a poor person's profession and often a weak incentive for protecting biodiversity. In order for it to be a route out of poverty the NTFP business needs to undergo commercialisation and enhancements to productivity, but these changes will tend to make it less compatible with biodiversity conservation (Belcher et al. 2005; Belcher and Schreckenberg 2007).

The response to disenchantment with ICDPs has sometimes been referred to as a 'backlash' against people-friendly conservation and pressure to return to fortress conservation (Wilshusen et al. 2002; Hutton et al. 2005; Lélé et al. 2010). Such a backlash can certainly be discerned in some significant writings of the time, such as Terborgh's (1999) *Requiem for Nature* and Oates' (1999) *Myth and Reality in the Rainforest*, in which they respectively explore the failures of conservation in Indonesia and West Africa. In reality there have been at least two different – and in some ways diametrically opposed – responses to the failures of ICDPs. Firstly, there is a critique of ICDPs that proposes that the weakness of the approach is rooted in its anthropocentrism. According to this thinking, it is an error of judgement to believe that development for humans should be the motive for conserving nature.

> Science and environmental ethics influence each other in a mutually benefi-cial way; science showed us that humans are part of the same evolutionary line as all other species, making decisions about how humans treat the diver-sity of life important (Rozzi 2009). Those decisions should be made with respect and humility, not the egoism of anthropocentrism.
>
> *(Miller 2014, p. 1)*

The position of Miller and colleagues is that if we prioritise sustainable development – the wise use of nature as a resource *for* humans – we are basically aligning with those who still think that progress is defined as economic growth, marketisation and ever increasing material consumption. They propose that we need a purer conservation motive based on the humility of recognising that we are part of nature and must respect nature.

The second response to the perceived ineffectiveness of ICDPs is really the antithesis of the first. Instead of arguing against anthropocentrism, it argues for more and better anthropocentrism. It invokes neoclassical economics and calls for market-based instruments to bring about more cost-effective conservation that will maximise benefits to humans (Ferraro and Kiss 2002). Not surprisingly, it is this response that gained most traction in the early 2000s and that I have included in Figure 7.1. On the one hand this is positioned as a move towards governance by non-state actors, through market mechanisms. On the other hand I position this as a move away from prioritising development and back towards prioritising conser-vation outcomes. I do this because the shift to market-based approaches has been argued on the basis of conservation effectiveness as the overarching priority for work undertaken with conservation funding.

In practice, the shift from fortress conservation to integrated conservation and then to market-based approaches does not involve a new narrative simply replacing an old one. For example, although ICDPs were widely considered ineffective by the late 1990s, they remain very popular (Blom et al. 2010) and a main focus for international donor spending on conservation. Whilst they might not now be called 'ICDPs', more than two-thirds of international donor funding for biodiversity conservation is for projects with twinned conservation and development objectives (Miller et al. 2014). Indeed, many so-called market-based interventions do not actually involve market transactions (Milne and Adams 2012) and rather resemble ICDPs dressed up in new clothes. There are several reasons for this persistence of old narratives and practices: firstly, new approaches require very considerable investment and there is rarely the capacity to introduce them everywhere; secondly, even if the capacity does exist, it is usually desirable to introduce innovation gradually as part of a learning process; thirdly, not all places are suitable to all approaches.

Even in locations where new practices are introduced, they still do not simply replace old practices. New approaches to conservation are not introduced into empty social and ecological spaces but into places with pre-existing skills, experiences, traditions, institutions, authorities and power relations. Inevitably, new ways of operating not only change the existing institutional landscape but also are adapted to it (Giddens 1984; Cleaver 2012). Thus, the introduction of decentralised conservation and ICDPs has often occurred in places where fortress conservation has a strong tradition, where forest bureaucracies resist giving up their economic interests, and where, as a result, pre-existing narratives and practices are not simply given up overnight.

In India, for example, Joint Forest Management was introduced by a forest service cadre trained and structured according to preceding practices based on exclusionary approaches. Back in the mid 1990s when Joint Forest Management was being introduced in Karnataka, I remember attending a two-day participatory planning event at a village in Dakshina Kannada district. Around the middle of the first day, I noticed that the forest department representative had disappeared and I subsequently found him asleep in the back of his vehicle. He had already had enough of sitting around on the floor talking to villagers: this was not what he was trained for and, perhaps more to the point, this was not an assignment that provided opportunities to supplement his income via informal means. He was not alone: I later discovered that many of those who had been assigned to JFM duties had put in requests to transfer back into the 'territorial' division of the forest department, where commercial opportunities abounded. Just as I have noted that ICDPs persist despite falling out of favour in some circles, so too the ideas, institutions and practices of fortress conservation persist. Dominant conservation narratives are highly resilient to change, especially where they are institutionalised within large bureaucracies.

I turn now to a case study from southern Tanzania which serves two main purposes. Firstly, it demonstrates what the trends identified in Figure 7.1 actually appear like on the ground – in particular, how the market-based approaches are superimposed on to integrated conservation and development approaches, resulting in hybrid narratives and institutions, rather than a simple succession in which a new set of ideas and practices replaces an old one. Secondly, the case shows how, even with innovative application of market-based initiatives, it is very difficult to use income generation as the primary mechanism for integrating conservation and development. By explaining in some detail why this is so difficult, I begin to make the case for a new shift in narrative – to 'just conservation'.

Conservation and development in Kilwa district, Tanzania[1]

Kilwa is a district in the Lindi region of Tanzania, bordered by the Indian Ocean to the east and the huge, 50,000 km² Selous Game Reserve inland to the west (Figure 7.2). The district covers 13,347 km² and has a population of 190,744 (2012 census), living in 93 villages, many of which have substantial village lands. Woodland covers about 70% of the territory, dominated by Miombo woodland, with some patches of East African coastal forest. More remote village lands often retain relatively intact forest (Ball and Makala 2014). Away from the coast, farming is the principal form of livelihood, dominated by shifting cultivation of maize, millet and rice for subsistence consumption although there is now a transition towards a cash crop economy with a boom in sesame production, encouraged by government price support mechanisms. Local tribes have kept very few livestock (apart from chickens) due to tsetse fly infestation but cattle numbers have recently increased greatly with the arrival of pastoral groups such as the Sukuma who have been relocated to Kilwa following eviction from game reserves in northern and eastern Tanzania. For example, the families I met living near to Ruhatwe village (adjacent to Kikole in Figure 7.2) had begun in Shinyanga district in the north. In 2008 the government had moved them 500km south to Mbeya district and in 2013 had moved them another 500km, this time east to Kilwa.

Analysis of Landsat images from 2000 and 2010 shows that actual deforestation rates, i.e. change from forest to agriculture, are only 0.2% per annum on average. This is because agriculture tends to be located in the most fertile river valleys and does not compete directly with remaining intact forests. The cutting of trees to produce charcoal (a superior cooking fuel to wood) is also not considered to be a major cause of deforestation, although it is predicted to be so in the future as the demand for charcoal from Dar es Salaam extends ever further (Ahrends et al. 2010; MCDI 2015). Timber logging is identified as a significant but highly selective activity. In 2004 policy was enacted to ban export of roundwoods from natural forests, greatly reducing the harvest in Kilwa.

---

1 This case study of Kilwa is heavily indebted to the work of many colleagues. At the Mpingo Conservation and Development Initiative particular thanks go to Jasper Makala, Glory Massao and Steve Ball; at the Autonomous University of Barcelona, thanks to Esteve Corbera and Kaysara Khatun; and at my own university, Nicole Gross-Camp and Oliver Springate-Baginski.

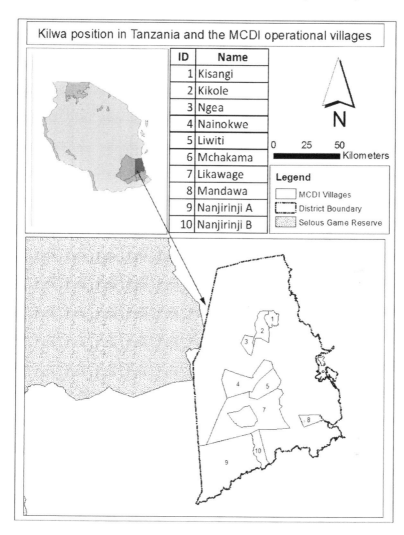

Kilwa position in Tanzania and the MCDI operational villages

ID	Name
1	Kisangi
2	Kikole
3	Ngea
4	Nainokwe
5	Liwiti
6	Mchakama
7	Likawage
8	Mandawa
9	Nanjirinji A
10	Nanjirinji B

N

0   25   50
▬▬▬▬ Kilometers

Legend
☐ MCDI Villages
⌐⌐⌐ District Boundary
▒ Selous Game Reserve

FIGURE 7.2   Map showing Kilwa district, Tanzania, including locations of the ten villages where the Mpingo Conservation and Development Initiative (MCDI) operates.

At the moment then, there is no rapid loss or degradation of forests as a result of agricultural expansion, charcoal production or timber logging. In fact the main threat to the Miombo woodland is now considered to be degradation rather than outright deforestation and a 2012 study found fire to be the largest driver of tree loss (Miya et al. 2012). The importance of fire needs to be explained in a bit of detail as it is central to understanding some of the recent efforts to integrate conservation and development. About 60% of the landscape burns each year, leading to tree mortality and retarding regeneration (MCDI 2012). Miombo woodland is a naturally fire-modified ecosystem, so the occurrence of fires is not always a bad thing. However, the frequency and intensity of fires is critical to the survival and species diversity of forest (Ryan and Williams 2011). In the absence of intense fires, Miombo will form closed canopy forest which is desirable for biodiversity and eco-system services; but with annual fire it tends towards grassland which is generally considered less desirable.

Fire is an essential method for clearing agricultural fields prior to planting. This is not a problem in itself but unfortunately fires often spread beyond farming areas to neighbouring woodlands. Fire is also used to prepare areas for both licensed and illegal game hunting, clearing vegetation to ensure better lines of sight for spotting and pursuing game (Khatun et al. 2016). It is not only the frequency of fire that matters, but also the intensity. Late dry season fires will often burn hotter due to the drier vegetation and these intense fires can top-kill up to 12% of larger tree stems (those with more than 5cm diameter at breast height) (Ryan and William 2011). This is a cause of some conflict between farming and forest conservation because farmers tend to wait until the dry season is quite well established before starting agricultural fires – it can actually be quite hard to establish fires early in the dry season when they would burn less intensely.

As elsewhere in the world, shifting cultivation has since colonial times been demonised as inefficient and destructive. During interviews in 2015, government officers in Kilwa district clearly expressed their hopes that land use planning pro-cedures could be used to restrict the areas available for villagers' farming so that more village lands could be designated for conservation-oriented uses. There is thus a clear tension between agriculture-led incomes and forest conservation. The sesame boom is increasing local incomes but it is a crop that requires frequent rota-tion (and frequent fires for clearance) due to problems with weeds and this puts it at odds with government plans to designate more village lands for conservation. In nearby Namtumbo district (also adjoining the Selous) villages have given up to 92% of their lands to conservation (changing the status of the land to Wildlife Management Areas) during land use planning exercises supported by international conservation NGOs (Noe and Kangalawe 2015). Such a massive contribution to wildlife conservation, in one of the poorest areas of Tanzania, is agreed during participatory processes at village level: it is technically voluntary. But this is still highly problematic because villagers are enticed to volunteer their land for conser-vation on the basis of strong expectations of future financial benefits that have not yet, and are unlikely to, materialise (Noe and Kangalawe 2015). It is a lesson that conservation has to proceed very carefully if it is to avoid injustices. To provide one more example from further away, the conversion of village lands to Wildlife Management Areas in Longido district, near Kilimanjaro, was also undertaken through consultation with local communities. But here, despite the benefits that villagers were led to expect, the formation of Wildlife Management Areas has led to more households becoming poorer and fewer households becoming wealthier, compared to villages that have not had their land redesignated in this way (PIMA 2016). These are in effect land grabs against poor villagers, carried out in the name of conservation.

Since 2004, the Mpingo Conservation and Development Initiative (MCDI, renamed from the Mpingo Conservation Project in 2012) has developed a series of activities to conserve and enhance the Miombo forests whilst also improving local livelihoods. Principal amongst these has been support for Participatory Forest Management (PFM) which operates in two ways under the 2002 Tanzania Forest Act. Joint Forest Management (JFM) allows villages to enter into co-management agreements with owners of non-village lands and in particular, state reserved forests. JFM has a limited presence in Kilwa in villages adjoining the Selous Game Reserve. Participatory Forest Management (PFM) enables villages to declare areas of their own village lands as community forests known as Village Land Forest Reserves; these are managed by Village Natural Resource Councils in conjunction with existing Village Councils. MCDI have supported Village Land Forest Reserve (VLFR) formation in 12 villages in Kilwa district to date: the first in Kikole village was initially just 454 hectares whilst one of the latest, in Nanjirinji, is 61,000 hectares. Tanzania's PFM policy allows sustainable timber harvesting from VLFR and villages retain 95% of the sale value. The forests contain high-value timbers, including the East African Blackwood, *Dalbergia melanoxylon* (Mpingo in Swahili) that is prized for manufacturing high-end musical instruments, including clarinets and bagpipes.

By 2008, 12.8% of Tanzania's forests were managed under PFM arrangements (Government of Tanzania 2013). The generalised outcomes mirror an interesting picture that has emerged across Africa, that forest decentralisation often achieves some positive forest conservation outcomes, but generally fails to deliver significant livelihood improvements. For example, Blomley et al. (2008) found some evidence that PFM leads to increased basal area of trees whilst Persha and Meshack (2016) also find some evidence that PFM helps to reduce forest degradation. However, the latter study finds no evidence of any livelihood impacts, mirroring previous research findings that PFM in Tanzania delivers few economic benefits due to low timber yields and values, the appropriation of benefits by local elite, and high operating costs for local communities (Blomley and Ramadhani 2006; Meshack et al. 2006; Lund and Treue 2008; Vyamana 2009; Burgess et al. 2010; Merger et al. 2012).

These are intriguing findings and I think they are hugely significant because they question both the assumptions that underpinned the integrated conservation and development narrative described above, as well as the subsequent critique and justification for a market-oriented approach. The former assumes that support for conservation is best achieved by increasing local incomes through support for livelihood activities. The latter assumes that this failed because success in delivering livelihood projects did not trigger support for conservation because the two outcomes were not causally linked (Salafsky and Wollenberg 2000). Both assumptions appear to be wrong in Tanzania and I strongly suspect elsewhere. The alternative picture that emerges is that support for forest conservation can be garnered even in the absence of significant livelihood improvements because PFM provides other things that people value and, in particular, devolution of decision-making.[2] It is for

---

2 Some of the evidence for this was summarised at the end of Chapter 3.

this reason that I propose we should be focusing on a change of narrative to 'just conservation' (Figure 7.1). This will ensure that we move away from prioritising income and livelihoods alone, to also focus on the wider range of practices and outcomes that are valued by local people.

Such a shift, from emphasising the need to boost incomes through forestry, to pursuing a broader range of justice outcomes, is not only desirable in normative terms but may also be more effective. One reason for this is that it is extremely difficult to deliver high economic returns to communities. Even in Kilwa district, where there are still some high-value timbers and where the rules of PFM allow communities to retain much of the sales price from these, it still proves difficult to achieve substantial contributions to incomes. In 2009, MCDI brokered a group-based Forest Stewardship Council certification (the first in Africa) for communities managing Village Land Forest Reserves. Whilst Forest Stewardship Council certification does not guarantee a price premium, it provides evidence of high social and environmental standards and it was hoped that this would lead to improved market demand, especially from musical instrument manufacturers. The potential income in Kilwa district is quite high, although the forest quality is highly variable and the quantity of forest available to each village also varies greatly. Mpingo logs can now be sold to contractors for $150/m^3$, of which 95% is retained in the village. Following sawmill processing into billets sized for musical instrument parts, the timber is sold for export at $15,000/m^3$, a price mark-up that reflects very high (c. 90%) wastage rates. Based on the range of local timbers, MCDI calculated a potential sustainable income of $25/ha/year for Village Land Forest Reserves, based on annual extraction rates of 1.5% of standing timber volume. In practice, however, sales have been much lower less than this due to low market demand – achieved revenue is closer to $1/ha/year. One problem is the competition from cheaper, non-sustainably logged timbers. Another is the long turnover times of musical instrument manufacturing. Makers often have large stocks of timber and may prefer to store billets for years before using them. This makes it slow to develop a market for Forest Stewardship Council certified instruments, although the first such clarinet was produced in 2011 by Hanson Clarinets, using Mpingo wood from Kilwa.

In 2010 MCDI received funding from the Norwegian Embassy for a pilot REDD+ project, with a view to securing an additional income stream for VLFR from selling carbon offsets (Ball and Makala 2014; Khatun et al. 2015). Based on a market price of $7/tonne of CO_2, REDD+ was estimated to yield annual sales of $2.1/ha of VLFR, of which about a third was expected as net revenue for villages. On completion of the pilot in late 2014, considerable advances had been made towards achieving carbon sales but a series of technical issues prevented actual sales. This is not uncommon. In fact, during that period none of Tanzania's nine pilot REDD+ projects were able to achieve sales of offsets. In MCDI's case, the delays stemmed from the need to adapt the project to new knowledge that emerged about the causes of forest degradation. In particular, it became clear that fire was the largest driver of forest degradation and this required a new approach to REDD+.

A system of community-based 'early burning' was developed whereby the frequency and, in particular, the intensity of fires was managed through a programme of systematic early dry season burning to prevent more intense, late season fires (Khatun et al. 2016). Early burning requires a considerable management effort, including for example the clearing of vegetation to produce fire breaks, in order to restrict the spread of fires. However, fire management for REDD+ takes place within Village Land Forest Reserves so only involves lands where access has already been restricted. The additional costs to local communities, in terms of restrictions on farming and the collection of forest products, are therefore minimal.

Early burning itself has proved challenging for reasons that include technique, timing and organisation (see Ball and Makala 2014 and MCDI 2015 for details). The technique for establishing fires early in the dry season proved more difficult than initially expected, the timing of burning is critical and yet unpredictable due to variability in dry season timings each year, and it is hard to quickly organise community and NGO staff mobilisation when conditions are judged to be just right. For these inter-linked reasons, early burning has not been executed fully to plan each year, but has required a learning process. Additionally, for carbon offsets to be saleable on the voluntary carbon market, there is a requirement for a completed Project Design Document and a Verified Carbon Standard. These involve lengthy and highly technical procedures to establish a robust and verifiable system for demonstrating carbon savings and as in other Tanzanian REDD+ pilots, it proved impossible to complete them within the project period.

To summarise the case so far, the history of conservation in Kilwa has involved a series of overlapping interventions and associated governance institutions, shaped in large part by the presence of a local NGO, MCDI. Traditional government regulation has involved gazettement of protected areas but has also involved rules that have removed rights to both wildlife and trees for local communities, including on village lands. PFM has restored decentralised local authority over selected areas of village land forests and can be seen as part of the global shift towards integrating conservation and development objectives through community-based initiatives. This shift has gone hand in hand with a broadening of governance to embrace a range of stakeholders including local communities, Mpingo Conservation and Development Initiative, Forest Stewardship Council, funders such as the Danish government and Comic Relief and private sector actors including sawmills and musical instrument manufacturers. REDD+ has worked with the local institutional platform developed as part of PFM, bringing in additional stakeholders such as the Norwegian government, the private sector carbon broker Carbon Tanzania, and research teams from the universities of Edinburgh and East Anglia in the UK. The result is a complex mosaic of governance involving the state, civil society, local and global NGOs, the private sector and international operating standards such as Verified Carbon Standard, United Nations REDD+ Safeguards and the Climate, Community and Biodiversity standards. With one hand this evolving complex of forest governance gives authority to local people, using PFM as the institutional basis to assign village communities rights over forest timber and carbon, and protecting local rights through global standards; but with the other hand it takes away local authority by imposing very technical requirements, calling for adherence to international rules and specialist consultants to support this – a process that serves to pull authority away from local institutions, investing power with ever more distant global stakeholders (Phelps et al. 2010).

In 2011 and 2014 we worked with MCDI to survey nine villages involved in PFM and/or REDD+ as well as six villages which were not. The nine participant villages included four that had been involved early in the scheme, starting between 2004 and 2009 (Kikole, Kisangi, Liwiti and Nainokwe), and five that were later entrants, beginning in 2010 or later (Likawage, Mandawa, Mchakama, Mitole and Ngea). The six 'control' villages (Mtyalambuko, Ngorongoro, Nakiu, Mtandi, Nandete and Mbwemkuru) were selected to be similar to the participant villages in two key respects: firstly, the population sizes of villages and secondly, the respective distances to the main Mtwara to Dar es Salaam road. Each round of surveys involved (a) participatory workshops in each village to assess forest governance performance and (b) 452 questionnaire interviews to explore household-level social-economic impacts of project interventions. In 2015 we undertook some further research in two villages, including more ethnographic methods for exploring local concerns in relation to environmental justice.

The participatory governance assessments involved meetings with around 20 villagers. A set of nine governance criteria were discussed, each with their own sets of indicators. Following discussion, participants used a simple assessment system for each criterion, whereby it was adjudged to have been well performed, partially performed or poorly performed (Springate-Baginski et al. 2015). These judgements were subsequently given numerical scores (+1, 0 and −1). Table 7.1 summarises the results, providing mean scores each criterion for both 2011 and 2014.

The findings suggest that villages with longer involvement in PFM have developed stronger local forest governance than later entrant and control villages. Three of the four early entry villages showed strong improvements across all criteria but one, between 2011 and 2014. One of the early entry villages – Liwiti – performed less well in 2014 having achieved the highest scores in 2011. This is down to some particular tensions that arose in this village, including the resignation of the village Chairperson after it was revealed that he had been involved with loggers and subsequently the resignation of 16 out of 25 Village Council members (Khatun et al. 2015). The later entry villages were also showing some signs of improving governance but the overall performance was judged to be quite low. The control villages adjudged their forest governance to be poor in many respects. This is an important finding because the conservation logic of PFM is premised on assumptions that participation will improve governance over time which will in turn enhance conservation. Furthermore, seen through an environmental justice lens, we would expect villagers to value this participation in its own right – i.e. not only for its instrumental value in achieving more effective forest outcomes.

The survey of household livelihoods found rising income across the participating villages. However, we knew that incomes were rising anyway, due to a boom

TABLE 7.1 Mean governance criteria scores by village category.

Criteria	Early involved villages			Later involved villages			Control villages		
	2011	2014	Change	2011	2014	Change	2011	2014	Change
1. User organisation & cohesion	0.9	0.9	*0.0*	0.2	0.3	*0.1*	0.0	−0.1	*−0.1*
2. Communication & awareness	0.4	−0.3	*−0.7*	−0.5	−0.4	*0.1*	−1.0	−0.8	*0.2*
3. Decision-making & implementation	0.1	0.3	*0.2*	−0.3	0.2	*0.5*	0.0	0.4	*0.4*
4. Forest management	0.4	1.0	*0.6*	−0.8	0.0	*0.8*	−0.8	−0.5	*0.3*
5. Forest product access & distribution	0.4	0.9	*0.5*	0.8	0.8	*0.0*	0.5	0.4	*−0.1*
6. Gender and equity consideration	0.0	0.0	*0.0*	0.3	0.0	*−0.3*	0.0	0.0	*0.0*
7. Economic / fund development	0.5	1.0	*0.5*	0.3	−1.0	*−1.3*	0.0	0.0	*0.0*
8. Conflict management	−0.3	0.8	*1.1*	0.3	1.0	*0.7*	0.5	−0.3	*−0.8*
9. Linkage and network development	−0.1	0.4	*0.5*	−0.5	−0.1	*0.4*	0.5	−0.3	*−0.8*
Overall mean criteria score	**0.3**	**0.5**	*0.2*	**0.0**	**0.1**	*0.1*	**0.0**	**−0.1**	*−0.1*

Source: Springate-Baginski et al. 2015.

Note: The maximum mean criteria score is 1.0 and the minimum is −1.0.

in the cultivation of sesame, a relatively lucrative cash crop. So what we wanted to know was whether the rate of income growth in PFM/REDD+ villages was different to that in control villages. When we undertook this 'difference in difference' statistical analysis we found no significant difference that could be attributed to the PFM/REDD+ interventions (Corbera et al. 2015). We ran models for three measures of material wealth: a count of household assets, total household income, and total household expenditure. In each case, the change over time for participating villages was not significantly different to changes in the matched controls. In other words, we found no evidence that conservation and development interventions had made households significantly materially richer.

In some ways this was not surprising because forestry income remains marginal compared to agriculture – relatively small changes to forestry income will not have a big impact on overall livelihoods. By Tanzanian standards, Kilwa represents a high-income case of PFM because of the high-value timber sales. However, even here the income from forestry, carried out sustainably for markets with Forest Stewardship Council chain of custody certification, brings relatively small total income. For example, Kikole village has only a small VLFR and from 2004 to 2014 the timber harvest had brought an income of $4913. That is a little over $10 per person or an annual average of $1 per person. Nainokwe village has a much larger VLFR and a smaller population, yielding $44 per person, or a little under $9 per person per year.

Some forest conservation benefits are received individually through wages paid for activities such as the clearing, marking and patrolling of VLFR boundaries and the early burning operations described above. However, the majority of income from timber sales is invested in public goods, including about 52% spent on the operating costs of the Village Natural Resource Committee and the remaining 48% invested in projects determined at village General Assembly meetings (Khatun et al. 2015). Across the four villages that had received income from timber sales by 2013, there has been general contentment with both the way that decisions were made about these spends and about the outcomes. Eighty-six per cent of spending was considered widely beneficial to the community and 89% of interviewees considered their communities to be better off as a result of PFM. Some respondents cited the environmental and social benefits, including the involvement in village governance, but most also referred to the benefits arising from income from timber sales. This suggests that whilst the economic benefits from PFM are too small to have a significant impact on household incomes, they are nonetheless highly valued. Communal income, spent according to locally determined priorities, is perceived to be important to the village. An interesting example comes from Nainokwe where the biggest single timber sale was recorded in 2011 (about $8395). Much of this was spent on building a house for the Village Executive Officer, a decision that led to concerns amongst external agencies, including one of the donors, Comic Relief, that profits were going to the local elite and not helping the poor. But when we interviewed non-elite villagers about this decision they did not view it like this at all – they considered it a wise investment because this officer's role was so important for village development (Khatun et al. 2015).

I will now turn to a more explicit consideration of the justice issues raised by villagers through the example of Kikole village. This case illustrates what has become apparent above – that focusing only on the economics of livelihoods is an insufficient basis for Participatory Forest Management or other interventions which seek to integrate conservation and development objectives. Instead, an environmental justice perspective is necessary to understand the fuller range of things that are valued by local people and which raise concerns for them. PFM involves a process of layering new institutions over old ones in ways that inevitably create tensions which play out as local conflicts. Such conflicts should not necessarily be viewed as negative; in the case of Kikole, they can be viewed as processes that can support transformation towards more just conservation. Whilst discussing PFM with villagers in Kikole, four issues were raised that I report here as being justice concerns: benefit distribution, land disputes, problems with wild animals and concerns over future forest tenure.

Kikole conducted the world's first Forest Stewardship Council certified mpingo harvest in 2009 and another in 2011. The distribution of benefits from these sales was widely appreciated, including the decision to invest in a borehole and in a house for the midwife. There were, however, two types of concern. Firstly, Kikole includes a main village and two sub-village hamlets, Nanyati and Mbunga, reachable by motorbike in the dry season but a difficult journey in the wet season. These outlying communities had not been successfully involved in PFM and did not consider themselves to be beneficiaries. Those we spoke to in the hamlets clearly articulated this as being against justice (*kinyume na haki*) and suggested alternative distributional principles including sharing income proportionately according to the population of the three settlements. Secondly, there were concerns about corruption. Funds for the midwife's house had been redirected from a new build to repair of an old building, leading to accusations that this was a scam that enabled local elite to gain by over-charging for materials. Furthermore, there is concern that illicit timber felling is continuing and that the village elite are complicit in this, as the following interview respondent complains:

'So one day the VNRC [Village Natural Resource Committee] had received information from a community member informing them that he had heard a chainsaw in the forest. So at that time the VNRC decided tomorrow they should go to patrol in the forest. I was among the ones who participated in the patrol. . . So the next day I was first to arrive in the village. As we were walking, the VEO [Village Executive Officer] followed us and insisted that we shouldn't go to the forest. They had even tried to bribe us with 20,000 shillings but we refused to take the money. When we reached the forest we managed to find the timber that had been harvested. So we decided to go back to the village and report what we had found. Then we reported to the village chairperson but his answer wasn't very pleasing. . . The community stayed in the forest for two days but they didn't have any food so they decided to come back and fetch food. When they came back I think the village chairperson saw them and immediately he called the business guy to go and take out the timber, so when the community returned back they found the timber was gone. As a result the village didn't get anything.'

Whilst such problems persist, the presence of PFM is nonetheless viewed as a significant step towards procedural justice within the village. Whilst the woman speaking above is articulating frustration that such events still occur, there is a general appreciation that the creation of the VNRC has provided the institutional basis to confront such practices. The crucial thing is that PFM is bringing poor governance into the limelight and providing a platform to confront it.

Land use conflicts have been a regular feature of both PFM and REDD+ in Kilwa district. In the absence of clear and agreed boundaries, and with conservation and development initiatives which create or increase the monetary values of forest timbers and carbon, disputes are inevitable and views can quickly crystallise across lines of inter-group conflict. As with the issue of corruption just discussed, PFM (and REDD+) brings more latent conflicts into the foreground – it is a catalyst rather than a root cause. There are three main land conflicts in Kikole. The first involves a boundary dispute with the neighbouring village, Kisangi. Lacking good forest within their own boundaries, Kisangi had requested some of Kikole's forests so that they could start their own Village Land Forest Reserve. Kikole granted this request but subsequently Kisangi had cut valuable trees beyond the gifted area and then disputed the agreed boundary. This has largely been resolved but it is interesting to consider the justices and injustices (from Kikole's perspective). In particular, the original decision to give forest land to Kisangi was considered right because (a) Kisangi did not have suitable forest of its own and would therefore miss out on PFM, (b) Kisangi had followed the correct procedure for requesting the land and, (c) the two villages have strong family ties across them. Thus, the granting of land was justified on an intertwined mix of distributional, procedural and relational grounds. Conversely, whilst Kisangi's abuse of this gift was viewed as a betrayal, the relational bonds remained sufficiently strong to want to seek a compromise resolution.

The second conflict is still live at time of writing and involves people of the Wamatumbi tribe who have recently come to Kikole from nearby Nambondo village, around 20km away. They have occupied an area of high forest that had been demarcated to be Kikole's second Village Land Forest Reserve, to enable participation in the REDD+ pilot. The Wamatumbi have been clearing the forest for sesame production and this has put a stop to the development of the new community forest. This forest clearance is clearly articulated as an injustice by those we spoke to, firstly, because permission to use the land had not been requested and secondly, because it was believed that village leaders had allowed this encroachment to occur in return for bribes.

The third conflict is with the Sukuma pastoralist people who had been relocated to the region in 2013 but were then left to their own devices to find suitable places to settle. Of the three conflicts, this is the most complex in some ways, indicated by differences in the claims made in public and in private. In a general assembly meeting, a strong line was adopted that the presence of the Sukuma was wrong and that they should be evicted. In private interviews, however, a greater range of views was apparent, including a principle of a right to land for all Tanzanians. Whilst such sympathies existed in private, they were overridden in public by strong procedural concerns. As with the Wamatumbi dispute, it has become widely believed that leaders have been unofficially 'taxing' the Sukuma and thereby profiting from their presence. Again, concerns about procedure are paramount and viewed as deeply connected to distributional outcomes. To reiterate the point made above, these are the kinds of everyday conflicts that make forest conservation so challenging, in this case eroding the legitimacy of an existing VLFR and preventing the creation of a second, much larger one.

In addition to conflicts between different groups of people, animals are also important actors in this landscape. Tanzania's elephant population has been decimated by poaching in recent years, falling from 109,051 in 2009 to 43,330 in 2014.

About 13,000 of these remaining elephants live in the Selous ecosystem where they roam an area almost twice the extent of the Game Reserve (Siege and Baldus 2000) and are common visitors to the village lands in Kilwa district. For villagers, elephants are a threat, causing injuries and deaths, as well as damage to crops. When discussing this problem, the theme that emerges most strongly concerns not being taken seriously by the District Forest Officer, resulting in government failure to pursue its responsibility to help the villagers. This perceived failure of recognition is really quite damaging to the relationship with local communities and to the prospects for a strong conservation partnership.

In 2015 we asked 60 villagers in Kikole whether they felt that it would be fair to further expand the area of village forest managed for conservation. We were surprised and admittedly disappointed to discover that 51 (85%) said it would be unfair. Villagers are mainly supportive of the existing conservation and development interventions introduced by MCDI and partners. They appreciate the economic benefits (even if small) and many are very astute in seeing that some of the internal tensions created are products of a constructive process of democratisation and a shift in power over forest governance. That being so, why would they not want more forest land to be designated for conservation through gazettement as Village Land Forest Reserve? The answer to this appears to be strongly linked to the perceived lack of recognition from district government and a sense that the district government does not prioritise villagers' interests. There were two main reasons given for not wanting an expansion of conservation. The first related to the dangers from wild animals, and it should again be stressed that this is not only a matter of crop damage, but also of threat to lives. The second is a concern about where they will be able to farm in future, when fertility declines in existing farmlands. Villagers are aware that the government wants to see the majority of village forests re-designated for conservation as part of an overarching strategy to spatially restrict agriculture and to discourage shifting cultivation techniques. This could pose significant problems, in addition to the threat of wild animals just mentioned. With a rising population and increasing dependence on land-hungry sesame crops for cash income, local livelihoods remain highly tied to extensive use of land. As one respondent put it, nobody has convincingly answered the question of 'how would we eat?' if access to farmland were restricted. It is a pertinent question: in our survey of livelihoods, only 17% of households in Kikole said that their self-produced food was sufficient to last them through the year – there is a regular 'hungry season' in Kilwa.

From conservation and development to just conservation

I believe that the case of Participatory Forest Management in Kilwa represents something of a crisis for the integrated conservation and development model, both in Tanzania and worldwide. This case represents a location that enjoys conditions which are in many ways conducive to success. Villages have huge territories, some of them with surviving forests containing valuable tree species. The rules of PFM in Tanzania allow villages to sell these timbers and retain 95% of the sale price. PFM has been supported by a specialised and long-serving local NGO that understands local conditions well and has provided continuity of advice and advocacy. This NGO has been innovative in its approaches, seeking market-based mechanisms to enhance revenue streams, for example taking on Forest Stewardship Council certification and carbon offsetting through a REDD+ pilot. In doing so it has secured financial support from a range of international donors that has covered the start-up and running costs of key initiatives. These are significant advantages that have helped to achieve some good outcomes for forest governance. But it is also clear that, even with such advantages, an approach to conservation and development which primarily emphasises economic development and livelihoods (the ICDP model, Figure 7.1) struggles to raise incomes.

To provide another brief example, in May 2016 I visited the Amani Nature Reserve in Tanzania's East Usambara mountains. Like Kilwa, this is widely considered a success story, with Joint Forest Management as an institutional basis for sharing revenues with surrounding villages, tourism bringing some regular income, strong local support for income-generating activities (e.g. the Tanzania Forest Conservation Group's support for butterfly farming) and extensive international support from donors and conservation NGOs. But there are some clear similarities to the experience in Kilwa. Villagers are generally supportive of the conservation work being done, but again, despite these advantageous conditions, the economic benefits arising from the reserve are very small, with revenue-sharing from tourism amounting to well under a dollar per person per year. More generally, a recent study finds that Joint Forest Management across Tanzania provides benefits in terms of governance improvements, but no significant benefits for livelihoods (Persha and Meshack 2016).

A conservation and development narrative tells us that providing livelihood benefits is a key strategy for achieving conservation effectiveness. But even given the most advantageous conditions, we see that achieving more than modest benefits is challenging. And even when modest benefits are highly appreciated locally, there is little to suggest that these alone would overcome prevailing tensions between conservation and livelihoods, such as the perceived conflicts between conservation and farming in Kilwa. One response to this problem is to try to find new ways of financing livelihood benefits, preferably with strong linkage to conservation. The currently popular suggestion is to employ an ecosystem services analysis to (a) better understand the monetary value of conservation services to the wider world and (b) work with the private sector to connect potential providers of these services (such as villages in Kilwa) with those who are willing buyers of the service (such as ethically minded bagpipers and those seeking to reduce their carbon footprint), and (c) to do this in ethical ways employing modes of operation that respect human rights. We have seen this evolution to market-based initiatives in Kilwa, through Forest Stewardship Council certification and then attempted entry into carbon offset markets. Significant progress has been made but still without producing large contributions to local livelihoods and certainly not providing a model that would be easy to apply widely. I will say more about this in the next chapter but for now it is sufficient to state that markets do not offer a simple solution to the demand for more economic benefits from conservation.

A new narrative of 'just conservation' calls for us to change the way in which we think about and respond to the social impacts of conservation. There are two central tenets to such an approach: a more pluralistic conception of what kinds of impacts are valued and contested by communities, and greater attention to how such impacts are distributed. A just conservation framing of the social aspects of conservation will not discount the importance of generating and distributing economic benefits to local people, but will develop a more sophisticated approach to analysing how these benefits connect with other valued social goals of fair procedure and recognition.

Conclusion

The case for making this change now seems overwhelming. Firstly, there is a normative case. In the introduction to this chapter, I cited Michael Soulé as saying that the goals of conservation reflect dominant norms regarding global social responsibilities. Indeed, we might say that if conservation fails to keep attuned to global norms it will lose any claim to a moral high ground and find its mandate compromised. Global social development norms have been evolving, moving away from a narrow focus on development defined in terms of livelihoods and income, and towards more pluralistic conceptions of human wellbeing. This is prominent, for example, in the shift in agenda that can be discerned between the Millennium Development Goals (MDGs) agreed in 2000 and the Sustainable Development Goals (SDGs) which succeeded them in 2015. The MDGs placed much emphasis on a small number of material indicators of poverty such as numbers of people living on less than a dollar a day. The SDGs by contrast emphasise broader conditions of human wellbeing and highlight equality across social divisions such as gender. To be aligned with SDGs, conservation will be better served by a broader, justice-oriented framing of social goals, than by a narrower livelihoods-oriented approach.

If for no other reason than to be better aligned with global moral commitments, conservation should adopt a broader and more equity-oriented framing of its social development goals. However, as has been argued throughout this book, there is another reason: this shift also promises to be instrumental in the generation of more effective conservation. Based on the content of this chapter, there are at least four supporting arguments for this claim.[3] Firstly, as just mentioned, the moral argument for just conservation crosses over into an instrumental one. Conservation depends on high-level political support and on massive public support. To maintain and enhance that support it needs to strive for continued legitimacy in both its biological and social agendas. Secondly, conservation also depends heavily on local

---

3 Some of the points made here have benefited greatly from discussion with Phil Franks at the International Institute of Environment and Development.

support, from those communities living in and around areas that are most valued for their biodiversity and charismatic species. As the case of Kilwa has shown, winning local support through economic benefits alone is unlikely to succeed outside of a minority of locations blessed with exceptional capacity to generate income from conservation-linked activities. It was widely known by the late 1990s that simply raising income does not lead to more conservation-oriented behaviours. The lesson learned was that to benefit conservation, this income must be linked to conservation such that future income was dependent on successful conservation. But as we have seen, this limits the range of relevant income-generating activities to ecotourism, sustainable harvesting of products such as timber and wildlife, and a few other activities such as beekeeping, butterfly farming and sale of carbon offsets. These conservation-linked livelihood activities are certainly a desirable part of conservation but have limited potential in many places. For social agendas to support conservation effectiveness it is therefore essential to go beyond income generation (Franks et al. 2016). Thirdly, the Kilwa case provides positive evidence of the scope for broadening the range of benefits for local communities. Villagers involved in Participatory Forest Management value comparatively small economic benefits when they are part and parcel of progress towards fairer systems of governance. In particular, they appreciate the restoration of rights and authority over areas of forest, the ability to make their own decisions about how to invest revenues and the institutional platform to confront corruption (even if they still have a long way to go to beat it). On the other hand the case also demonstrates the perceived failures of recognition that undermine trust between villagers and local government, exemplified by claims that district foresters do not take seriously the threat to human lives posed by wildlife. The Kilwa case does not suggest that conservation practice should ignore income generation and livelihoods, but rather that these efforts will be more effective if embedded in a broader social justice agenda that includes attention to procedure and recognition. Fourthly, economic benefits will achieve greater conservation outcomes where their distribution is seen to be equitable – bearing in mind that what is considered equitable distribution might vary from context to context. This argument is increasingly supported by wider studies. Sticking with evidence from Tanzania, studies of Marine Protected Areas have found that lack of participation of legitimate stakeholders has led to elite capture of benefits and to local communities losing interest and disengaging (Gustavsson et al. 2014; Katikiro et al. 2015). Similarly a study of Tanzania's terrestrial conservation and development initiatives, including Joint Forest Management and Wildlife Management Areas, finds that failures to recognise local tenure rights leads to the poor being disadvantaged (Patenaude and Lewis 2014). A picture is emerging therefore of the inter-linkage between participation, recognition and the distribution of costs of benefits, and of how this nexus of justice concerns determines local engagement with conservation.

8

CONSERVATION, MARKETS AND JUSTICE

Introduction

Regulation by governments and inter-governmental agreements remains an important way of protecting biodiversity. Examples include the national laws which govern protected areas, currently covering more than 15% of the earth's terrestrial surface, and the global Convention on International Trade in Endangered Species of Wild Fauna and Flora (CITES). But regulation is increasingly used in combination with alternative governance techniques and is not always desirable or sufficient. For example, blanket regulations to prevent farming in ecologically sensitive areas might be hard to enforce, might be impossible to obey in the absence of supporting measures, and might result in small farmers disproportionately bearing the costs of conservation. Similarly, rules that simply forbid access to a forest or marine reserve might not be reasonable where livelihoods and cultures are dependent on resources within that area. This chapter considers the opening up of conservation governance to include a wider range of approaches and, correspondingly, a wider set of actors which includes the private sector. This shift from 'government' to 'governance' is nowhere more controversial than in its attempts to harness market forces for the advancement of conservation, often in tandem with government regulatory frameworks. For some this is a welcome move because it brings the private sector on board, prompts new sources of conservation funding, provides mechanisms for more efficient allocation of scarce funds, and ultimately meets a utilitarian goal to maximise conservation outcomes for humanity. For critics, however, this is a deeply flawed agenda which threatens to undermine more durable forms of caring for the environment and at the same time creates the conditions for further transfers of wealth and power from poor to rich.

In England, almost 70% of all farmland is now managed under voluntary agreements in which landowners receive payments for environmentally sensitive farming practices that include the objective to conserve biodiversity. About 6 million hectares is under Environmental Stewardship agreements in which farmers receive annual payments depending on management options and location. The majority of this land is managed under the 'entry level' Stewardship scheme and lowland farms receive £30 per hectare annually for a five-year agreement period (Silcock et al. 2012; DEFRA 2013). This is a government rather than a market-based scheme, although it involves a shift from regulatory to incentive-based governance in which uptake is, in principle at least, voluntary. It would require a significant further step to link incentives to markets in ways that would allow the laws of supply and demand (rather than governments) to determine who provides the environmental services, where they are provided, and at what price. The most notable examples of market-based environmental governance are cap-and-trade schemes such as the tradeable permit system for NO_x and SO_2 emissions which was introduced under the 1990 US Clean Air act. Here, government regulation provides the 'cap' on total emissions and this determines the 'total emissions permits' issued to polluters. The permits then become a tradeable commodity, allowing emission reductions to be made efficiently – the idea is that those able to make cuts at the lowest cost will sell their emission permits to those who can't. Carbon offset trading and biodiversity offsetting follow a similar rationale of seeking out least-cost opportunities for environmental improvements.

The success of incentive and market-based approaches remains very much debated. Some claim there is "evidence that incentives such as PES [Payments for Ecosystem Services] may be one of the only effective ways to motivate conservation amongst impoverished local communities" (Shoreman-Ouimet and Kopnina 2015, p. 322). But more systematic reviews of the evidence suggest that such claims may be premature (Samii et al. 2014). Cap and trade market systems have also had mixed outcomes. Whilst trading of air pollution permits in the US is often cited as a success story, the carbon offset market has been blighted by falling market prices for carbon, threatening the benefits to be received by those who have become carbon offset sellers (Corbera and Martin 2015). Biodiversity offsets pose a more technical challenge about the extent to which substitute sites of biodiversity can ever really be equivalent to the development sites that they are intended to offset.

I begin this chapter with a broad overview of the rationale for incentive and market-based approaches to conservation governance, including payments for ecosystem services, green consumerism and biodiversity offsets. I then consider two main types of concern about market-based conservation: one that market-based incentives undermine other forms of motivation to care for nature; and the other that markets enable powerful actors to dispossess others of their control over natural resources. These generalised lines of critique are informative but it is also important to recognise that real cases of 'market-based' conservation often do not conform to generic blueprints, and nor do the on-the-ground experiences of the people involved in them. For that reason, I proceed to take a more empirical, place-based approach to exploring the challenges and opportunities of linking conservation, markets and justice. I employ cases from Bolivia, China and Rwanda that provide a flavour of the differences in the interventions themselves and in the ways that interventions play out locally. In doing so, two main arguments emerge. Firstly, market-based approaches can have both positive and negative effects locally, depending on contextual conditions. Sometimes markets can be utilised strategically by communities to advance their own environmental justice agendas but in other circumstances they can undermine such agendas. Secondly, I pick up on an argument that has been present throughout the book, that whilst justice (or equity) and effectiveness are sometimes considered to be competing objectives, they are in fact interdependent.

The case for market-based conservation

Broadly speaking there are three explanations for the current popularity of incentive and market-based approaches to conservation: one linked to science, one to political norms and one to experience. In terms of science, there has been considerable research into the role of biodiversity in ecosystem services and an accompanying effort to understand the economic value of these services (e.g. Kumar 2010). Putting a price on ecosystem services has provided the rationale for paying for conservation through incentive schemes, and also the means by which services can be exchanged on markets. In terms of politics, the receptivity of policymakers to market-based approaches is almost certainly influenced by the existing dominance of neoliberal political ideologies. In terms of experience, the case for market-based conservation has been a response to disillusionment with the hitherto popular approach of integrated conservation and development projects (ICDPs).

As discussed in the last chapter, one of the key weaknesses of ICDPs was that the interventions they financed were not sufficiently well linked to the conservation outcomes they were intended to bring about (Salafsky and Wollenberg 2000). ICDPs sought to win hearts and minds of people living near to protected areas by supporting their livelihoods through rural development projects. There was an assumption that such activities would make people less poor, less dependent on park resources or just better disposed towards park protection. But, at best, many ICDPs were irrelevant to conservation because they simply involved projects that had no effect on local protected areas; at worst, they subsidised the very activity (agriculture) which was threatening biodiversity in the first place. An appealing solution was to stop using funds to pay for development projects and instead pay people directly for services to conservation (Ferraro 2001; Wunder 2001).

Payments for ecosystem services

The call for 'direct payments' for conservation was soon replaced by the model of Payments for Ecosystem Services (PES), defined along the lines of a scheme that is: (a) voluntary; (b) where an ecosystem service is bought by one party from another party; and (c) where payment is conditional on delivery of that service

(Wunder 2005). In theory, PES can bring efficiency gains to conservation through better targeting – targeting those locations where the most conservation can be achieved and targeting those people who can provide conservation services at least cost. In principle then, you can get more conservation for your bucks by finding those willing to 'sell cheap', thereby achieving a greater aggregate welfare gain. Such cost-effectiveness gains are the main argument in favour of PES and market-based approaches, although advocates also point to a possible pro-poor benefit. PES contracts tend to manifest between public sector service buyers and relatively marginalised groups of service sellers who rely disproportionately more on environmental services for their daily lives. This provides the opportunity to transfer wealth from rich to poor, and to those who have historically borne the burden of biodiversity conservation (Pagiola et al. 2005). A good way to think about this is the relative position of more and less wealthy people in a watershed. Poorer people tend to live upstream in remoter, often forested and hilly locations with small-scale farming systems. Downstream settlements are more likely to include large-scale farmers, industries and towns. PES provides a mechanism for the relatively wealthy downstream stakeholders to pay upstream stakeholders to protect the watershed.

PES schemes were initially envisaged as market-based approaches in which willing buyers and willing providers of services such as biodiversity conservation could interact in new market places, allowing laws of supply and demand to efficiently allocate conservation funding. What has tended to emerge, however, is non-market incentive programmes that resemble the above-mentioned Environmental Stewardship Scheme in the UK. The Chinese Sloping Lands Conversion Program (SLCP, also known as 'Grain for Green') is one of the biggest examples. After a series of droughts and floods affected the watersheds of the Yellow and Yangtze rivers in the late 1990s, the government introduced a scheme to incentivise private landholders to convert croplands and barren wastelands to forest plantations, initially providing payment in grain, and later in cash (Bennett 2008). The SLCP is far from perfect, having attracted criticism for not being truly voluntary (Bennett 2008), low tree survival rates in some areas (Changjin and Chen 2005) and negative impacts on some livelihoods (Xu et al. 2010). But the scale of afforestation remains impressive: by the end of 2013, the SLCP had involved more than 100 million farmers and the National Forestation Committee claims that 25.8 million hectares of land has been converted to forest (Feng and Xu 2015).

Such large-scale, government-funded PES schemes have now become more popular in the tropics. Examples include: Costa Rica's national scheme to pay farmers to conserve forests; Mexico's payments for hydrological services and carbon forestry schemes; Ecuador's *Socio Bosque* payments for forest conservation; and Namibia's community-based wildlife conservation payments (Calvet-Mir et al. 2015). In addition to large-scale national schemes, there are many regional and local PES schemes funded by governments, multilateral organisations and NGOs. These schemes typically incentivise biodiversity conservation as one of a number of environmental goals, including carbon storage, prevention of soil erosion and flooding, and enhanced water quality.

Biodiversity offsetting

Biodiversity offsetting has its origins in 1970s legislation in the US which was designed to ensure no net loss of wetlands (Bonneuil 2015). It has since been adopted in Australian states such as New South Wales and Victoria and is beginning to enter into government policy in the tropics. For example, biodiversity offsets are now a requirement for certain types of project in Brazil, Colombia, Mexico and Peru (Villaroya et al. 2014). Biodiversity offsets work to the principle of 'no net loss' of biodiversity. They are considered a last resort in a mitigation hierarchy in which 'avoidance' of adverse impacts on biodiversity is always the first preference, followed by 'minimisation' and 'rehabilitation' and finally 'offsetting', to compensate for any remaining, unavoidable biodiversity loss (BBOP 2012). 'No net loss' policies can be mandatory, such as the above-mentioned US legislation requiring no net loss of wetlands. Such legislation creates markets for biodiversity credits that can be purchased in 'banks' to offset the adverse impacts on biodiversity caused by development projects. Some actors can create units of credit and deposit these in the bank (e.g. 'wetland banking' in the US), whilst developers can pay to withdraw these. In effect then, offsets are a way to ensure that developers internalise the costs of adverse biodiversity impacts (Bull et al. 2013).

Advocates of biodiversity offsets work from the premise that some developments (such as new mining sites) are all but inevitable and that using the full range of the mitigation hierarchy might be the only way to ensure no loss of biodiversity. Some large environmental NGOs such as the Nature Conservancy and Conservation International have supported the development of offsetting on the basis of the need for innovative solutions that are 'outcome-based, financially sustainable and compatible with economic development' (cited in Coralie et al. 2015). But for others, biodiversity offsetting is a 'licence to trash' (Vidal 2014). Offsetting requires that nature is thought of as a set of commensurate units that can be exchanged for each other – such that a loss of woodland here can be adequately offset by a gain in woodland there. But critics argue that equivalence is not achieved in practice and that net losses of biodiversity persist (Maron et al. 2015). For example, Kormos et al. (2014) review offsetting projects in the Republic of Guinea, Sierra Leone and Cameroon which are intended to offset destruction to chimpanzee and gorilla populations by creating alternative habitats elsewhere. The authors note the serious ethical questions that arise from e.g. 'offsetting chimpanzees' but also note significant uncertainties over whether such offsets will avoid net loss.

Green consumerism

Certification systems such as the Forest Stewardship Council (FSC) standards facilitate market exchanges in which willing buyers of environmental services (i.e. green consumers) interact with service providers who want to enhance their reputation and market standing. As of September 2015, FSC certifies nearly 184 million hectares of forest, of which more than 80% is in North America and Europe (www.info.fsc.org). The Marine Stewardship Council certified 275 fisheries in 36 countries with its Fisheries Standard for sustainable fishing, amounting to 10% of annual global harvest from wild capture fisheries (www.msc.org). Systems of standards and labelling enable consumers to express their preferences through market transactions, using their 'dollar vote' to make purchases that support their moral beliefs and exerting the option to exit markets that are considered unethical (withdrawing purchase of products and sale of labour).

The case against market-based conservation

Amongst social scientists in particular, there is widespread feeling that putting a price on nature may be wrong, that profiting from such commodification is even more morally hazardous, and that enticing resource-poor farmers to join in is worse still. In an attempt to clarify the reasons underlying these concerns I consider two main sets of objections: concerns about the impact of putting a price on nature, and concerns about the underlying injustices that such pricing reveals.

Putting a price on nature

Is commodifying nature harmful? For Michael Sandel (2012) one of the dangers of putting a price on things which previously lay outside of the market is that it might diminish the value of the goods or services themselves. For example, if we put a price on an educational award such as a first class degree in biodiversity conservation such that anyone with sufficient means can buy one, then we clearly diminish the value of this good. But this loss of intrinsic value is not so obvious for goods such as biodiversity, a walrus, a DNA sequence, a unit of wetland or a tonne of carbon. We can put a price on them, trade them, and even if their market price approaches zero, they seem to retain their intrinsic quality. For example, the market price for certified emission reductions (carbon offsets) was 20 Euros in 2008 but had collapsed to about half a Euro by late 2015. But this does not change the underlying quality of a tonne of carbon.

However, commodification may still determine the ways in which we value environmental goods and services and the reasons why we care about them. Motivational crowding theory (Frey and Jegen 2001) holds that under certain conditions, the establishment of monetary motives (such as through a PES) can displace higher-order, not-for-profit motives which stem from altruism and cultural norms of responsibility towards nature and fellow citizens (Neuteleers and Engelen 2015). Such a switch to financial motives may be less sustainable than ethically motivated behaviour because payments may be for a limited period only, and might be dependent on market prices. The most famous example of motivational 'crowding out' comes from a study at an Israeli nursery, where financial incentives were used to try and resolve the problem of parents arriving late to pick up their children. A system of fines was introduced such that a late pick-up landed parents with a bill. The initiative proved counter-productive, leading to increasing lateness. The explanation for this was that the commodification of timeliness by rendering it as something commensurate with a cash amount undermined the moral value previously attached to it (Gneezy and Rustichini 2000). Worryingly, it appears that this crowding out of the moral motive for being on time was not reversed after the fines were stopped. Money, it seems, really can corrupt.

In addition to switching between moral and economic motives, financial incentives have also been shown, in some circumstances, to be more immediately counter-productive. They can induce the opposite of the desired behavioural change, resulting for example in less recycling rather than more. One explanation for this is that humans place high value on autonomy – we are psychologically pre-disposed towards preferring to develop our own internally generated justification for our choices about how to behave (Bowles and Polanía-Reyes 2012). A person who is vigilant about adopting a green lifestyle does so of their own free will and determination and the contribution to their subjective wellbeing flows as much from this self-determination as from the outcome it leads to (we value means as well as ends). The introduction of financial incentives can 'over-justify' the activity and in doing so reduce the wellbeing gain the individual derives from it.

Bowles and Polanía-Reyes (2012) review a large body of experimental evidence and find that such crowding-out effects are indeed commonplace. However, they also find cases of 'crowding in', where the introduction of a financial incentive complements and encourages ethical motives. This is of particular interest to conservation because they find that 'crowding in' is particularly prevalent in cases where management of common pool resources are involved. We don't know much about why crowding in occurs in some cases, but one part of this seems to be that financial incentives lead people to try something new and that this turns out to be so effective or satisfying that they decide it is worthwhile even without payment. For example, whilst on a field trip with undergraduate students, I talked with the manager of Morley Farms Ltd in Norfolk, UK. He explained how he initially adopted a range of conservation practices on his farms because of the financial payments gained through the Environmental Stewardship scheme. However he has since seen the benefits from some of these activities and they have become management practices that he is proud of – he would now continue at least some of them even if the payments were removed.

Another concern, raised by Michael Sandel, is that bringing more and more of society and nature into market arrangements can exacerbate inequality and increase poverty. It's an argument that I introduced in Chapter 1 – in a world in which very few of the things that we value are subject to market exchange, the difference between having money and not having money is not that important. In a world in which everything is bought and sold, having money is everything. It's a simple but profound argument about the kind of society we really want to live in and what, fundamentally, are the appropriate ways to protect those subjected to the indignity of poverty.

Accumulation and dispossession

The concern about motivational crowding is based on a body of theory about how markets directly determine moralities, changing how people think about what is right and wrong, with potential consequences for both social and ecological outcomes. This remains a comparatively niche topic of academic inquiry into environmental problems, albeit an important one in my view. There is a much larger literature that considers the problems of commodification from the perspective of Marxist theory about capitalist accumulation. In this literature, commodification and market-based approaches are viewed as symptomatic of a systemic political project arising from the structure and power dynamics of the global economy. Commodification of nature serves to incorporate more and more goods and services into this global system (carbon, wetlands, biodiversity, ecosystem services), rendering more lands and people vulnerable to the accumulation of resources by global centres of high consumption. This process of accumulation for the rich through dispossession from the poor (Harvey 1996) has already been touched upon in relation to theories of unequal ecological exchange discussed in Chapter 5 but it is helpful to develop a more particular discussion here of whether market-based approaches serve to perpetuate and deepen the injustices of unequal exchange.

Marx envisaged that the capitalist mode of production failed to invest sufficiently in the conditions of production, including the ecological basis of the agricultural and manufacturing economy. He observed for example the declining fertility of European farmland with an interest in how the capitalist classes responded to this threat to their continued accumulation of wealth. Unsurprisingly perhaps, the response was not to invest more in constructing the conditions of production, or to seek changes to the social relations of production that led to this lack of investment. Such responses would have reduced their profit margins and slowed their accumulation of wealth. Instead the solution was to use imperial power to commandeer sources of nitrate fertiliser from beyond domestic borders. Famously, this included the nineteenth-century plunder of guano from the Pacific coast of South America, sustained through military force played out in wars involving Peru, Chile and Bolivia (Clark and Foster 2009). In this way, the 'metabolic rift' identified by Marx (Foster 1999) was temporarily fixed by actions that on the one hand dispossessed less powerful nations of their resources and authority, and on the other enabled capitalist classes in the European core to sustain their accumulation.

Fast forwarding 150 years, O'Connor (1998) describes the 'metabolic rift' as the second contradiction of capitalism, in which barriers to accumulation are produced by shortages of resources, by the need to invest in pollution reduction and remediation, and by the social movements that place environmental problems on political agendas. Such concerns have of course intensified since Marx's time, with growing understanding of problems such as biodiversity loss, climate change and nitrogen cycles. This expanded range of environmental problems can also be seen to be linked to an expanding range of 'fixes', especially by opening new commodity frontiers at which contemporary mechanisms of dispossession operate (Muradian et al. 2012). These includes new frontiers of energy production, such as demand for lithium (e.g. Chile, Argentina, Bolivia), demand for land for biofuels (e.g. US, China, Brazil), new frontiers of climate change mitigation, including demand for CO_2 storage in forests and soils in the global South (e.g. Kenya, Uganda, DRC), and new frontiers for biodiversity, including habitat creation for biodiversity offsetting (e.g. US, Australia). These have collectively been described as forms of 'green grabbing' (Fairhead et al. 2012), with resource-specific variations such as 'accumulation by decarbonization' (Bumpus and Liverman 2010). There is now deep concern that the economic valuation of ecosystem services, and their incorporation into global commodity circuits, enhances the risks of dispossession for local communities (Kosoy and Corbera 2010; Büscher et al. 2012; McAfee 2012; Li 2014; Matulis 2014).

Market-based approaches to environmental problems are widely seen as a product of alliances between states and industry, with the immediate ambition being to respond to political pressures to act, but to do so in ways that minimise domestic actions and protect profits for industry. For example, this is a broadly accepted analysis of how market-based 'flexible mechanisms' entered into the 1997 Kyoto Protocol, strongly promoted by the United States in cahoots with the corporate fossil fuel lobby (Grubb et al. 1999; Spash 2010). Furthermore, we can now see the risks of dispossession that such markets create for the many thousands of smallholders and communities in the global South who, as a result, manage their private or communal lands for the sale of carbon credits. Whilst market prices for carbon have continued to decline, governments and environmental NGOs continue to promote entry to this market to some of the most economically vulnerable people on the planet (Corbera and Martin 2015).

Evidence from actually existing market-based conservation interventions

Attempts to generalise the findings of empirical studies of market-based conservation do not clearly support one view or the other. Indeed, systematic reviews conclude that there is insufficient evidence of the effects of green and ethical certification (Blackman and Rivera 2011; Steering Committee of the State-of-Knowledge Assessment of Standards and Certification 2012; Romero et al. 2013) or PES (Pattanayak et al. 2010; Miteva et al. 2012; Samii et al. 2014; Wunder 2013). On the positive side, there are findings that PES, certification and biodiversity offsetting do not always dispossess local communities and, to the contrary, can be instrumental to improved land tenure security for local people. Such cases have been highlighted in research into the impacts of forest certification (Steering Committee of the State-of-Knowledge Assessment of Standards and Certification 2012), PES schemes (Tacconi et al. 2010), REDD+ pilot projects (Hoang et al. 2013; Maraseni et al. 2014; Khatun et al. 2015) and biodiversity offsetting (Hackett 2015).

Equally, however, there are case studies that find otherwise. In Uganda, for example, afforestation programmes to serve the carbon market have been associated with aggressive dispossessions around Mount Elgon (Cavanagh and Benjaminsen 2014; Lyons and Westoby 2014). More widely, there are concerns about whether market-based approaches will ever serve the interests of the poor, even in cases where violent dispossessions do not occur. Certification systems such as FSC and Rainforest Alliance, for example, have achieved only low uptake among small-holders in developing countries because the costs of entry are high relative to realistic benefits (Marx and Cuypers 2010; Auer 2012; Gullison 2003; McDermott et al. 2015; Pinto and McDermott, 2013). Contrary to the claimed potential to be pro-poor, PES schemes have also been found to favour wealthier and larger farm-ers because entry to schemes is limited by whether a household has sufficient land (Porras et al. 2008), or literacy (Zbinden and Lee 2005). Such barriers to entry can be particularly limiting for women (Boyd 2002; Lee et al. 2015).

Despite these mixed and sometimes contradictory research findings, academic debate about market-based environmentalism has become somewhat polarised across an ideological chasm. On one side of this chasm are advocates of market efficiency, drawing on neoclassical economic theory to claim greater effective-ness and efficiency. On the other are critics of neoliberalism who employ Marxist analysis to reveal class-based injustices associated with capital accumulation and dispossession. I try to avoid these polarities, arguing for a more place-based understanding of how specific interventions play out in practice, with a particular focus on how market-based interventions constrain and enable local stakehold-ers' pursuit of environmental justice. This fits with an emerging body of research that takes a more empirical approach to studying neoliberal environmentalism, examining the process and outcomes of particular market-based interventions, rather than viewing all such cases as symptoms of a single, underlying, global political project (Hackett 2015). The distinction is between studying a theoreti-cal, imagined model of neoliberalism and studying actually existing instances of its practice (Castree 2008).

In his study of conservation offsets in a First Nation community in Alberta, Hackett (2015) confirms that the commodification of nature provides mechanisms that can serve accumulation and dispossession. But he does not find this to be an intrinsic quality of the tools or an inevitable outcome. In some contexts, includ-ing his own case of a Cree First Nation community, market-based tools such as biodiversity offsets are perceived by communities as opportunities to pursue their own political and cultural agendas, and in particular to enhance tenure security and fend off dispossession. In light of such observations, the interesting questions are not only about whether market-based approaches are inherently just or unjust, but about the conditions under which different stakeholders are empowered to use such techniques to further their own justice claims. I use three case stud-ies to explore some of these conditions and how they mediate experiences of market-based interventions in particular contexts. First, I consider a case study from Bolivia in which local communities have initially enjoyed some success in the strategic use of forest certification and marketing to secure their territorial claims, but have subsequently struggled to align commercial forestry with their vision of a just environmental future. Secondly, I present a case from China where community members were also able to use market-based opportunities to secure land tenure on their own terms and have subsequently faced fewer problems aligning this with community preferences. Finally, I return to the Rwanda case study used in previous chapters to explore how a trial PES scheme provides some preliminary evidence about the conditions under which market-based interventions effect local motivation to protect a park.

'Capitalism is undermining community': forests and markets in Lomerio, Bolivia

Lomerio is an indigenous territory in the Santa Cruz Department of Bolivia and home to around 7000 Chiquitano people who live in 29 communities. The area is characterised by lowland forests at the intersection of the more humid Amazonian ecosystem and the drier Chaco ecosystem. The Chiquitano people combine different nations and languages which were brought together in Jesuit missions such as Concepción and eventually forged a collective identity and a single claim to an ancestral territory. During the rubber boom of the late nineteenth and twentieth centuries, the Chiquitano were brutally exploited as forced labourers on plantations. It is not unusual for elders to describe their own parents as having been slaves and exploitation by large landowners continued into the late twentieth century, even after the Chiquitano had escaped the mission towns and (re-)established their territory. The Chiquitano began organised resistance through formation of an Agrarian Peasant Union in 1964 and later formed the Indigenous Organisation of the Native Communities of Lomerio (CICOL) in 1983. After a long struggle, CICOL and partners eventually succeeded in gaining a 259,188 hectare Native Communal Territory in 2006. In this same year Evo Morales became Bolivia's first indigenous president, pursuing de-colonial agendas and providing a boost to those indigenous nations who were seeking autonomy. The 2009 constitution saw Bolivia officially transformed into a plurinational state that recognises indigenous cultures and lists 37 official state languages. Respect for mother earth (*pachamama*) is enshrined in this constitution which also asserts good living (*buen vivir*) as a goal of the state, an explicit attempt to de-colonialise Bolivia and embrace appropriate non-Western development philosophy (Alcoreza 2013). The constitution also allows for indigenous peoples to make the transition from having communal territories under central state authority to being fully autonomous territories and nations.

At the time of writing, 20 indigenous nations have submitted claims for autonomy but all but one of these claims have been delayed and there is widespread concern that the political momentum for indigenous rights is faltering. Having submitted their application, the Chiquitano now need a letter from the Minister for Autonomy to confirm that their claim is constitutional, which is currently where the process has stalled. Once they have this, there would be a referendum and finally a law to create their autonomous territory and 'nation'.

The current delay in the process can be attributed to three main issues. Firstly, there is a perceived change in national government priorities, away from indigenous rights and towards use of natural resources for economic growth. Secondly, there is concern that given autonomy over natural resources, indigenous peoples will quickly enter into exploitative contracts with private mining and forestry companies, as has been happening in Venezuela, for example. Thirdly, divisions are appearing within communities, catalysed by local government support for an anti-autonomy faction; this occurs because autonomy threatens loss of departmental and municipal government revenues. Nevertheless, there appears to be a momentum to try to resolve these concerns and this was illustrated by the high profile given to the Chiquitano case during the May 2016 meeting of the UN Permanent Forum on Indigenous Issues in New York.

A complex picture has emerged in which, for the Chiquitano elders, environmental justice is inextricably linked with completing a long struggle for territorial autonomy. The General Chief of CICOL points out that this is a struggle which has cost lives and that it is the only way to de-colonialise and achieve freedom. He is also aware that Bolivia and the Chiquitano are of interest to others around the world because they are developing an alternative model for conserving the planet. Market-based natural resource projects have become deeply entwined in this story and reveal an important dilemma about market-based approaches. On one horn of this dilemma, market-based natural resource management might be the only realistic way to make autonomy work. It might be the economic platform that allows the Chiquitano to pursue environmental justice. Chief Anacleto acknowledges this, stating that 'we have used natural resources to meet our social needs, now they must meet our productive needs' (General Chief Anacleto Pena, pers. com.). But on the other horn of the dilemma, entry into timber and mining markets has been seen to undermine an equally fundamental basis for autonomy: community. This dilemma was in evidence at a round table meeting to discuss the relationship between environmental justice and autonomy (Inturias et al. 2016). Arguing against an immediate granting of autonomy, the ex-director of Bolivia's La Autoridad de Bosques y Tierra (ABT) expressed the issue very bluntly: 'capitalism is undermining community'. Whilst Chief Anacleto supports immediate autonomy he does share this concern, saying that 'community vision is lost to market forces'. Equally, the Vice Minister for Autonomy observes the same problem: 'some people are still part of the community but have adopted capitalist ways and individualism. So there is an internal struggle.'

Two examples help to illustrate the difficulties for the Chiquitano as they try to resolve tensions between conservation, markets and justice. Firstly, Lomerio became the first local forest enterprise to be certified in Bolivia, gaining Rainforest Alliance 'Smart Wood' certification in 1996 (Markopoulos 1998). This market-based intervention was used to further the Chiquitano's bigger strategic agenda to secure their territory. Entry into certified timber markets enabled them to argue that they were using their forests both economically and sustainably and generated support to oust illegal timber operators. In this way, the Chiquitano utilised the market-based opportunity as a means to present themselves to government in a way that strengthened their case for a native territory. But despite being widely touted as a success story at the time, the enterprise was clearly a failure and the Puquio sawmill was ultimately unsustainable. It was dogged by problems of quality control and moreover by financial failures. Looking back, the elders tell us that a key problem was a tension between communalism and individuals, and in particular a feeling that elders were not respected by the kind of business model which was promoted by external project planners. What was needed to make the business work was a market model in which benefits were distributed only according to current effort (i.e. those who worked at the mill got paid) and remaining revenue was reinvested. But that model was not considered fair according to the elders, some of whom felt that it failed to reward those who had struggled for decades to bring the community to the point where it was able to benefit from its own resources. As McDaniel (2003) observed, the market model simply didn't fit with a communal vision of what constitutes appropriate distribution of benefits:

> The Chiquitano administrator who distributes the project funds to family and friends is rewarded with status and prestige for his generosity, and his actions make perfect sense in the indigenous economy based on reciprocity. However, this type of economic behaviour quickly leads to bankruptcy in the market economy where managers must invest capital carefully, and accumulate cash rather than distribute it freely.
>
> *(McDaniel 2003, p. 338)*

Indeed, a retrospective evaluation of this suggests it was not just about distributing to family and friends, but about taking an alternative, longer-term, view of who had contributed to making the enterprise possible and therefore what a just distribution of benefits should be. The misfit between community and market logics of justice led to problems for those who worked in the sawmill – they say that they suffered from witchcraft being exercised against them and this was a significant factor in the sawmill's demise. As previewed above, the market-based approach to sustainable forestry offered an attractive basis for autonomous management of territorial resources, but it actually led to internal conflict, undermining the sense of community that is an equally vital condition for autonomy and its linked objective of environmental justice.

The second example is more recent, based on sustainable harvesting of timbers within forest management units. Again, there is nothing to suggest that this process has not been carried out with the best of intentions, including the aspiration that sustainable forestry can become one element of an autonomous economy. Each community has been allocated areas of forest within larger 'Forest Plan' units and they are able to negotiate contracts with private sector companies within a set of fairly stringent regulations. The results so far suggest that this is unlikely to provide the sustainable economy that is hoped for. One case is that of Santa Rosario, one of the communities falling under Lomerio's North Plan.

Members of the community say that they have basically been 'taken for a ride' in their dealings with both companies and the state. One of the problems is that they negotiate weak contracts, with low timber prices that fail to properly account for the most valuable species. They also lose out because of lack of clarity about how volumes of timber will be calculated, and they then experienced 'disappearance' of 50 m^3 of timber during its transport to the sawmill. Worse still, there were errors in tree selection in their first harvest in 2010/11, resulting in the government inspector imposing a fine of 63,000 bolivianos (about \$10,000). They were supposed to leave one in five trees standing for regeneration purposes but had not done so, and had also cut some trees that were below the minimum allowed diameter. They claimed that they had been poorly advised and that this was the company's fault, but the company refused to accept any fault and walked away. So at this point, Santa Rosario's forest enterprise had generated a very large debt. To pay this back they had to enter into a contract with a second company who agreed to pay the fine as part of the payment. Subsequent harvests occurred in the remaining plan area in 2014 and 2015, enabling them to clear their debt but not to make any profit. Having done this, however, Santa Rosario will need to wait at least 40 years before another harvest.

Here and in other communities, the reason for harvesting all available timbers straight away was not purely about paying off debts. It was also about the kind of contracts acceptable to the private sector, and an acknowledgement that if trees are not harvested legally, they are likely to be harvested illegally by others. Santa Rosario has arrived where it is, with little prospect of future forestry income, based on a set of perceived injustices: being taken for a ride contractually by companies; being harshly treated by authorities for what it claims to be a legitimate mistake; and being unable to protect its forests against illegal logging. It is largely villagers themselves who sell to the illegal trade, so the situation reflects the broader concern of a tension between community activity and individual gain. In this case it seems that individualism is indeed undercutting community and, with it, the opportunity for communal forestry to be part of a future vision for autonomy and justice.

For the Chiquitano, environmental justice must be founded on autonomy. This poses a serious challenge because to flourish as an autonomous territory they need a strong economy and a strong community. But the road to a strong resource-based economy is fuelling internal tensions between individual and community due to the exposure to a market economy. CICOL's leader describes an 'epidemic of division' within indigenous movements throughout Bolivia, which is in part orchestrated by bureaucracies whose power and revenues are threatened by autonomy, but also by internal struggles arising from marketisation. This is not the end of the story – it is not a story of how markets have defeated dreams of autonomy and justice. But it is a case that illustrates the significance of commodifying nature and transforming local relationships with natural resources from subsistence to market exchange. This is not only a change in economic relations but also of social relations and this changes the range of possible futures and possible justices and injustices. In December 2015

Evo Morales spoke at the Paris UNFCCC negotiations, describing capitalism as 'the formula that has destroyed our species' and calling for a new relationship with nature based on respect for mother earth. It is somewhat ironic then, that in Bolivia, indigenous nations are feeling they have to enter into commercial forestry in order to further their territorial claims. In many ways this is a case of mal-recognition, in which a group has to emulate dominant norms in order to gain respect from those in power. In some ways, the case of the Chiquitano resembles that of the Cree described by Hackett (2015). They were able to use a market-based governance technique proactively to advance their own territorial claims and take a significant step towards their vision of social and environmental justice. But in the case of the Chiquitano, the need to assimilate to individualistic market norms has proven divisive.

'PES is supporting community forestry': the case of Xinqi village, China

Xinqi is a village in Tengchong County in Yunnan Province, near to China's border with Myanmar. It is considered a success story, having strategically utilised national policies to build on its own traditions of collective forestry, and 80% of its territory is now afforested. Villagers managed to tailor China's forest tenure reforms to fit with their own governance preferences: whereas in much of China these reforms involve privatisation of forest use rights, Xinqi protested against this and succeeded in persuading county foresters to allow them to pursue forest commercialisation through collectivised management. It is a case study that demonstrates the array of governance hybridisations that occur, combining elements of Maoist collectivisation, government incentive schemes, commercialisation and marketisation, forest privatisation, amongst others. The reality is that 'neoliberal' and 'market-based' governance techniques rarely appear in pure and unaccompanied forms.

In Tengchong County as a whole, 118,000 households were allocated private-use forests during reforms introduced in 2005 (Jintao et al. 2012), but Xinqi had practised collective forestry since the 1960s and successfully opposed privatisation for all but a small percentage of its forestland. At the same time, a pilot system of harvest quotas was introduced in which villages were given annual sales quotas, enabling Xinqi to move towards greater commercialisation of its community forestry. In 2015 the village had: 4332 hectares of plantation forests, mainly pine; 730 hectares of camellia forest, for oil extraction; and 913 hectares of walnuts. About a third is managed collectively by the village, another third is managed collectively by smaller 'production teams' and the remaining third has been privatised, with use rights allocated to individual households.

Villagers report positive changes in this period and the village director estimated that more than 70% of household income comes from forest-related enterprises, including the sawmill, transportation, agro-forestry, mushroom harvesting and camellia oil extraction. In 2002, the village handed use rights to the 730 hectares of camellia forest to an association of village elders. Now over 500 elder residents (over 60 years of age) are members of the association, collectively earning about 500,000 yuan per year. This is distributed to individuals based on days contributed, as well as special payments during the Spring Festival, to those over 85 years old and to any household that has to cope with a funeral. But money is also invested in public goods such as support for a Confucian temple, street cleaning and celebrations. The next step for the village is to become a 'Forest Association' which would in effect allow them to operate like a private company.

A couple of decades ago, Xinqi was a predominantly agricultural community using slash-and-burn techniques to grow buckwheat on its surrounding hills. The government of China wanted villagers to stop shifting cultivation in order to increase forest cover and enhance ecosystem services such as flood, drought and landslide prevention. They used incentives under the Sloping Land Conversion Program (SLCP), helping villagers get through the eight or so year transition period between planting trees and beginning to generate forest revenues. And they introduced tenure and market reforms to support this process. The outcome, according to most villagers we spoke to, is a largely sustainable system of forestry that they consider a superior livelihood to the one they have given up. The one downside that is openly acknowledged by villagers is the risk of fire. In effect, each household holds substantial forest assets, much of it coniferous, with the risk that a large fire could hit their livelihoods very hard.

There are some key lessons we should take from this case. Firstly, market-based approaches need to be understood contextually, as particular instances of hybrid governance techniques, introduced into particular places with their own histories, cultures, ecological capacities and institutions. In Lomerio, we saw evidence of a misfit between the particular forms of governance introduced and the socio-ecological contexts into which they were dropped. In Xinqi, there was sufficient flexibility in tenure reforms and incentive schemes to enable villagers to adapt commercial forestry operations to their long-established capacity for community forestry. They could enter relatively slowly into schemes such as the Sloping Land Conversion Program, beginning with just a few hundred hectares and then expanding their forest operations as they saw the benefits. Above all, villagers in Xinqi were able to play a significant part in negotiating the terms of tenure reforms and their subsequent entry into commercial forestry markets. Crucially, this involved tailoring the programme to fit with their own forest governance traditions and expertise, an option that had not been available in Lomerio. In Lomerio, entry into commercial forestry operations opened up divisions between young and old, along lines of preference for individual versus community enterprise. In Xinqi, we also discerned an element of this, with suggestion that young people prefer individual over collective management. But according to the village director, community forestry also delivers what the young need. He told us that prior to 2000 the young were unable to get into universities as the schools could not achieve sufficient examination results for scholarships. Since 2000, with schools improved due to forest-based incomes, he says more than 100 have gone to university.

Xinqi was quite fortunate to have been involved during a pilot phase of forest tenure reforms, prior to extension throughout China. At that stage there was greater flexibility to experiment with different models and this is part of the reason that village leaders could successfully challenge privatisation. It is unlikely that such a protest would be successful now that the privatisation model has been fully adopted and includes the expectation that 70-90% of village forests will be allocated to household use rights. In parts of Tibet, for example, pressure from the Chinese government to privatise forests is posing a threat to indigenous communities.

Fairness and crowding-in: Nyungwe National Park, Rwanda

In 2009 I worked with partners in the Rwanda Development Board and the Wildlife Conservation Society to introduce a trial Payments for Ecosystem Services scheme in four cells (clusters of 3 to 5 villages) adjacent to the Nyungwe National Park. These communities entered into voluntary contracts in which they agreed to provide specified conservation services in return for cash payments. Payments were conditional on and in proportion to verified service provision. Some services involved reductions of activities within the park which park authorities had categorised as threats to biodiversity, notably hunting with snares, cutting trees and gold mining. Other services involved increasing pro-conservation activities on village lands, including tree and bamboo planting, and organised efforts to reduce conflicts with wild animals (Gross-Camp et al. 2012). Specific performance indicators were negotiated, with each community following a baseline study, and these indicators were monitored by teams of community members and project staff. Changes were monitored in relation to the 2009 baseline and against control locations. The first control was a set of four cells which had no PES scheme but where we undertook a similar level of additional monitoring (e.g. with forest transects to observe snares, mines and tree felling). The second control was the rest of the park, where there was no PES and no additional monitoring. Here, there were no visits by special monitoring teams and we relied on existing park-wide monitoring data conducted by the park authority.

A generalised linear model showed significantly lower levels of threats to biodiversity in the park in trial PES cells than in the first set of controls (those where we conducted similarly intensive monitoring) (Martin et al. 2014b). However, whilst cells with the PES had lower levels of these activities, we found no significant difference in the rate of reductions in these activities over a 30-month monitoring period; the four trial cells and four control cells saw similar rates of threat reduction over time. This suggested that something was influencing human activity in both the trial and the control cells. In an attempt to explain this, we proposed the null hypothesis that the PES was ineffective and that the changes we were seeing simply reflected a park-wide reduction in human activities over time. We tested this using a time series of geo-referenced monitoring data collected by park rangers as part of a pre-existing park-wide monitoring effort. The result found a small but significant *increase* in threats in the rest of the park (Figure 8.1).

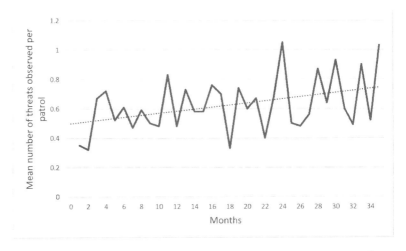

FIGURE 8.1 Observed threats for the whole of Nyungwe NP over a 35 month period. The mean threat count is the mean of the total observations of snares, tree-felling and mines seen per ranger patrol outing.

Source: Martin et al. 2014b.

Thus we rejected the null hypothesis and were left with the finding that the reduction in threats to biodiversity was likely to result from the increased levels of monitoring as much as the PES itself (Martin et al., 2014b). Subsequent interviews bolstered this interpretation: 50% of respondents in the four original control cells stated that the presence of guards was the main reason for reduced activity in park. Respondents also tended to state that there had been a significant increase in interaction with the park authority, suggesting that they had perceived the project monitoring teams to have been park guards.

From the perspective of a PES trial, this seems to be a rather negative finding. It suggests that we achieved much the same result in control cells, at considerably less cost, simply by increasing the presence of park guards (monitoring). However, the use of a simple impact evaluation methodology misses a very important difference between the cells. In essence, the method described looks at the different rates of change over time for different types of case (the 'difference-in-difference' approach). It tells us that the effectiveness is similar in the PES cases and the with-monitoring control cases. Given that the PES cases are more expensive, this could lead to the conclusion that they are less cost-efficient because it costs more for each unit of extra conservation. However, it would be wrong to assume that the outcome is the same in both cell types. Yes, the change in use of the park is statistically similar but, crucially, the reasons for this change are different. In surveys undertaken before and after the trial, we asked respondents about the factors that prevent people entering the park to use resources. We found a significant shift in the control cells towards thinking that law enforcement was the main reason, whereas in PES cells respondents were significantly more likely to cite their participation in park management and environmental education about the importance of the park (Martin et al. 2014b).

The main effect of the PES may then be to change *motives* for conserving the park, away from motives based on fear of punishment, to motives based on inclusion and understanding of the importance of conservation. This is interesting for at least two reasons. Firstly, referring back to the discussion of motivational crowding, it suggests that the introduction of a monetary incentive scheme might actually work to 'crowd in' not-for-profit motives in this case. This remains admittedly quite speculative but it does tie in with some examples from agri-environmental incentive schemes in Europe. It also appears to resonate with motivational crowding theory which finds that crowding in is more likely to occur in situations where incentive schemes are seen as participatory and not as a threat to autonomy (Frey and Jegen 2001; d'Adda 2011). Secondly, this suggests a relatively unexplored link between environmental justice and conservation effectiveness. If we assume that motives based on inclusion and learning are more sustainable (and more desirable) than motives based on fear; and if we assume that attention to local justice issues helps to foster these superior conservation motives, then we can cautiously make a case that advancing a local sense of justice is also a means to advancing conservation effectiveness.

Discussion and conclusions

Just as the design of market-based schemes is highly varied, so too is the range of contexts in which they are implemented. This is one reason why it remains important to learn from specific place-based cases, as proposed by Castree (2008). The cases that have appeared in this chapter, and indeed others I am familiar with, confirm that so-called market-based approaches to conservation are in reality a set of hybridised governance initiatives which combine regulatory approaches with incentive schemes. In the case of Payments for Ecosystem Services schemes such as the Sloping Land Conversion Program in China and Environmental Stewardship in England, there is rarely a market base at all because services are purchased not through market supply and demand but through government or third sector procurement. Strictly speaking, most PES schemes are incentive schemes rather than market-based approaches although they are widely considered to belong to neoliberal, market-based ideologies of environmental management. The reason for this is that they establish a price for ecosystem services even where that price is not determined through the market. Certification and standards such as those operated by the Forest Stewardship Council and Rainforest Alliance are more firmly market-based. So too have been the forest tenure and licensing reforms in China that for most communities involve incentive payments for managing 'ecological forests' but also a requirement to manage 'economic forests' for market sales.

For communities, the difference between incentive and market-based approaches is critical. Whereas incentive schemes put a price on activities which protect biodiversity and ecosystem services, true market-based approaches also introduce market-oriented notions of environmental justice, including procedures for resource allocation and individualistic and meritocratic principles for benefit distribution. In Lomerio, it is not the pricing of nature per se that challenges and divides the community, it is the introduction of market-based social relations, placing individuals and communities in competition with each other, in stark contrast to the communitarianism that is needed to complete the goal of territorial autonomy. These concerns are very explicitly articulated in claims that capitalism destroys 'the community' and even 'the species'. In Xinqi, the population is nearly all from the majority Han ethnic group and already strongly integrated into the pro-market transitions that have swept through China. Nevertheless, community leaders still understood that commercialisation of forestry would work best if they could retain communitarian and culturally appropriate principles of justice, including forms of benefit distribution that aligned with the strong respect for elders that flows from Confucian philosophy. They have achieved some balance between these local norms of environmental justice and the demands of market efficiency. In this case, they achieved this because of the ability to negotiate the terms of tenure reform.

One of the key concerns I have with market and incentive-based approaches is that they are heralded for promoting personal freedoms due to the voluntary nature of participation, but the reality is rarely so clear-cut. Communities entering our PES trial in Rwanda went through an extensive consultation period before deciding to participate but even then it is hard to ignore the fact that these were 'community' level decisions and dominated by particular sectors of the community, such as men rather than women. It is also important to be aware that offers of cash incentives, in communities where cash is in short supply, inevitably constitute a 'hard to refuse' offer. In Lomerio, there was a compulsion to enter into commercial forestry as a means of strengthening territorial claims. The community felt compelled to begin a commercial forest enterprise as a means of securing possession of their territory; but in doing so they opened up new mechanisms of dispossession and new territorial struggles. But here the adverse impacts of markets are not fully captured by the discourse of 'accumulation and dispossession'. Also important are the conflicting and divisive notions of justice that have taken root within the community through the assimilation of a market logic.

There is a tendency to think that it is impossible to maximise equity and effectiveness outcomes simultaneously. In some respects this is almost certainly true. For example, Sven Wunder (2001) uses the hypothetical example of having a limited fund to incentivise forest protection in the Amazon. To maximise effectiveness it might be best to spend the entire fund incentivising a few very large landowners, thus minimising transaction costs. To maximise equity it might be considered best to spread the fund around many less wealthy small farmers, but introducing large transaction costs. But at a finer scale, we see that equity and effectiveness are often inter-twined. In Lomerio, perceptions of inequity led to problems with witchcraft that ultimately led the sawmill business to fail. In Xinqi, the ability to maintain local principles of equity, such as ensuring benefits for elders, has been an important feature of effective transition from shifting cultivation to forestry. In Nyungwe, a strongly participatory approach appears to have played a role in 'crowding-in' motives for protecting the national park. In these more positive cases, the ability to negotiate the design of interventions to better align them with local conceptions of environmental justice seems to be significant.

9

CONSERVATION AND JUSTICE

Researching and assessing progress

Introduction

I have previously highlighted the need for social justice concerns to be integrated into the objectives of conservation practice. I have also developed in some detail what I consider to be the key issues of conservation justice and the ways in which we might set out to inquire about these. In this concluding chapter I focus on how these ideas might inform the ways in which conservation is researched, monitored and measured. It is generally accepted that conservation practice will be more effective and more efficiently targeted where it is based on good evidence (Sutherland et al. 2004). But the choice of what evidence to collect is very much framed by how the goals of conservation are characterised in the first place. In keeping with the argument of this book, the goals should be the inter-connected objectives of biodiversity conservation and social justice, and justice should be conceived as multi-dimensional.

The challenge of researching justice

In Chapter 4 I explored the tensions between contextual and more universal and objective approaches to the study of justice and wellbeing. In Figure 9.1 I summarise these approaches in a way that highlights the challenge for developing forms of research which will provide useful evidence for those wanting to assess progress towards more just conservation. The lower part of the figure represents what policymakers and practitioners want: forms of objective assessment of the social effects of conservation along different dimensions of justice (distribution, participation, recognition). This demand for 'justice research as objective assessment' contrasts with the bulk of justice research in universities (upper part of Figure 9.1) which is oriented towards either contextual social science methods or humanities-based normative ethics.

FIGURE 9.1 A typology of environmental justice research

Social scientists ask a range of questions about the kinds of injustices perceived by groups and individuals and about the causes and consequences of the justice claims that arise from those injustices. These are mainly questions that are, in principle, amenable to empirical social science research: questions that explore the justice claims and practices of individuals, groups and social movements (e.g. Schlosberg 2009; Walker 2012; He and Sikor 2015); questions that explore the subjective realm of beliefs and motives (Konow 2001; Fisher 2012); questions about the psychological and discursive roots of injustice in inter-subjective encounters (Escobar 1998; Neumann 2004; Mignolo 2009); political economy questions about the economic and political interests that drive moral claims (Fraser 1995; Harvey 1996); and ecological economics questions about how the metabolism of the global economy generates patterns of injustice, including conflicts arising along resource frontiers (Temper et al. 2015; Martínez Alier et al. 2016).

The second type of environmental justice research identified in Figure 9.1 is a more normative approach in which the object is to arrive at generalised principles or procedures for determining what the right course of action is in any given situation. Whilst such an approach might well be guided by empirical knowledge about the kinds of conditions humans and non-humans experience, this type of research primarily falls under philosophy, with attention to disciplines of reason rather than disciplines of field observation. Environmental ethics looks to establish moral codes and benchmarks that can be action guiding, in contrast to the social science approach which is more concerned with describing and analysing than with guiding. Individual philosophers tend to subscribe to one tradition of moral philosophy with its own particular stance on where one should look to find guidance. In Chapter 1, I described three main Western traditions. *Duty-based* (or deontological) ethics seeks to identify moral rules that can be used to guide the way that we live. These rules might be produced by human reasoning or by attention to divine instruction and lead to complementary sets of duties and rights. In conservation, rights-based approaches have led to the Conservation Initiative on Human Rights. *Utilitarianism* seeks guidance from the consequences of our actions, defining a good action as one which enhances aggregate utility – or which leads to the greatest happiness. Such an emphasis on maximising desired outcomes has dominated attempts to define and measure conservation effectiveness. For *Virtue ethics* the right thing to do is to act in the way a virtuous person would act. Assuming that conserving biodiversity is part of a virtuous life, the challenge would be to develop a society in which people could become, through self-development, good people – people who want to care for nature rather than people who obey rules or worry about consequences.

If we could all agree on one of these approaches to ethics, we could establish a single, consensual tradition of ethics, identify a set of derivative principles, and use these as indicators for the kind of 'objective assessment' identified as the third type of environmental research in Figure 9.1. But in practice, of course, traditions and principles of justice will remain intractably plural (as discussed in Chapter 4) and we will always need an empirical, social scientific approach to understand the particular contexts that surround justice claims. The extent of this challenge will vary from case to case. In some instances the normative principles will be clear and widely agreed. For example, the environmental justice campaign against toxic waste in the US draws on a principle that is well established through civil rights movements: that it is morally wrong to discriminate against people because of the colour of their skin. Furthermore, objective assessment of such discrimination is made possible through statistical analysis of actual locations of environmental harms (such as toxic waste disposal sites). But whilst measuring distributional harms can be relatively straightforward, claims about procedure and recognition often require more qualitative inquiry.

At the same time, the trajectory of what counts as robust evidence in conservation circles has shifted away from in-depth, qualitative work. The trend is towards quantitative research that employs experimental or quasi-experimental designs in order to establish robust counter-factuals. The strength of these methods is the ability to establish the difference between what has happened in practice and what would have happened in the absence of the conservation intervention. This is important. When we undertake research into the effects of conservation interventions we need to be able to measure those outcomes that were actually caused by the conservation intervention, rather than outcomes that may have resulted from a range of other contextual factors. For example, prior to the development of 'counter-factual' methods in conservation, there was a tendency to exaggerate the effectiveness of protected areas in reducing deforestation by over 65% (Andam et al. 2010). Firstly, research was not sensitive to choice of locations of protected areas – they are often located in more remote areas where deforestation would be low even without the protected area status. Secondly, methods did not account for the possibility of spillover effects – that deforestation was simply shifted to areas neighbouring the protected area.

This search for a more robust understanding of the effects of conservation interventions should be very much welcomed; it will begin to cross over from the measurement of conservation effects to the measurement of social effects. However, I want to use the rest of this concluding chapter to highlight two main ways in which more contextual and plural approaches to research must contribute to evidence of the effects of conservation on justice. Firstly, I pick up on the idea of justice research being empirical and contextual and say a bit more about how this might be approached. In doing so, I propose an inter-disciplinary approach that combines elements of all parts of Figure 9.1. With respect to justice assessment, the idea is that such in-depth exploration of how people perceive justice and injustice will commonly be needed to complement broader-based assessment tools. Research questions about environmental justice will rarely be well served by quantitative impact assessment methods in isolation. Some distributional questions can be explored in this way, such as whether there is discrimination against particular groups of people in the location of toxic waste sites. But exploration of how individuals perceive the legitimacy of a conservation intervention, and how this feeds into perceived injustice and resentment, often requires a case study approach.

Secondly, I consider the parallel need to progress towards a more generalised set of indicators of conservation justice that can be used to assess progress and to guide practice. This is admittedly quite a painful idea for a social scientist who is steeped in the contextual approaches that I will describe below. My first instinct is to think that coming up with generalised indicators of conservation justice, potentially to be used to assess performance across tens of thousands of locations, would be to deny the plurality of justice conceptions that I have argued for and would run counter to my advocacy of an empirical and contextual approach. Wouldn't any set of indicators be biased towards some people's conceptions of justice at the expense of others? Would it not itself be guilty of failure to recognise cultural difference? I think this is a real danger but, on the other hand, I also think the case for developing indicators is a compelling one. The way forward that I describe is to take a deliberative approach in which a broad range of stakeholders pursue a process of dialogue to agree a set of principles and indicators that we can work with.

An empirical approach – to support justice assessment

I propose that a case-based contextual study of environmental justice should explore three types of questions which involve elements from each part of Figure 9.1. Firstly, it will seek to empirically identify different claims to environmental justice, the situations in which these are formed and articulated, and the positionality of social actors making the claims. Secondly, it will seek to identify dominant conceptions of justice that have shaped key policies and/or interventions. Thirdly, it will look for evidence of outcomes, including the more measurable harms and benefits for different groups of people.

A contextual analysis can perform at least two useful purposes. Firstly, it can relate a dominant conception of justice to alternative conceptions seen in the claims of other social actors. For example, in the case study of PES in Rwanda described in Chapter 8, we found that local respondents mostly preferred an egalitarian approach to distributing payments (each household receiving the same amount). However, dominant ideas about PES hold that differentiated payment, according to a household's contribution to service provision and/or the associated opportunity costs (foregone income) would be fairer and more efficient (Martin et al. 2014a). So here an empirical study of local conceptions of justice discovers that local and global norms about payment mechanisms are not aligned, with potential for failures of legitimacy and loss of support. Secondly, an empirical approach can examine the fit between these dominant norms and other commonly articulated norms relating to social and ecological objectives. For example, Sikor et al. (2014) argue that conservation interventions designed on a utilitarian basis are likely to be incompatible with an objective to deliver pro-poor outcomes. This second analytical step serves to connect a contextual analysis to more objective benchmarks of justice, as I proposed in Chapter 4. Thus, Sikor et al. (2014) connect their empirical observation of conceptions of justice with established norms of being pro-poor. Similarly, in a study of Uganda's Bwindi Impenetrable National Park (Martin et al. 2015), I relate empirical observation of the distribution of costs and benefits with justice benchmarks derived from capability thresholds. This step of connecting empirical observation with contextually relevant benchmarks of justice enables justice assessment to be judgemental and action-guiding. It enables one to ask how appropriate a particular dominant norm (and its associated policy/project design) is in the context in which it is employed (Sikor et al. 2014).

The approach I am proposing is very dependent on the idea of 'conceptions of environmental justice'. It seeks to observe and describe a dominant conception of justice which frames policy and practice whilst also exploring the tensions this creates with alternative, often local, conceptions of justice. Such tensions were central to the discussion of 'justice as motive' in Chapter 3, in which I argued that convergence and divergence between different views of fairness was a determinant of how legitimate a conservation intervention was seen to be. A 'conception of environmental justice' can be analysed by decomposing it into four main elements: subjects, dimensions, harms and principles. This builds on a similar framework introduced by Sikor et al. (2014), the main difference being the inclusion of 'harms' as a separate component.

- *Subjects* refers to the 'who' of a justice conception: who are the subjects who deserve to be protected by norms of justice or who have duties of protection? This might be: individuals within a nation state, or within the world; communities as well as individuals; future as well as current people; non-humans as well as humans; eco-systems as well as species.

- *Dimensions* could be described as the 'what' of a justice conception. What kinds of values and concerns should be considered within a justice analysis? As discussed in Chapter 1, the kinds of concerns expressed are usefully classified into the justice dimensions of distribution, procedure and recognition.
- *Harms* refers to the nature of any suffering inflicted upon specified subjects of injustice. I separate this from dimensions because articulations of injustice can often view different harms arising from the same dimension; this occurs primarily because of the interrelationship between different dimensions. For example, inequitable distribution of benefits (or costs) can be viewed as lead-ing to harm to human wellbeing, but among conservation practitioners it is often viewed as leading to harms to conservation effectiveness and thus harms to nature or to the greater good of humanity. Likewise, some view proce-dural injustices as intrinsic harms to human rights or agency, whilst others view harms more instrumentally, in terms of how lack of participation can be a cause of inequitable distribution. Finally, there is a debate about failures of recognition as to whether the harm done is primarily psychological (for example to self-esteem) or whether it is primarily material, and to what extent harm related to recognition, participation and distribution are inter-twined (see Chapter 6).
- *Principles* or criteria refer to the specific rules applied to these different dimen-sions of justice concerns. For example, there are many different ways of thinking about the 'right' way to distribute benefits from a park. Distribution might be considered 'just' based on principles of egalitarianism, meritocracy, need, and so on.

This decomposed view of conceptions of justice can be applied widely: to the analysis of dominant conceptions of environmental justice in mainstream policymaking and practice; to the analysis of conceptions employed in specific project interventions; and to the different conceptions articulated by different stakeholder groups.

Developing a broader-scale justice assessment approach

Whilst the need to consider equity and justice has been progressively acknowledged in policy circles over nearly half a century, there has been relatively little progress in attempts to collect relevant evidence that can guide and measure progress. If we go back to the 1972 Stockholm Conference on the Human Environment, the resulting Declaration states:

> Man [sic] has the fundamental right to freedom, equality and adequate con-ditions of life, in an environment of a quality that permits a life of dignity and

wellbeing, and he bears a solemn responsibility to protect and improve the environment for present and future generations. In this respect, policies promoting or perpetuating apartheid, racial segregation, discrimination, colonial and other forms of oppression and foreign domination stand condemned and must be eliminated.

(Declaration of the United Nations Conference on the
Human Environment, 1972, Principle 1)

Fifteen years after the Stockholm conference, the influential Brundtland Report on *Our Common Future* (WCED 1987) actually defined sustainable development in terms of equity, as did the subsequent *Blueprint for a Green Economy* (Pearce et al. 1989). These works invoked the popular and ancient idea of inter-generational responsibility but also argued that sustainability required *intra-generational* equity. Sustainability therefore required equity both between and within generations. This argument became embodied in the so-called social pillar of sustainability (along with the economic and environmental pillars) at the 1992 United Nations Conference on Environment and Development. The Convention on Biological Diversity (CBD) was one of the outcomes of this summit and sets out three objectives:

The objectives of this Convention, to be pursued in accordance with its relevant provisions, are the conservation of biological diversity, the sustainable use of its components and the fair and equitable sharing of the benefits arising out of the utilisation of genetic resources.

(United Nations 1992, Article 1)

The CBD's 10th Conference of Parties in 2010 led to the 'Nagoya Protocol on Access to Genetic Resources and the Fair and Equitable Sharing of Benefits Arising from their Utilization' and subsequently the Aichi Targets which include Target 11:

By 2020, at least 17 per cent of terrestrial and inland water, and 10 per cent of coastal and marine areas, especially areas of particular importance for biodiversity and ecosystem services, are conserved through effectively and equitably managed, ecologically representative and well connected systems of protected areas and other effective area-based conservation measures, and integrated into the wider landscapes and seascapes.

(CBD 2010, Aichi Target 11)

The idea that biodiversity can and should be conserved *through* equitable management resonates very clearly with the argument that equity and justice may be instrumental to conservation success. Given the relatively short, decade-long, timescale of the target, it might also be assumed that there are existing ways and processes for measuring equity outcomes against this target, and perhaps even baselines against which progress can be evaluated. I proceed to argue that despite decades of talking about equitable biodiversity conservation, there has in fact been hardly any progress towards its assessment and management. As it stands, there is no way of judging progress towards the equity component of Aichi Target 11.

Prior to the Aichi Targets, the CBD Programme of Work on Protected Areas was agreed in 2004 and included the following goals and targets:

Goal 4.2: To evaluate and improve the effectiveness of protected areas management

Target: By 2010, frameworks for monitoring, evaluating and reporting protected areas management effectiveness at sites, national and regional systems, and transboundary protected area levels adopted and implemented by Parties.

(CBD, 2000, Programme of Work, Goal 4.2)

A key response to this goal was the development of the Protected Area Management Effectiveness (PAME) evaluation tool which uses six sets of indicators to monitor PA effectiveness: context, planning, input, processes, outputs and outcomes (Hockings et al. 2006).

Within the target period, PAME was conducted in over 8000 protected areas within 140 countries (Leverington et al. 2010).

Goal 2.1: To promote equity and benefit sharing

Target: Establish by 2008 mechanisms for the equitable sharing of both costs and benefits arising from the establishment and management of protected areas.

(CBD, 2000, Programme of Work, Goal 2.1)

This target was partly met (albeit slightly late) by the 2010 Nagoya Protocol. But it is interesting to note the comparative status of the goal. Whilst 'effectiveness' (Goal 4.2) is something for which there has been a longstanding mandate and associated 'mechanisms', 'equity' (Goal 2.1) is at a more fledgling stage despite its apparent importance within the original 1992 CBD. The fact that the mandate and mechanisms for equitable management of biodiversity were only beginning to be addressed within the CBD in the late noughties is one reason why there are no equity or justice assessment tools that have gained any degree of traction within the conservation policymaking and practitioner communities. There is certainly nothing that comes close to PAME in terms of resourcing, uptake and global synthesis. The data for global implementation of the CBD Programme of Work finds progress on Goal 2.1. to be poor: 42% of PAs have not even begun a process of developing mechanisms, a further 33% report having only just begun a process, and less than 3% report having completed this target (Figure 9.2). The corresponding figures for Goal 4.2 are a bit better, with 21.8% not having started and 11.0% having completed.

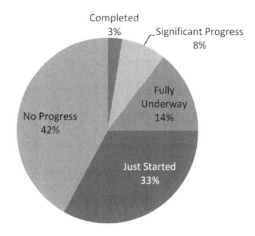

FIGURE 9.2 Progress on CBD Programme of Work Goal 2.1 to promote equity and benefit sharing.

Source: Data from www.cbd.int/protected/implementation (accessed 15/7/15).

Given that member states reported so little progress on the Programme of Work equity target (2000 to 2010), it is clearly over-ambitious for the Aichi programme (2010 to 2020) to target the achievement of equitable management by 2020. This is not just due to the current absence of assessment tools, but also because there is an important step to be made before such tools can be developed. There needs to be a process to determine *how* equity will be framed and assessed. The terms equity and justice are multi-dimensional and contested, making their evaluation especially difficult. Without careful consideration of how they are to be framed there is an inherent danger that any assessment might reflect and bolster particular ideologies rather than recognising plural values and cultures.

Developing a framework for assessing equity and justice in conservation is challenging because of the need to integrate the views of justice held by multiple stakeholders. However, if we are serious about assessing progress towards equitable or just conservation, we have little choice but to attempt this. Since 2015, I have been part of a team convened by the International Institute of Environment and Development in order to develop such a framework. This has involved a process of consultation with a range of conservation stakeholders, including: policymakers such as the International Union for the Conservation of Nature; monitoring specialists, notably the World Conservation Monitoring Centre; large conservation international NGOs such as WWF, Fauna and Flora International and Conservation International; activists including the Forest Peoples Programme; national NGOs, governments and communities in field testing sites in Kenya, Tanzania and Uganda; and academics from several universities. As I write, the draft framework produced through this consultation process (Figure 9.3) is about to be presented at the 2016 World Parks Congress in Hawaii, for further discussion and development. The hope is to produce a framework for assessing equity that has sufficient consensus to serve as a basis for developing assessment tools. The framework adopts the term 'equity' rather than justice because this is the language that has currency within mainstream conservation and in particular, features in the CBD's Aichi targets. Nonetheless, the framework essentially employs an environmental justice approach, incorporating principles relating to the three dimensions of recognition, procedures and distribution (Franks et al. 2016) (Figure 9.3).

Recognition

1. Recognition and respect for human rights
2. Recognition and respect for statutory and customary property rights
3. Recognition and respect for the rights of Indigenous Peoples, women and marginalised groups
4. Recognition of different identities, values, knowledge systems and institutions
5. Recognition of all relevant actors and their diverse interests, capacities and powers to influence
6. Non-discrimination by age, ethnic origin, language, gender, class and beliefs

Procedure

7. Full and effective participation of all relevant actors in decision making
8. Clearly defined and agreed responsibilities of actors
9. Accountability for actions and inactions
10. Access to justice, including an effective dispute-resolution process
11. Transparency supported by timely access to relevant information in appropriate forms
12. Free, prior and informed consent for actions that may affect the property rights of Indigenous Peoples and local communities

Distribution

13. Identification and assessment of costs, benefits and risks and their distribution and trade-offs
14. Effective mitigation of any costs to Indigenous Peoples and local communities
15. Benefits shared among relevant actors according to one or more of the following criteria:
    - Equally between relevant actors or
    - According to contribution to conservation, costs incurred, recognised rights and/or the priorities of the poorest
16. Benefits to present generations do not compromise benefits to future generations

Enabling conditions

1. Legal, political and social recognition of all protected area governance types
2. Relevant actors have awareness and capacity to achieve recognition and participate effectively
3. Alignment of statutory and customary laws and norms
4. An adaptive, learning approach

FIGURE 9.3 Equity framework for protected areas: principles and enabling conditions.

Source: Franks, Martin and Schreckenberg, 2016.

The framework in Figure 9.3 identifies a set of equity principles that can be used in the assessment and governance of protected areas, as well as a set of broader 'enabling conditions' covering factors beyond the control of the protected area stakeholders, for example national rules of tenure (see McDermott et al., 2013). The framework can potentially be applied to all stages of protected areas, from prior assessment and establishment, through to ongoing governance and management both of protected areas and related activities. It can also potentially be applied at the level of individual protected areas as well as at system level, such as a national network of protected areas.

Some of the partners in this process have themselves been active in developing tools that can monitor some aspects of equity and justice. For example, WWF have adapted the Management Effectiveness Tracking Tool (a simple questionnaire-based assessment system, Coad et al. 2013) to assess the distribution of social benefits from protected areas (Stephenson and McShane, 2015). IIED have been developing a more intensive process of assessing the distribution of social costs and benefits: the Social Assessment of Protected Areas (SAPA) tool (Franks and Small, 2016). IUCN has been a partner in developing SAPA and has also been developing a framework and methodology for evaluating the governance of protected areas; this includes a focus on issues related to the allocation of rights and decision-making (see Borrini-Feyerabend et al. 2013). These are all important and welcome contributions that will make a difference if they gain traction in conservation practice. However, it remains the case that there are dedicated and widely used tools for evaluating and tracking management effectiveness, but nothing equivalent for justice or equity. The draft equity framework in Figure 9.3 is therefore an important initiative. Until we have clearer agreement about what we mean by equity and justice it will be extremely hard to develop assessment tools, and without such tools, 'evidence-based conservation' will continue to work from only a partial picture.

Conclusion

The Conservation Evidence database (ConservationEvidence.com, accessed 18/3/16) returned 1525 results using the search term 'effectiveness' but none at all using either 'equity' or 'justice'. To be strictly accurate, I did get one return for 'justice', but this turned out to be a study conducted by a researcher named D. Justic. This is symptomatic of a wider problem that whilst much is said about the importance of equity and justice in relation to conservation, the capacity to research and monitor this aspect remains low. This may well be partly down to political will but it is also at least partly caused by some disjuncture between the kinds of research which are prioritised and the kinds of research that are needed. Mainstream 'conservation evidence' research very much favours econometric impact evaluation methods that are hard to apply to the measure of some types of justice effect. These methods rely on large-scale data from government surveys or remotely sensed images and have less use for in-depth case study work. For this reason they are mainly applied to measuring progress in conservation outcomes and sometimes the distributional dimension of justice outcomes.

For a more broad-based understanding of conservation justice we will need to develop empirical, contextual methods of inquiry and this will require the more intensive case study approaches described above. But at the same time, we also need to establish some level of consensus about what constitutes 'just conservation', as a basis for developing principles and indicators that can be used for a more coarse-grained but wider-scale assessment of the performance of conservation. Only then can we set targets for equity or justice that are in any way credible and useful.

REFERENCES

Adams, W. M., Aveling, R., Brockington, D., Dickson, B., Elliott, J., Hutton, J. et al. (2004). Biodiversity conservation and the eradication of poverty. *Science* 306: 1146–1149.

Agnew, D. J., Pearce, J., Pramod, G., Peatman, T., Watson, R., Beddington, J. R. et al. (2009). Estimating the worldwide extent of illegal fishing. *PLoS ONE* 4(2): e4570.

Agrawal, A., & Redford, K. (2009). Conservation and displacement: an overview. *Conservation and Society* 7(1): 1–10.

Ahrends, A., Burgess, N. D., Milledge, S. A.H., Bulling, M. T., Fisher., Smart, J. C. R., Clarke, G. P. et al. (2010). Predictable waves of sequential forest degradation and biodiversity loss spreading from an African city. *Proceedings of the National Academy of Sciences* 107(33): 14556–14561.

Alcoreza, R. P. (2013). Buen Vivir as a model for state and economy. In Lang, M. & Mokrani, D. (eds) *Beyond Development, Alternative Visions from Latin America*. Quito: Fundación Rosa Luxemburg, Abya Yala Ediciones.

Alkire, S. (2007). Measuring freedoms alongside wellbeing. In Gough, I. and McGregor, J. A. (eds) *Wellbeing in Developing Countries: From Theory to Research*. Cambridge: Cambridge University Press.

Allison, E. H., Ratner, B. D., Åsgård, B., Willmann, R., Pomeroy, R. & Kurien, J. (2012). Rights-based fisheries governance: from fishing rights to human rights. *Fish and Fisheries* 13: 14–29.

Almudi, T. & Berkes, F. (2010). Barriers to empowerment: fighting eviction for conservation in a southern Brazilian protected area. *Local Environment* 15(3): 217–232.

Alroy, J. (2008). Dynamics of origination and extinction in the marine fossil record. *Proceedings of the National Academy of Sciences* 105(Supplement 1): 11536–11542.

Armstrong, A. (2014). *Ethics and Justice for the Environment*. London: Routledge.

Ashayeri, S. & Newing, H. (2012). Meat, markets, pleasure and revenge: multiple motivations for hunting in Bamu National Park, Fars Province, Iran, *Parks* 18(1): 125–133.

Auer, M. (2012). Group forest certification for smallholders in Vietnam: an early test and future prospects. *Human Ecology* 40(1): 5–14.

Baker, J., Milner-Gulland, E. J. & Leader-Williams, N. (2012). Park gazettement and integrated conservation and development as factors in community conflict at Bwindi Impenetrable Forest, Uganda. *Conservation Biology* 26(1): 160–170.

Ball, S. & Makala, J. (2014). *Making REDD+ Work for Communities and Forests: Three Shared Lessons for Project Designers*. London: International Institute of Environment and Development.

Barnosky, A. D., Matzke, N., Tomiya, S., Wogan, G. O. U., Swartz, B., Quental, T. B., Marshall, C. et al. (2011). Has the Earth's sixth mass extinction already arrived? *Nature* 471: 51–57. doi:10.1038/nature09678.

Barrett, S. & Graddy, K. (2000). Freedom, growth, and the environment. *Environment and Development Economics* 5(4): 433–456.

BBOP (2012). *Business and Biodiversity Offsets Programme. Executive Summary of BBOP Standard, Technical Handbooks and Resource Papers*. Washington DC: BBOP.

Beaune, D. (2015). What would happen to the trees and lianas if apes disappeared? *Oryx* 49(3): 442–446.

Beaune, D., Fruth, B., Bollache, L., Hohmann, G. & Bretagnolle, F. (2013). Doom of the elephant-dependent trees in a Congo tropical forest. *Forest Ecology and Management* 295 (May): 109–117.

Beckmann, V. (2014). Conservation, protected areas and economic development of remote rural areas. In Frieder, F., Dünkel, R., Herbst, M. & Schlegel, T. (eds) *Think Rural! Dynamiken des Wandels in peripheren ländlichen Räumen und ihre Implikationen für die Daseinsvorsorge*. Wiesbaden: VS Verlag für Sozialwissenschaften.

Belcher, B. & Schreckenberg, K. (2007). Commercialisation of non-timber forest products: a reality check. *Development Policy Review* 25(3): 355–377.

Belcher, B., Ruíz-Pérez, M. & Achdiawan, R. (2005). Global patterns and trends in the use and management of commercial NTFPs: implications for livelihoods and conservation. *World Development* 33(9): 1435–1452.

Bennett, M. T. (2008). China's sloping land conversion program: institutional innovation or business as usual? *Ecological Economics* 65(4): 699–711.

Bentham, J. (2009). *Utilitarianism*. Charleston: BiblioBazaar.

Berger, J. (2008 [1972]). *Ways of Seeing*. London: Penguin.

Bigg, T. (2012). Five things we've learnt from Rio+20. http://www.iied.org/five-things-we-ve-learnt-rio20 Accessed 30/08/2016.

Bird, K., Hulme, D., Moore, K. & Shepherd, A. (2002). *Chronic Poverty and Remote Rural Areas*. CPRC Working Paper No. 13. Chronic Poverty Research Centre, International Development Department, School of Public Policy. Birmingham: University of Birmingham.

Blackman, A. and Rivera, J. (2011). Producer-level benefits of sustainability certification. *Conservation Biology* 25(6): 1176–1185.

Blom, B., Sunderland, T. & Murdiyarso, D. (2010). Getting REDD to work locally: lessons learned from integrated conservation and development projects. *Environmental Science & Policy* 13(2): 164–172.

Blomley, T. & Ramadhani, H. (2006). Going to scale with participatory forest management: early lessons from Tanzania. *International Forestry Review* 8(1) (March): 93–100.

Blomley, T., Pfliegner, K., Isango, J., Zahabu, E., Ahrends A. & Burgess, N. (2008). Seeing the wood for the trees: an assessment of the impact of participatory forest management on forest condition in Tanzania. *Oryx* 42: 380–391. doi:10.1017/S0030605308071433.

Bohman, J. (2007). Beyond distributive justice and struggles for recognition freedom, democracy, and critical theory. *European Journal of Political Theory* 6(3): 267–276.

Bonneuil, C. (2015). Tell me where you come from, I will tell you who you are: a genealogy of biodiversity offsetting mechanisms in historical context. *Biological Conservation* 192: 485–491.

Borie, M. & Hulme, M. (2015). Framing global biodiversity: IPBES between mother earth and ecosystem services. *Environmental Science & Policy* 54: 487–496.

Borras Jr., S. M., Hall, R., Scoones, I., White, B. & Wolford, W. (2011). Towards a better understanding of global land grabbing: an editorial introduction. *Journal of Peasant Studies* 38(2): 209–216.

Borrini-Feyerabend, G., Dudley, N., Jaeger, T., Lassen, B., Broome, N. P. & Phillips, A. (2013). *Governance of Protected Areas: From Understanding to Action.* Gland: International Union for the Conservation of Nature.

Bowles, S. & Polania-Reyes, S. (2012). Economic incentives and social preferences: substitutes or complements? *Journal of Economic Literature* 50(2): 368–425. doi:10.1257/jel.50.2.368.

Boyd, E. (2002). The Noel Kempff project in Bolivia: gender, power, and decision-making in climate mitigation. *Gender & Development* 10(2): 70–77.

Brand, U. & Vadrot, A. B. M. (2013). Epistemic selectivities and the valorisation of nature: the cases of the Nagoya Protocol and the Intergovernmental Science-Policy Platform for Biodiversity and Ecosystem Services (IPBES). *Law, Environment and Development Journal* 9(2): 202.

Brandon, K. & Wells, M. (2009). Lessons for REDD+ from protected areas and integrated conservation and development projects. In *Realising REDD+ National strategy and policy options.* Bogor: CIFOR.

Brandon, K. & Wells, M. (1992). *People and Parks: Linking Protected Area Management with Local Communities.* Washington DC: World Bank.

Brock, G. (2009). *Global Justice: A Cosmopolitan Account.* Oxford: Oxford University Press.

Brockington, D. (2004). Community conservation, inequality and injustice: myths of power in protected area management. *Conservation and Society* 2(2): 411–432.

Brockington, D. (2003). Injustice and conservation—is 'local support' necessary for sustainable protected areas? *Policy Matters* 12: 22–30.

Brockington, D. (2002). *Fortress Conservation: The Preservation of the Mkomazi Game Reserve, Tanzania.* Bloomington: Indiana University Press.

Brockington, D. & Wilkie, D. (2015). Protected Areas and Poverty. Phil. Trans. R. Soc. B 370: 20140271. http://dx.doi.org/10.1098/rstb.2014.0271.

Brockington, D. & Igoe, J. (2006). Eviction for Conservation: A Global Overview. *Conservation and Society* 4(3): 424–470.

Brosius, J. P. & Hitchner, S. L. (2010). Cultural diversity and conservation. *International Social Science Journal* 61: 141–168.

Bruckner, M., Wiebe, K. S., Giljum, S., Lutz, C. & Polzin, C. (2012). Carbon and materials embodied in the international trade of emerging economies. *Journal of Industrial Ecology* 16: 636–646.

Bruner, A. G., Gullison, R. E., Rice, R. E. & Da Fonseca, G. A. (2001). Effectiveness of parks in protecting tropical biodiversity. *Science* 291: 125–128.

Bulkeley, H., Castán Broto, V. & Maassen, A. (2014). Low-carbon transitions and the reconfiguration of urban infrastructure. *Urban Studies:* 51(7), 1471–1486..

Bull, J. W., Suttle, K. B., Gordon, A., Singh, N. J. & Milner-Gulland, E. J. (2013). Biodiversity offsets in theory and practice. *Oryx* 47(3): 369–380.

Bullard, R. D. (1990). *Dumping in Dixie: Race, Class, and Environmental Quality.* Boulder, CO: Westview.

Bumpus, A. G. & Liverman, D. M. (2010). Carbon colonialism? Offsets, greenhouse gas reductions, and sustainable development. *Global Political Ecology* 203.

Burgess, N. D., Bahane, B., Clairs, T., Danielsen, F., Dalsgaard, S., Funder, M., Zahabu, E. et al. (2010). Getting ready for REDD+ in Tanzania: a case study of progress and challenges. *Oryx* 44(3): 339–351.

Büscher, B., Sullivan, S., Neves, K., Igoe, J. & Brockington, D. (2012). Towards a synthesized critique of neoliberal biodiversity conservation. *Capitalism Nature Socialism* 23(2): 4–30.

Business and Biodiversity Offsets Programme (BBOP) (2012). *Standard on Biodiversity Offsets*. BBOP, Washington DC. http://bbop.forest-trends.org/guidelines/Standard.pdf Accessed 30/8/2016.

Butchart, S. H. M., Walpole, W., Collen, B., Van Strien, A., Scharlemann, J. P. W., Almond, R. E. A., Baillie, J. E. M. et al. (2010). Global biodiversity: indicators of recent declines. *Science* 328(5982) (28 May): 1164–1168.

Butterfield, N. J. (2007). Macroevolution and macroecology through deep time. *Palaeontology* 50(1): 41–55.

Cadotte, M. W., Cardinale, B. J. and Oakley, T. H. (2008). Evolutionary history and the effect of biodiversity on plant productivity. *Proceedings of the National Academy of Sciences* 105(44): 17012–17017.

Callicott, J. B. (1994). *Earth's Insights: A Multicultural Survey of Ecological Ethics from the Mediterranean Basin to the Australian Outback*. Berkeley: University of California Press.

Calvet-Mir, L., Corbera, E., Martin, A., Fisher, J. & Gross-Camp, N. (2015). Payments for ecosystem services in the tropics: a closer look at effectiveness and equity. *Current Opinion in Environmental Sustainability* 14: 150–162.

Cardinale, B. J., Duffy, J. E., Gonzalez, A., Hooper, D. U., Perrings, C., Venail, P. & Narwani, A. (2012). Biodiversity loss and its impact on humanity. *Nature* 486: 59–67.

Castree, N. (2008). Neoliberalising nature: the logics of deregulation and reregulation. *Environment and Planning A* 40(1): 131–152.

Castree, N. (2004). Differential geographies: place, indigenous rights and 'local' resources. *Political Geography* 23(2): 133–167.

Cavanagh, C. & Benjaminsen, T. A. (2014). Virtual nature, violent accumulation: the 'spectacular failure' of carbon offsetting at a Ugandan national park. *Geoforum* 56: 55–65.

Cavendish, W. (2000). Empirical regularities in the poverty–environment relationship of rural households: evidence from Zimbabwe. *World Development* 28(11): 1987–2000.

Cavendish, W. & Campbell, B. M. (2000). *Poverty, Environmental Income and Rural Inequality: A Case Study from Zimbabwe*. Bogor: CIFOR.

CBD (2014). *Global Biodiversity Outlook 4*. https://www.cbd.int/gbo4/ Accessed 30/08/2016.

CBD (2010a). *Global Biodiversity Outlook 3*. https://www.cbd.int/doc/publications/gbo/ gbo3-final-en.pdf Accessed 30/08/2016.

CBD (2010b). *Aichi Biodiversity Targets*. https://www.cbd.int/sp/targets/ Accessed 29/08/2016.

CBD (2006). *Global Biodiversity Outlook 2*. https://www.cbd.int/doc/gbo/gbo2/cbd-gbo2-en.pdf Accessed 30/08/2016.

Chambers, R. (1983). *Rural Development: Putting the Last First*. London: Longman.

Changjin, S. and Chen, L. (2005). The Status of Payments for Watershed Environmental Services of Forests in China and Its Institutional Analysis. IIED Project Desk Study I-The Study of Policies and Legislations Affecting Payments for Watershed Environmental Services, draft. RCEEE for IIED-funded Watershed Protection Services, unpublished.

Chapin, M. (2004). A challenge to conservationists. *WorldWatch*. 17(6): 17–31.

Chhatre, A. & Agrawal, A. (2009). Trade-offs and synergies between carbon storage and livelihood benefits from forest commons. *Proceedings of the National Academy of Sciences* 106(42): 17667–17670.

Chum, H., Faaij, A., Moreira, J., Berndes, G., Dhamija, P., Dong, H., Gabrielle, B. et al. (2011). Bioenergy. In Edenhofer, O., Pichs-Madruga, R., Sokona, Y., Seyboth, K., Matschoss, P., Kadner, S. and Zwickel, T. (eds) *IPCC Special Report on Renewable Energy Sources and Climate Change Mitigation*. Cambridge: Cambridge University Press. http://dx.doi.org/10.1017/CBO9781139151153.006.

CIHR (Conservation Initiative on Human Rights) (2010). http://www.iied.org/conservation-initiative-human-rights Accessed August 2016.

Cinner, J. E., Huchery, C., MacNeil, M. A., Graham, N. A., McClanahan, T. R., Maina, J., Maire, E. et al. (2016). Bright spots among the world's coral reefs. *Nature* 535(7612): 416–419.

Clark, B. & Foster, J. B. (2009). Ecological imperialism and the global metabolic rift: unequal exchange and the guano/nitrates trade. *International Journal of Comparative Sociology* 50(3–4): 311–334.

Cleaver, F. (2012). *Development through Bricolage: Rethinking Institutions for Natural Resources Management*. New York: Routledge.

Coad, L., Leverington, F., Burgess, N. D., Cuadros, I. C., Geldmann, J., Marthews, T. R., . . . & Zamora, C. (2013). Progress towards the CBD protected area management effectiveness targets. *Parks* 19(1): 13–24.

Coleman, E. A. (2009). Institutional factors affecting biophysical outcomes in forest management. *Journal of Policy Analysis and Management* 28: 122–146.

Coleman, E. A. & Steed, B. C. (2009). Monitoring and sanctioning in the commons: an application to forestry. *Ecological Economics* 68: 2106–2113.

Colquitt, J. A., Conlon, D. E., Wesson, M. J., Porter, C. O., Ng, K. Y. (2001). Justice at the millennium: a meta-analytic review of 25 years of organizational justice research. *Journal of Applied Psychology* 86: 425.

Coolsaet, B. (2016). Towards and agroecology of knowledges. *Journal of Rural Studies*, 47 (October): 165–171..

Coralie, C., Guillaume, O. & Claude, N. (2015). Tracking the origins and development of biodiversity offsetting in academic research and its implications for conservation: a review. *Biological Conservation* 19 (December): 492–503.

Corbera, E. and Martin, A. (2015). Carbon offsets: Accommodation or resistance? *Environment and Planning A* 47(10): 2023–2030.

Corbera, E., Martin, A., Villasenor, A. Springate-Baginski, O. (2015). Combining REDD, PFM and FSC Certification in SE Tanzania: An Analysis of Livelihoods Impacts through Household Panel Data (2011-2014). Unpublished report for Mpingo Conservation and Development Initiative.

Corbera, E., Brown, K. & Adger, W. N. (2007). The equity and legitimacy of markets for ecosystem services. *Development and Change* 38(4): 587–613.

Costanza, R., De Groot, R., Sutton, P., Van der Ploeg, S., Anderson, S. J., Kubiszewski, I. Farber, S. et al. (2014). Changes in the global value of ecosystem services. *Global Environmental Change* 26 (May): 152–158.

Costanza, R., D'Arge, R., De Groot, R., Farberk, S., Grasso, M., Hannon, B., Limburg, K. (1997). The value of the world's ecosystem services and natural capital. *Nature* 387 (May) 253–260.

Coulthard, G. S. (2007). Subjects of empire: indigenous peoples and the 'politics of recognition' in Canada. *Contemporary Political Theory* 6: 437–460.

Cracknell, J., Miller, F. & Williams, H. (2013). *Passionate Collaboration? Taking The Pulse of the UK Environmental Sector*. http://www.greenfunders.org/passionate-collaboration/ Accessed 1/09/2016.

Cripps, E. (2010). Saving the polar bear, saving the world: can the capabilities approach do justice to humans, animals and ecosystems? *Res Publica* 16(1): 1–22. doi:10.1007/s11158–010–9106–2.

Cronon, W. (1996). The trouble with wilderness; or, getting back to the wrong nature. *Environmental History* 1(1): 7–28.

Crosby, A. W. (1986). *Ecological Imperialism: The Biological Expansion of Europe, 900–1900.* Cambridge: Cambridge University Press.

D'Adda, G. (2011). Motivation crowding in environmental protection: evidence from an artefactual field experiment. *Ecological Economics* 70: 2083–2097.

Dalton, R. J. (2005). The greening of the globe? Cross-national levels of environmental group membership. *Environmental Politics* 14: 441–459.

Davis, A. & Ruddle, K. (2012). Massaging the misery: recent approaches to fisheries governance and the betrayal of small-scale fisheries. *Human Organization* 71(3): 244–254.

Dawson, N. & Martin, A. (2015). Assessing the contribution of ecosystem services to human wellbeing: a disaggregated study in Western Rwanda. *Ecological Economics* 117: 2–72.

Dawson, N., Martin, A. & Danielsen, F. (2016a). Assessing equity in protected area governance: approaches to promote just and effective conservation, under review, *Conservation Letters.*

Dawson, N., Martin, A. & Sikor, T. (2016b). Green revolution in Sub-Saharan Africa: implications of imposed innovation for the wellbeing of rural smallholders. *World Development* 78 (February): 204–218.

De Boer, J., Schösler, H. & Boersema, J. J. (2013). Climate change and meat eating: an inconvenient couple? *Journal of Environmental Psychology* 33: 1–8.

DEFRA (2013). *Developing the Potential for Payments for Ecosystem Services: An Action Plan.* London: Department for Environment, Food and Rural Affairs.

Deininger, K. & Byerlee, D. (2011). *Rising Global Interest in Farmland: Can It Yield Sustainable and Equitable Benefits?* Washington DC: World Bank.

Deutsch, M. (2000). Justice and conflict. In Deutsch, M. and Coleman, P. (eds.) *The Handbook of Conflict Resolution: Theory and Practice.* San Francisco: Jossey-Bass Publishers, pp. 41–64.

Dobson, A. (2003). Social justice and environmental sustainability: ne'er the twain shall meet? In Agyeman, J., Bullard, R. D. and Evans, B. (eds) *Just Sustainabilities. Development in an Unequal World.* London: Routledge.

Doyal, L. & Gough, I. (1991). *A Theory of Human Need.* London: Palgrave Macmillan.

Doyal, L. and Gough, I. (1984). A theory of human needs. *Critical Social Policy* 10: 6–38.

Dryzek, J. S. (2000). *Deliberative Democracy and Beyond: Liberals, Critics, Contestations.* Oxford: Oxford University Press.

Duffy, R. (2014). Waging a war to save biodiversity: the rise of militarized conservation. *International Affairs* 90: 819–834.

Duffy, R. (2000). *Killing for Conservation: Wildlife Policy in Zimbabwe.* Melton, Suffolk: James Currey.

Ellis, F. & Biggs, S. (2001). Evolving themes in rural development 1950s–2000s. *Development Policy Review* 19(4): 437–448.

Embassy, L. (2009). HMG floats proposal for marine reserve covering the Chagos Archipelago [Online]. http://www.telegraph.co.uk/news/wikileaks-files/london-wikileaks/8305246/hmg-floats-proposal-for-marine-reserve-covering-the-chagos-archipelago-british-indian-ocean-territory.html Accessed 26/06/2013.

Escobar, A. (1998). Whose knowledge, whose nature? Biodiversity, conservation, and the political ecology of social movements. *Journal of Political Ecology* 5(1): 53–82.

Estes, J. A., Terborgh, J., Brashares, J. S., Power, M. E., Berger, J., Bond, W. J., Carpenter, S. R. et al. (2011). Trophic downgrading of Planet Earth. *Science* 333(6040) (15 July): 301–306.

Ewing B., Moore, D., Goldfinger, S., Oursler, A., Reed, A. & Wackernagel, M. (2010). *The Ecological Footprint Atlas 2010.* Oakland: Global Footprint Network.

Fairhead, J., Leach, M. & Scoones, I. (2012). Green grabbing: a new appropriation of nature? *Journal of Peasant Studies* 39(2): 237–261.

FAO, WFP & IFAD. (2012). *The State of Food Insecurity in the World 2012*. Rome: FAO.

Fehr, E. & Falk, A. (2002). Psychological foundations of incentives. *European Economic Review* 46: 687–724.

Feng, L. and Xu, J. (2015). Farmers' willingness to participate in the next-stage grain-for-green project in the Three Gorges Reservoir Area, China. *Environmental Management* 56(2): 505–518.

Ferraro, P. J. (2001). Global habitat protection: limitations of development interventions and a role for conservation performance payments. *Conservation Biology* 15: 990–1000.

Ferraro, P. J. & Hanauer, M. M. (2011). Protecting ecosystems and alleviating poverty with parks and reserves: 'win-win' or tradeoffs? *Environmental and Resource Economics* 48: 269.

Ferraro, P. & Simpson, R. D. (2005). Cost-effective conservation when eco-entrepreneurs have market power. *Environment and Development Economics* 10(5): 651–663.

Ferraro, P. J. & Kiss, A. (2002). Direct payments to conserve biodiversity. *Science* 298(5599) (29 November): 1718–1719. Fisher, J. (2012). No pay, no care? A case study exploring motivations for participation in payments for ecosystem services in Uganda. *Oryx* 46(1): 45–54.

Forest Peoples Programme (2014). The Batwa Petition before Uganda's Constitutional Court. http://www.forestpeoples.org/topics/rights-land-natural-resources/news/2014/07/batwa-petition-uganda-s-constitutional-court Accessed 14/10/14.

Foster, J. B. (1999). Marx's theory of metabolic rift: classical foundations for environmental sociology. *American Journal of Sociology* 105(2) (September): 366–405.

Franks, P. and Small, R. (2016). *Social Assessment for Protected Areas (SAPA). Methodology Manual for SAPA Facilitators*. London: IIED.

Franks, P., Martin, A. & Schreckenberg, K. (2016). *From Livelihoods to Equity for Better Protected Area Conservation*, IIED Policy Brief (August).London: International Institute of Environment and Development.

Fraser, N. (2000). Rethinking recognition. *New Left Review* 3: 107–120.

Fraser, N. (1997). *Justice Interruptus: Critical Reflections on the 'Postsocialist' Condition*. Cambridge: Cambridge University Press.

Fraser, N. (1995). From redistribution to recognition? Dilemmas of justice in a 'post-socialist' age. *New Left Review* I(212) (July–August): 68–93.

Fredericks, S. E. (2013). *Measuring and Evaluating Sustainability: Ethics in Sustainability Indexes*. London: Routledge.

Frey, B. S. & Jegen, R. (2001). Motivation crowding theory. *Journal of Economic Surveys* 15: 589–611.

Friedlingstein, P., Andrew, R. M., Rogelj, J., Peters, G. P., Canadell, J. G., Knutti, R., Luderer, G., et al. (2014). Persistent growth of CO2 emissions and implications for reaching climate targets. *Nature Geoscience* 7(10): 709–715.

Friedman-Rudovsky, J. (2011). Dreams of a lithium empire. *Science* 334(6058): 896–897.

Fukuyama, F. (2012). The drive for dignity. *Foreign Policy* (12 January), http://www.npr.org/2012/01/13/145157969/foreign-policy-the-struggle-for-dignity.

Gadgil, M. & Guha, R. (1992). *This Fissured Land: An Ecological History of India*. Oxford: Oxford University Press.

Giddens, A. (1984). *The Constitution of Society*. Berkeley: University of California Press. Global Footprint Network and WWF (2014). http://www.footprintnetwork.org/en/index.php/gfn/page/living_planet_report_2014_facts Accessed 31/08/2016.

Global Forest Expert Panel (2012). *Understanding Relationships between Biodiversity, Carbon, Forests and People: The Key to Achieving REDD+ Objectives*. IUFRO World Series Vol. 31.

Gneezy, U. & Rustichini, A. (2000). A fine is a price. *Journal of Legal Studies* 29(1) (January): 1–17.

Gorenflo, L. J., Romaine, S., Mittermeier, R. A. & Walker-Painemilla, K. (2012). Co-occurrence of linguistic and biological diversity in biodiversity hotspots and high bio-diversity wilderness areas. *Proceedings of the National Academy of Sciences* 109(2)1: 8032–8037.

Gough, I. (2007). Wellbeing and welfare regimes in four countries. In *WeD International Conference 2007, Wellbeing in International Development*, 28-30 June 2007. Bath: University of Bath.

Gough, I. (2004). Human well-being and social structures: relating the universal and the local. *Global Social Policy* 4(3): 289–311.

Gough, I. R., McGregor, J. A. & Camfield, L. (2007). Theorising wellbeing in international development. In Gough, I. R. & McGregor, J. A. (eds) *Wellbeing in Developing Countries: From Theory to Research*. Cambridge: Cambridge University Press.

Government of India (1952). National Forest Policy of India, New Delhi.

Government of Tanzania (2013). *National Strategy for Reduced Emissions from Deforestation and Forest Degradation (REDD+)*. Dar es Salaam: Vice-President's Office, Government of Tanzania.

Gross-Camp, N. D., Few, R. & Martin, A. (2015a). Perceptions of and adaptation to environmental change in forest-adjacent communities in three African nations. *International Forestry Review* 17(2) (June): 153–164.

Gross-Camp, N. D., Martin, A., McGuire, S. & Kebede, B. (2015b). The privatization of the Nyungwe National Park Buffer Zone and implications for adjacent communities. *Society and Natural Resources* 28(3): 296–311.

Gross-Camp, N. D., Martin, A., McGuire, S. & Kebede, B. (2012). Payments for ecosystem services in an African protected area: exploring issues of legitimacy, fairness, equity and effectiveness. *Oryx* 46 (1) (January): 24–33.

Grubb, M., Vrolijk, C. and Brack, D. (1999). *The Kyoto Protocol. A Guide and Assessment*. London: Royal Institute of International Affairs, Energy and Environmental Programme.

Guardian (2016). Ecuador drills for oil on edge of pristine rainforest in Yasuni. https://www.theguardian.com/environment/2016/apr/04/ecuador-drills-for-oil-on-edge-of-pristine-rainforest-in-yasuni Accessed 30/08/2016.

Guardian (2013). Ecuador approves Yasuni national park oil drilling in Amazon rainforest. https://www.theguardian.com/world/2013/aug/16/ecuador-approves-yasuni-amazon-oil-drilling Accessed 30/08/2016.

Guha, R. (1989). *The Unquiet Woods: Ecological Change and Peasant Resistance in the Himalaya*. Oxford: Oxford University Press.

Guha, R. & Martínez Alier, J. (2013). Varieties of Environmentalism: Essays North and South. London: Routledge.

Gullison, R. E. (2003). Does forest certification conserve biodiversity? *Oryx* 37(2): 153–165.

Gustavsson, M., Lindström, L., Jiddawi, N. S. & De la Torre-Castro, M. (2014). Procedural and distributive justice in a community-based managed Marine Protected Area in Zanzibar, Tanzania. *Marine Policy* 46: 91–100.

Hackett, R. (2015). Offsetting dispossession? Terrestrial conservation offsets and First Nation treaty rights in Alberta, Canada. *Geoforum* 60: 62–71.

Hagen, J. B. (1992). *An Entangled Bank: The Origins of Ecosystem Ecology*. New Brunswick, NJ: Rutgers University Press.

Halappa, G. S. (1964). *History of Freedom Movement in Karnataka*, Vol. 2. Bangalore: Govt. of Mysore Publications, pp. 175–179. Cited in Nadkarni, M. V., S. A. Pasha &

L. S. Prabhakar (1989). *Political Economy of Forest Use and Management*. New Delhi: Sage Publications.

Hall, J. M., Burgess, N. D., Rantala, S., Vihemaeki, H., Jambiya, G., Gereau, R. E., Makonda, F. et al. (2014). Ecological and social outcomes of a new protected area in Tanzania. *Conservation Biology* 28(6): 1512–1521.

Hamilton, J. T. (1995). Testing for environmental racism: prejudice, profits, political power? *Journal of Policy Analysis and Management* 14(1): 107–132.

Hardin, G. (1968). The tragedy of the commons. *Science* 162(3859) (December): 1243–1248.

Harrison, M., Roe, D., Baker, J., Mwedde, G., Travers, H., Plumptre, A., Rwetsiba, A. & Milner-Gulland, E. J. (2015). *Wildlife Crime: A Review of the Evidence on Drivers and Impacts in Uganda*. London: IIED.

Harvey, D. (2007). *A Brief History of Neoliberalism*. Oxford: Oxford University Press.

Harvey, D. (1996). *Justice, Nature, and the Geography of Difference*. Hoboken, NJ: Wiley-Blackwell.

Harvey, D. I., Kellard, N. M., Madsen, J. B. & Wohar, M. E. (2010). The Prebisch-Singer hypothesis: four centuries of evidence. *Review of Economics and Statistics* 92(2): 367–377.

Hayes, T. & Persha, L. (2010). Nesting local forestry initiatives: revisiting community forest management in a REDD+ world. *Forest Policy and Economics* 12: 545–553.

He, J. & Sikor, T. (2015). Notions of justice in payments for ecosystem services: insights from China's Sloping Land Conversion Program in Yunnan Province. *Land Use Policy* 43: 207–216.

Hegde, P. (1988). *Chipko and Appiko: How the People Save the Trees*. London: Quaker Press.

Hoang, M. H., Do, T. H., Phamb, M. T., Van Noordwijk, M. & Minang, P. A. (2013). Benefit distribution across scales to reduce emissions from deforestation and forest degradation (REDD+) in Vietnam. *Land Use Policy* 31 (March): 48–60.

Hockings, M. (2006). *Evaluating Effectiveness: A Framework For Assessing Management Effectiveness of Protected Areas*. IUCN: Gland.

Holland, T. G., Peterson, G. D. & Gonzalez, A. (2009). A cross-national analysis of how economic inequality predicts biodiversity loss. *Conservation Biology* 23: 1304–1313.

Honneth, A. (2004). Recognition and justice outline of a plural theory of justice. *Acta Sociologica* 47: 351–364.

Hornborg, A. (1998). Towards an ecological theory of unequal exchange: articulating world system theory and ecological economics. *Ecological Economics* 25: 127–136.

Huckle, J. & Martin, A. (2001). *Environments in a Changing World*. Oxford: Pearson Education.

Hutton, J., Adams, W. M. & Murombedzi, J. C. (2005). Back to the barriers? changing narratives in biodiversity conservation. *Forum for Development Studies* 32(2): 341–370.

Hvalkof, S. (2000). Outrage in rubber and oil: extractivism, indigenous peoples, and justice in the Upper Amazon. In Zerner, C. (ed.) *People, Plants and Justice: The Politics of Nature Conservation*. New York: Columbia University Press.

IEA (2008). *World Energy Outlook 2008*. https://www.iea.org/media/weowebsite/2008-1994/WEO2008.pdf Accessed 25/08/2016.

ILO (2014). *Key Indicators of the Labour Market*, 8th edition. Geneva: International Labour Office.

Inturias, M., Rodríguez, I., Baldelomar, H. & Pena, A. (2016). Justicia ambiental y autonomia indigena de base territorial en Bolivia: un dialogo político desde la Nacion Indigena Monkoxi de Lomerio. Bolivia: Ministerio de Autonomias.

IPCC (2014). *Climate Change 2014: Synthesis Report*. Contribution of Working Groups I, II and III to the Fifth Assessment Report of the Intergovernmental Panel on Climate Change [Core Writing Team, R. K. Pachauri and L. A. Meyer (eds)]. Geneva: IPCC.

IUCN (2014). *The Promise of Sydney* http://worldparkscongress.org/about/promise_of_sydney.html Accessed 02/09/2016.

Jintao, X., Yufang, S., Sun, X. & Siikamaki, J. (2012). *Overview of China's Tenure Reform, 1992–2012. Rights and Resources Initiative.* http://rightsandresources.org/wp-content/uploads/2014/01/doc_4926.pdf Accessed 31/08/2016.

Jorgenson, A. K. (2009). The sociology of unequal exchange in ecological context: a panel study of lower-income countries, 1975–2001. *Sociological Forum* 24: 22–46.

Kareiva, P. & Marvier, M. (2012). What is conservation science? *BioScience* 62(11): 962–969.

Kari-Oka 2 Declaration (2012). http://www.ienearth.org/kari-oca-2-declaration/ Accessed 20/08/2016.

Kashwan, P. (2013). The politics of rights-based approaches in conservation. *Land Use Policy* 31:.613-626.

Katikiro, R. E., Macusi, E. D. & Deepananda, K. A. (2015). Challenges facing local communities in Tanzania in realising locally-managed marine areas. *Marine Policy* 51: 220–229.

Kay, J. J. & Schneider, E. (1995). Embracing complexity, the challenge of the ecosystem approach. In Westra, L. & Lemons, J. (eds) *Perspectives on Ecological Integrity.* Dordrecht: Kluwer, pp. 49–59.

Kerr, J. (2002). Watershed development, environmental services, and poverty alleviation in India. *World Development* 30(8): 1387–1400.

Khatun, K., Corbera, E. & Ball, S. (2016). Fire is REDD+: offsetting carbon through early burning activities in South-Eastern Tanzania. *Oryx* 51(1): 43–52.

Khatun, K., Gross-Camp, N., Corbera, E., Martin, A., Ball, S. & Massoa, G. (2015). When participatory forest management makes money: insights from Tanzania on governance, benefit sharing, and implications for REDD+. *Environment and Planning* A 47(10) (October): 2097–2112.

Kinzig, A., McShane, T. O., Hirsch, P. D., Trung, T. C., Songorwa, A. N., Monteferri, B. & Mutekanga, D. (2011). Hard choices: Making trade-offs between biodiversity conservation and human well-being. *Biological Conservation* 144: 966–972.

Klein, N. (2015). *This Changes Everything: Capitalism vs. The Climate.* London: Penguin Books.

Kloosters, D. (2000). Institutional choice, community, and struggle: a case study of forest co-management in Mexico. *World Development* 28(1) (January): 1–20.

Konow, J. (2001). Fair and square: the four sides of distributive justice. *Journal of Economic Behavior and Organization* 46: 137–164.

Kormos, R., Kormos, C. F., Humle, T., Lanjouw, A., Rainer, H., Victurine, R. et al. (2014). Great apes and biodiversity offset projects in Africa: the case for national offset strategies. *PLoS ONE* 9(11): e111671.

Kosoy, N. & Corbera, E. (2010). Payments for ecosystem services as commodity fetishism. *Ecological Economics* 69: 1228–1236.

Krausmann, F., Erb, K. H., Gingrich, S., Haberl, H., Bondeau, A., Gaube, V., Lauk, C. et al. (2013). Global human appropriation of net primary production doubled in the 20th century. Proceedings of the National Academy of Sciences 110(25): 10324–10329.

Kuhlken, R. (1999). Setting 'the woods on fire: rural incendiarism as protest. *Geographical Review* 89: 343–363.

Kumar, K. (2014a). Confronting extractive capital: social and environmental movements in Odisha. *Economic and Political Weekly* 49(14): 66–73.

Kumar, K. (2014b). The sacred mountain: confronting global capital at Niyamgiri. *Geoforum* 54: 196–206.

Kumar, P. (2010). *The Economics of Ecosystems and Biodiversity: Ecological and Economic Foundations.* London and Washington DC: UNEP/Earthprint.

Land Matrix (2016). http://landmatrix.org/en/get-the-idea/web-transnational-deals/ Accessed 18/08/2016.

Laurance, W. F. (2004). The perils of payoff: corruption as a threat to global biodiversity. Trends in Ecology & Evolution 19(8) (August): 399–401.

Laurance, W. F., Useche, D. C., Rendeiro, J., Kalka, M., Bradshaw, C. J., Sloan, S. P., Laurance, M. et al. (2012). Averting biodiversity collapse in tropical forest protected areas. *Nature* 489: 290–294.

Leavy, J. & Smith, S. (2010). Future farmers: youth aspirations, expectations and life choices. Future Agricultures Discussion Paper No. 13: 1–15.

Lee, J., Martin, A., Kristjanson, P. & Wollenberg, E. (2015). Implications on equity in agricultural carbon market projects: a gendered analysis of access, decision making, and outcomes. *Environment and Planning A* 47(10): 2080–2096.

Lélé, S., Springate-Baginski, O., Lakerveld, R., Deb, D. & Dash, P. (2013). Ecosystem services: origins, contributions, pitfalls, and alternatives. *Conservation and Society* 11(4): 343–358.

Lélé, S., Wilshusen, P., Brockington, D., Seidler, R. and Bawa, K. (2010). Beyond exclusion: alternative approaches to biodiversity conservation in the developing tropics. *Current Opinion in Environmental Sustainability* 2: 94–100.

LenkaBula, P. (2008). Beyond anthropocentricity: Botho/Ubuntu and the quest for economic and ecological justice in Africa. *Religion and Theology* 15(3): 375–394.

Lenzen, M., Moran, D., Kanemoto, K., Foran, B., Lobefaro., L. & Geschke, A. (2012). International trade drives biodiversity threats in developing nations. *Nature* 486: 109–112.

Leopold, A. (2013 [1949]). *A Sand County Almanac & Other Writings on Conservation and Ecology*. No. 238 Library of America Series.

Leverington, F., Costa, K. L., Pavese, H., Lisle, A. & Hockings, M. (2010). A global analysis of protected area management effectiveness. *Environmental Management* 46(5): 685–698.

Li, T. M. (2014). What is land? Assembling a resource for global investment. *Transactions of the Institute of British Geographers* 39: 589–602.

Li, T. M. (2007). Practices of assemblage and community forest management. *Economy and Society* 36(2): 263–293.

Lund, J. F. and Treue, T. (2008). Are we getting there? Evidence of decentralized forest management from the Tanzanian Miombo Woodlands. *World Development* 36(12) (December): 2780–2800.

Lyons, K. and Westoby, P. (2014). Carbon colonialism and the new land grab: plantation forestry in Uganda and its livelihood impacts. *Journal of Rural Studies* 36: 13–21.

McAfee, K. (2012). The contradictory logic of global ecosystem services markets. *Development and Change* 43: 105–131.

McAfee, K. (1999). Selling nature to save It? Biodiversity and green developmentalism. *Environment and Planning D* 17(2) (April): 133–154.

McCallum, M. L. (2007). Amphibian decline or extinction? Current declines dwarf background extinction rate. *Journal of Herpetology* 41(3): 483–491.

McDaniel, J. M. (2003). Community-based forestry and timber certification in Southeast Bolivia. *Small-scale Forest Economics, Management and Policy* 2(3): 327–341.

McDermott, C. L., Irland, L. C. and Pacheco, P. (2015). Forest certification and legality initiatives in the Brazilian Amazon: lessons for effective and equitable forest governance. *Forest Policy and Economics* 50: 134–142.

McDermott, M., Mahanty, S. & Schreckenberg, K. (2013). Examining equity: a multidimensional framework for assessing equity in payments for ecosystem services. *Environmental Science & Policy* 33: 416–427.

Mace, G. M., Reyers, B., Alkemade, R. Biggs, R., Chapin, F. S., Cornell, S. E., Díaz, S., Jennings, S., Leadley, P. & Mumby, P. J. (2014). Approaches to defining a planetary boundary for biodiversity. *Global Environmental Change* 28 (September): 289–297.

McGregor, A. & Sumner, A. (2010). Beyond business as usual: what might 3-D wellbeing contribute to MDG momentum? *IDS Bulletin* 41: 104–112.

Madsen, B., Carroll, N., Kandy, D. & Bennett, G. (2011). *2011 Update: State of Biodiversity Markets Offset and Compensation Programs Worldwide*. http://www.forest-trends.org/publication_details.php?publicationID=2848 Accessed 29/08/2016.

Maisels, F., Strindberg, S., Blake, S., Wittemyer, G., Hart, J., Williamson, E.A., et al. (2013). Devastating decline of forest elephants in Central Africa. *PLoS ONE* 8(3): e59469.

Maraseni, T. N., Neupane, P. R., Lopez-Casero, F. & Cadman, T. (2014). An assessment of the impacts of the REDD+ pilot project on community forests user groups (CFUGs) and their community forests in Nepal. *Journal of Environmental Management* 136: 37–46.

Marglin, S. A. (2010). *Dismal Science: How Thinking Like an Economist Undermines Community*. Cambridge, MA: Harvard University Press

Markopoulos, M. (1998). *The Impacts of Certification on Community Forest Enterprises: A Case Study of the Lomerío Community Forest Management Project, Bolivia*. London: International Institute for Environment and Development (IIED).

Maron, M., Gordon, A., Mackey, B. G., Possingham, H. P. & Watson, J. E. (2015). Conservation: stop misuse of biodiversity offsets. *Nature* 523: 401–403.

Marris, E. (2014). Rethinking predators: Legend of the Wolf. *Nature* 507(7491): 158–160.

Martin, A., Coolsaet, B., Corbera, E., Dawson, N. M., Fraser, J. A., Lehman, I. & Rodríguez, I. (2016). Justice and conservation: the need to incorporate recognition. *Biological Conservation* 197: 254–261.

Martin, A., Akol, A. & Gross-Camp, N. (2015). Towards an explicit justice framing of the social impacts of conservation. *Conservation and Society* 13: 166–178.

Martin, A., Gross-Camp, N., Kebede, B., Mcguire, S. & Munyarukaza, J. (2014a). Whose environmental justice? Exploring local and global perspectives in payments for ecosystem services scheme in Rwanda. *Geoforum* 54: 167–177.

Martin, A., Gross-Camp, N., Kebede, B. & Mcguire, S. (2014b). Measuring effectiveness, efficiency and equity in an experimental Payments for Ecosystem Services trial. *Global Environmental Change* 28 (September): 216–226.

Martin, A., Akol, A. and Phillips, J. (2013a). Just conservation? in Sikor, T. (ed.) *The Justices and Injustices of Ecosystem Services*. Routledge: London, pp. 69-91.

Martin, A., McGuire, S. and Sullivan, S. (2013b). Global environmental justice and biodiversity conservation. *Geographical Journal* 179: 122–131.

Martínez Alier, J. (2014). The environmentalism of the poor. *Geoforum* 54: 239–241.

Martínez Alier, J. (2012). Environmental justice and economic degrowth: an alliance between two movements. *Capitalism Nature Socialism* 23(1): 51–57

Martínez Alier, J. (2009a). Social metabolism, ecological distribution conflicts, and languages of valuation. *Capitalism Nature Socialism* 20(1): 58–87.

Martínez Alier, J. (2009b). Socially sustainable economic de-growth. *Development and Change* 40 (6): 1099–1119.

Martínez Alier, J. (2003). *The Environmentalism of the Poor: A Study of Ecological Conflicts and Valuation*. Cheltenham: Edward Elgar.

Martínez Alier, J., Temper, L. and Demaria, F. (2016). Social metabolism and environmental conflicts in India. Nature, Economy and Society (pp. 19–49).

Marx, A. and Cuypers, D. (2010). Forest certification as a global environmental governance tool: what is the macro-effectiveness of the Forest Stewardship Council? *Regulation & Governance* 4(4): 408–434.

Marx, K. 2005. *Early Writings*. London: Penguin.

Matheny, G. (2005). Utilitarianism and animals. In Singer, P. (ed.) *In Defense of Animals: The Second Wave*. London: Wiley-Blackwell.

Matulis, B. S. (2014). The economic valuation of nature: a question of justice? *Ecological Economics* 104 (August): 155–157.

Merchant, C. (1980). *The Death of Nature: Women, Ecology, and Scientific Revolution*. London: Bravo.

Merger, E., Held, C., Tennigkeit., T. & Blomley, T. (2012). A bottom-up approach to estimating cost elements of REDD+ pilot projects in Tanzania. *Carbon Balance and Management* 7(1): 9.

Meshack, C. K., Adhikari, B., Doggart, N. and Lovett, J. C. (2006). Transaction costs of community-based forest management: empirical evidence from Tanzania. *African Journal of Ecology* 44: 468–477.

Mignolo, W. D. (2009). Epistemic disobedience, independent thought and de-colonial freedom. *Theory, Culture & Society* 26(7–8): 1–23

Mignolo, W. D. (2007). Delinking, *Cultural Studies* 21(2): 449–514.

Mikkelson, G. M., Gonzalez, A. & Peterson, G. D. (2007). Economic inequality predicts biodiversity loss. *PLoS ONE* 2(5): e444.

Millennium Ecosystem Assessment (2005). *Synthesis Report*. World Resources Institute. http://www.millenniumassessment.org/en/Synthesis.html Accessed 28/08/2016.

Miller, B., Soulé, M. E. and Terborgh, J. (2014). 'New conservation' or surrender to development? *Animal Conservation* 17: 509–515.

Miller, R. L. (2013). *Justice for Earthlings: Essays in Political Philosophy*. Cambridge: Cambridge University Press.

Miller, D. C., Agrawal, A. and Roberts, J. T. (2013). Biodiversity, governance, and the allocation of international aid for conservation. *Conservation Letters* 6(1): 12–20.

Miller, T. R., Minteer, B. A. and Malan, L. C. (2011). The new conservation debate: the view from practical ethics. *Biological Conservation* 144(3): 948–957.

Mills, J. H. & Waite, T. A. (2009). Economic prosperity, biodiversity conservation, and the environmental Kuznets curve. *Ecological Economics* 68: 2087–2095.

Milne, S. & Adams, B. (2012). Market masquerades: uncovering the politics of community-level payments for environmental services in Cambodia. *Development and Change* 43: 133–158.

Minang, P.A. & Van Noordwijk, M. (2013). Design challenges for achieving reduced emissions from deforestation and forest degradation through conservation: leveraging multiple paradigms at the tropical forest margins. *Land Use Policy* 31: 61–70.

Minteer, B. A. and Miller, T. R. (2011). The new conservation debate: ethical foundations, strategic trade-offs, and policy opportunities. *Biological Conservation* 144: 945–947.

Miteva, D. A., Pattanayak, S. K. and Ferraro, P. J. (2012). Evaluation of biodiversity policy instruments: what works and what doesn't? *Oxford Review of Economic Policy* 28(1): 69–92.

Miya, M., Ball, S. M. J., and Nelson, F. D. 2012. *Drivers of Deforestation and Forest Degradation in Kilwa District*. Mpingo Conservation and Development Initiative. Kilwa: Tanzania.

Moorman, R. H. (1991). Relationship between organizational justice and organizational citizenship behaviors: do fairness perceptions influence employee citizenship? *Journal of Applied Psychology* 76: 845–855.

Moran, D. D., Lenzen, M., Kanemoto, K. & Geschke, A. (2013). Does ecologically unequal exchange occur? *Ecological Economics* 89 (May): 177–186.

Morris, T. (2013). A brief history of the Ilois experience. http://www.zianet.com/tedmorris/dg/iloishistory-final-a4.pdf Accessed 30/08/2016.

Moseley, W. G. (2001). African evidence on the relation of poverty, time preference and the environment. *Ecological Economics* 38(3) (September): 317–326.

Mosse, D. (2003). *The Rule of Water: Statecraft, Ecology and Collective Action in South India.* New Delhi: Oxford University Press.

Mpingo Conservation and Development Initiative (2015). *Combining REDD, PFM and FSC certification in South-Eastern Tanzania: final report of NGO REDD+ pilot projects, Tanzania.* www.mpingoconservation.org Accessed 23/8/16.

Mpingo Conservation and Development Initiative (2012). *Combining REDD, PFM and FSC certification in South-Eastern Tanzania: project revision proposal 2012.* www.mpingo conservation.org Accessed 23/8/16.

Muradian, R., Walter, M. and Martínez Alier, J. (2012). Hegemonic transitions and global shifts in social metabolism: implications for resource-rich countries. Introduction to the special section. *Global Environmental Change* 22(3): 559–567.

Myers, N., Mittermeier, R. A., Mittermeier, C. G., Da Fonseca, G. A. B. & Kent. J. (2000). Biodiversity hotspots for conservation priorities. *Nature* 403 (February): 853–858

Myers, R., Sanders, A. J., Larson, A. M. & Ravikumar, A. (2016). *Analyzing Multilevel Governance in Indonesia: Lessons for REDD+ from the Study of Landuse Change in Central and West Kalimantan* (Vol. 202). Bogor: CIFOR.

Nadkarni, M. V., Pasha, S. A. & Prabhakar, L. S. (1989). *Political Economy of Forest Use and Management.* New Delhi: Sage Publications.

Naeem, S., Duffy, J. E. and Zavaleta, E. (2012). The functions of biological diversity in an age of extinction. *Science* 336 (6087) (June): 1401–1406.

Nepstad, D., Schwartzman, S., Bamberger, B., Santilli, M., Ray, D., Schlesinger, P., Lefebvre, P. et al. (2006). Inhibition of Amazon deforestation and fire by parks and indigenous lands. *Conservation Biology* 20: 65–73.

Neumann, R. P. (2004). Moral and discursive geographies in the war for biodiversity in Africa. *Political Geography* 23(7) (September): 813–837.

Neumeyer, E. (2011). *Sustainability and Inequality in Human Development.* Human Development Research Paper, 2011/04. New York: UNDP.

Neuteleers, S. & Engelen, B. (2015). Talking money: how market-based valuation can undermine environmental protection. *Ecological Economics* 117: 253–260.

Noe, C. and Kangalawe, R. Y. (2015). Wildlife Protection, community participation in conservation, and (dis) empowerment in Southern Tanzania. *Conservation and Society* 13(3): 244.

Norgaard, R. B. (2010). Ecosystem services: from eye-opening metaphor to complexity blinder. *Ecological Economics* 69: 1219–1227.

Norton, B.G. (2005). *Sustainability: A Philosophy of Adaptive Ecosystem Management.* Chicago: University of Chicago Press.

Nussbaum, M. C. (2011*). Creating Capabilities: The Human Development Approach.* Cambridge, MA: Harvard University Press.

Nussbaum, M. (2006). *Frontiers of Justice: Disability, Nationality, Species Membership.* Cambridge, MA: Harvard University Press.

Oates, J. F. (1999). *Myth and Reality in the Rain Forest: How Conservation Strategies Are Failing in West Africa.* Berkeley: University of California Press.

Ocampo, J. A. & Parra-Lancourt, M. N. (2010). The terms of trade for commodities since the mid-19th century. *Journal of Iberian and Latin American Economic History* 28(1): 11–43.

O'Connor, J. R. (ed). (1998). *Natural Causes: Essays in Ecological Marxism.* New York: Guilford Press.

O'Connor, M. (1993). On the misadventures of capitalist nature. *Capitalism Nature Socialism* 4(3): 7–40.

OECD (2015). *Material Resources, Productivity and the Environment.* Paris: OECD.

Ohenjo, N., Willis, R., Jackson, D., Nettleton, C., Good, K. & Mugarura, B. (2006). Health of indigenous people in Africa. *The Lancet* 367: 1937–1946.

Oldekop, J., Holmes, G., Harris, W. E. & Evans, K. L. (2015). A global assessment of the social and conservation outcomes of protected areas. *Conservation Biology* 30(1) (February): 133–41.

O'Riordan, T. (1981). *Environmentalism*. London: Pion Books.

Ostrom, E. (1990). *Governing the Commons. The Evolution of Institutions for Collective Action*. Cambridge: Cambridge University Press.

Ostrom, E. & Nagendra, H. (2006). Insights on linking forests, trees, and people from the air, on the ground, and in the laboratory. *Proceedings of the National Academy of Sciences* 103(51): 19224–19231.

Outhwaite, W. (2009). *Habermas: A Critical Introduction*. Palo Alto, CA: Stanford University Press.

Oxfam (2014). *Working for The Few: Political Capture and Economic Inequality*. https://www.oxfam.org/en/research/working-few Accessed 30/08/2016.

Pagiola, S., Arcenas, A. & Platais, G. (2005). Can payments for environmental services help reduce poverty? An exploration of the issues and the evidence to date from Latin America. *World Development* 33(2): 237–253.

Parsons, C. (2007). *How to Map Arguments in Political Science*. Oxford: Oxford University Press.

Pascual, U., Phelps, J., Garmedia, E., Brown, K., Corbera, E., Martin, A., Gomez-Baggethun, E. et al. (2014). Social equity matters in payments for ecosystem services. *BioScience* 64(11) (November): 1027–1036.

Pascual, U., Muradian, R., Rodríguez, L. C. & Duraiappah, A. (2010). Exploring the links between equity and efficiency in payments for environmental services: a conceptual approach. *Ecological Economics* 69: 1237–1244.

Patenaude, G. & Lewis, K. (2014). The impacts of Tanzania's natural resource management programmes for ecosystem services and poverty alleviation. *International Forestry Review* 16(4): 459–473.

Pattanayak, S. K., Wunder, S. & Ferraro, P. J. (2010). Show me the money: do payments supply environmental services in developing countries? *Review of Environmental Economics and Policy* req006.

Pattberg, P. & Mert, A. (2013). The future we get might not be the future we want: analyzing the Rio+20 outcomes. *Global Policy* 4(3): 305–310.

Pearce, D. (2002). An intellectual history of environmental economics. *Annual Review of Energy and the Environment* 27 (November): 57–81.

Pearce, D. W., Markandya, A. and Barbier, E. B. (1989). *Blueprint for a Green Economy*. London: Earthscan.

Peluso, N. L. and Lund, C. (2011). New frontiers of land control: Introduction. *Journal of Peasant Studies* 38(4): 667–681.

Persha, L. & Meshack, C. (2016). *A Triple Win? The Impact of Tanzania's Joint Forest Management Programme On Livelihoods, Governance and Forests*. 3ie Impact Evaluation Report 34. New Delhi: International Initiative for Impact Evaluation.

Persha, L., Agrawal, A. & Chhatre, A. (2011). Social and ecological synergy: local rulemaking, forest livelihoods, and biodiversity conservation. *Science* 331(6024): 1606–1608.

Phelps, J., Webb, E. L. and Agrawal, A. (2010). Does REDD+ threaten to recentralize forest governance? *Science* 328(5976): 312–313.

Piketty, T. (2014). *Capital in the Twenty-First Century*. Cambridge, MA: Harvard University Press.

PIMA (2016). *Poverty and Ecosystem Service Impacts of Tanzania's Wildlife Management Areas*. The Pima Project research dissemination note. May. London: UCL.

Pinto, L. F. G. & McDermott, C. (2013). Equity and forest certification: a case study in Brazil. *Forest Policy and Economics* 30: 23–29.

Plumptre, A. J., Kayitare, A., Rainer, H., Gray, M., Munanura, I., Barakabuye, N., Asuma, S. et al. (2004). The Socio-Economic Status Of People Living Near Protected Areas in the Central Albertine Rift. New York: Wildlife Conservation Society (WCS).

Plumptre, A. J., Masozera, M., Fashing, P. J., McNeilage, A., Ewango, C. Kaplin, B. A. & Liengola, I. (2002). *Biodiversity Surveys of the Nyungwe Forest of Southwest Rwanda: Final Report*. Bronx, NY: Wildlife Conservation Society.

Pogge, T. (2002). Cosmopolitanism: a defence. *Critical Review of International Social and Political Philosophy* 5(3): 86–91.

Polanyi, K. (1944). *The Great Transformation: Economic and Political Origins of our Time*. New York: Rinehart.

Porras, I. T., Grieg-Gran, M. and Neves, N. (2008). *All That Glitters: A Review of Payments for Watershed Services in Developing Countries*. Natural Resource Issues No. 11. London: IIED.

Porter-Bolland, L., Ellis, E. A., Guariguata, M. R., Ruiz-Mallén, I., Negrete-Yankelevich, S. & Reyes-García, V. (2012). Community managed forests and forest protected areas: an assessment of their conservation effectiveness across the tropics. *Forest Ecology and Management* 268: 6–17.

Povinelli, E. A. (2002). *The Cunning of Recognition: Indigenous Alterities and the Making of Australian Multiculturalism*. Durham, NC: Duke University Press.

Pretty, J., Adams, B., Berkes, F., De Athayde, S. F., Dudley, N., Hunn, E., Maffi, L. et al. (2009). The intersections of biological diversity and cultural diversity: towards integration. *Conservation and Society* 7(2): 100.

Pulido, L. (2000). Rethinking environmental racism: white privilege and urban development in Southern California. *Annals of the Association of American Geographers* 90(1): 12–40.

Rainforest Trust (2014). https://www.rainforesttrust.org/ Accessed November 2014.

Rasmussen, L., Christensen, A., Danielsen, F., Dawson, N., Martin, A., Mertz, P., Sikor, T., Thongmanivong, S., Xaydongvanh, P. (2016). From food to pest: conversion factors determine switches between ecosystem services and disservices. *Ambio*, forthcoming.

Rawls, J (1971). *A Theory of Justice*. Cambridge, MA: Harvard University Press.

Raworth, K. (2012). A safe and just space for humanity: can we live within the doughnut. *Oxfam Policy and Practice: Climate Change and Resilience* 8(1): 1–26.

Redpath, S. M., Young, J., Evely, A., Adams, W. M., Sutherland, W. J., Whitehouse, A., Amar, A. et al. (2013). Understanding and managing conservation conflicts. *Trends in Ecology & Evolution* 28: 100–109.

Republic of Rwanda (2011). *Rwanda Biodiversity Policy*. Kigali: Republic of Rwanda.

Republic of Rwanda (2004). *National Land Policy*. Kigali: Republic of Rwanda.

Rice, J. (2007). Ecological unequal exchange: consumption, equity, and unsustainable structural relationships within the global economy. *International Journal of Comparative Sociology* 48(1): 43–72.

Richards, P. (1985). *Indigenous Agricultural Revolution: Ecology and Food Production in West Africa*. London: Hutchinson.

Robbins, P., McSweeney, K., Chhangani, A. K. & Rice J. L. (2009). Conservation as it is: illicit resource use in a wildlife reserve in India. *Human Ecology* 37:559–575.

Robeyns, I. (2003). Is Nancy Fraser's critique of theories of distributive justice justified? *Constellations* 10: 538–554.

Rockström, J., Steffen, W., Noone, K., Persson, Å., Chapin, F. S., Lambin, E. F., Lenton, T. M. et al. (2009). A safe operating space for humanity. *Nature* 46:, 472–475.

Rodríguez, I. (2016). Historical reconstruction and cultural identity building as a local pathway to 'living well' amongst the Pemon of Venezuela. In White, S. and Blackmore. C. (eds) *Cultures of Wellbeing*. London: Palgrave Macmillan, pp. 260–280.

Rodríguez, I., Sletto, B., Bilbao, B., Sánchez-Rose, I., Leal, A. (2013). Speaking of fire: reflexive governance in landscapes of social change and shifting local identities. *Journal of Environmental Policy & Planning 15:* 1–20.

Rodríguez, I. (2007). Pemon perspectives of fire management in Canaima National Park, Southeastern Venezuela. *Human Ecology* 35: 331. doi:10.1007/s10745–006–9064–7.

Roe, D. (2008). The origins and evolution of the conservation-poverty debate: a review of key literature, events and policy processes. *Oryx* 42(04): 491–503.

Romero, C., Putz, F. E., Guariguata, M. R., Sills, E. O., Cerutti, P. O. and Lescuyer, G. (2013). *An Overview of Current Knowledge about the Impacts of Forest Management Certification: A Proposed Framework for Its Evaluation.* Occasional Paper 99. Bogor: CIFOR.

Ryan, C. M. and Williams, M. (2011). How does fire intensity and frequency affect miombo woodland tree populations and biomass? *Ecological Applications* 21(1): 48–60.

Sachs, J. D., Baillie, J. E. M., Sutherland, W. J., Armsworth, P. R., Ash, N., Beddington, J., Blackburn, T. M. et al. (2009). Biodiversity conservation and the Millennium Development Goals. *Science* 325(5947) (18 September): 1502–1503.

Said, E. (1978). *Orientalism.* New York: Pantheon Books.

Salafsky, N. & Wollenberg, E. (2000). Linking Livelihoods and Conservation: A Conceptual Framework and Scale for Assessing the Integration of Human Needs and Biodiversity. *World Development* 28(8): 1421–1438.

Saldanha, I. M. (1996). Colonialism and professionalism: A German forester in India. *Environment and History* 2(2): 195–219.

Samii, C., Lisiecki, M., Kulkarni, P., Paler, L. and Chavis, L. (2014). Effects of payment for environmental services (PES) on deforestation and poverty in low and middle income countries: a systematic review. *Campbell Systematic Reviews* 10(11).

Sandel, M. (2012). *What Money Can't Buy: The Moral Limits of Markets.* London: Penguin.

Sandel, M. J. (1998). *Liberalism and the Limits of Justice,* Cambridge: Cambridge University Press.

Schellnhuber, H. J., Rahmstorf, S. & Winkelmann, R. (2016). Why the right climate target was agreed in Paris. *Nature Climate Change* 6(7): 649–653.

Scherl, L. M. & Emerton, L. (2008). Protected areas contributing to poverty reduction. In *Protected Areas in Today's World: Their Value and Benefits for the Welfare of the Planet.* Technical Series 36. Montreal: Secretariat of the Convention on Biological Diversity, pp. 4–17.

Schlosberg, D. (2013). Theorising environmental justice: the expanding sphere of a discourse. *Environmental Politics* 22: 37–55.

Schlosberg, D. (2009). *Defining Environmental Justice: Theories, Movements and Nature.* Oxford: Oxford University Press.

Schlosberg, D. (2004). Reconceiving environmental justice: global movements and political theories. *Environmental Politics* 13(3) (Autumn): 517–540.

Schlosberg, D. & Carruthers, D. (2010). Indigenous struggles, environmental, justice, and community capabilities. *Global Environmental Politics* 10(4) (November): 12–35.

Schroeder, R. A. (2008). Environmental justice and the market: the politics of sharing wildlife revenues in Tanzania. *Society and Natural Resources* 21(7): 583–596.

Sen, A. (2009). *The Idea of Justice.* London: Penguin.

Sen, A. (2007). *Identity and Violence: The Illusion of Destiny.* London: Penguin.

Shoreman-Ouimet, E. & Kopnina, H. (2015). Reconciling ecological and social justice to promote biodiversity conservation. *Biological Conservation* 184: 320–326.

Short, J. R. (1991). *Imagined Country: Environment, Culture, and Society.* Syracuse: Syracuse University Press.

Siege, L. & Baldus, R. D. (2000). From decline to recovery: the elephants of the Selous. Tanzania Wildlife Discussion Paper, Vol. 27.

Sikor, T. (2013). *The Justices and Injustices of Ecosystems Services.* Routledge: London.

Sikor, T., Martin, A., Fisher, J. and He, J. (2014). Toward an empirical analysis of justice in ecosystem governance. *Conservation Letters* 7: 524–532.

Silcock, P., Allen, B. & Hart, K. (2012). *Land Stewardship in England post 2013: CAP Greening And Agri-Environment*. Wormington: Cumulus Consultants.

Singer, P. (1975). *Animal Liberation: A New Ethics for Our Treatment of Animals*. New York: HarperCollins.

Smith, A. (2008 [1776]). *The Wealth of Nations*. Oxford: Oxford University Press.

Soulé, M. E. (1985). What is conservation biology? *BioScience* 35: 727–734.

Spash, C. L. (2010). The brave new world of carbon trading. *New Political Economy* 15(2): 169–195.

Springate-Baginski, O., Mwendo, F., Massao, G. and Ball, S. (2015). *REDD+ Village Governance: Three Years in Review 2011 –2014*. Unpublished report for Mpingo Conservation and Development Initiative.

Springer, J., Gastelumendi, J., Oviedo, G., Walker Painemilla, K., Painter, M., Seesink, K., Schneider, H. et al. (2010). The conservation initiative on human rights: promoting increased integration of human rights in conservation. *Policy Matters* 17: 81–83.

Steering Committee of the State-of-Knowledge Assessment of Standards and Certification. (2012). *Toward sustainability: The roles and limitations of certification*. Resolve Inc.: Washington DC.

Steffen, W. & Smith, M. S. (2013). Planetary boundaries, equity and global sustainability: why wealthy countries could benefit from more equity. *Current Opinion in Environmental Sustainability* 5(3): 403–408.

Stephenson, P. J. and McShane, T. (2015). *WWF Global Conservation Programme Report*. Gland: WWF International.

Stepp, J. R., Cervone, S., Castaneda, H., Lasseter, A., Stocks, G. and Gichon, Y. (2004). Development of a GIS for global biocultural diversity. *Policy Matters* 13: 267–270.

Stiglitz, J., Sen, A. K. & Fitoussi, J. P. (2009). The Measurement of Economic Performance and Social Progress Revisited: Reflections and Overview. http://www.insee.fr/fr/publications-et-services/dossiers_web/stiglitz/doc-commission/RAPPORT_anglais.pdf Accessed 01/09/2016.

Strassburg, B. B. N., Vira, B., Mahanty, S., Mansourian, S., Martin, A., Dawson, N. M., Gross-Camp, N. et al. (2012). Social and economic considerations relevant to REDD+. In *Understanding Relationships between Biodiversity, Carbon, Forests and People: The Key to Achieving REDD+ Objectives*. IUFRO World Series Vol. 31.

Sullivan, S. (2013). Banking nature? The spectacular financialisation of environmental conservation. *Antipode* 45: 198–217.

Sullivan, S. (2009). Green capitalism, and the cultural poverty of constructing nature as service-provider. *Radical Anthropology* 3: 18–27.

Sullivan, S. (2002). How sustainable is the communalising discourse of 'new' conservation? The masking of difference, inequality and aspiration in the fledgling 'conservancies' of Namibia. In Chatty, D. and Colchester, M. (eds) (2002). *Conservation and Mobile Indigenous People: Displacement, Forced Settlement and Sustainable Development*. Oxford: Berghahn Press.

Sutherland, W. J., Pullin, A. S., Dolman, P. M. & Knight, T. M. (2004). The need for evidence-based conservation. *Trends in Ecology & Evolution* 19(6): 305–308.

Tacconi, L., Mahanty, S. & Suich, H. (2010). *Payments for Environmental Services, Forest Conservation and Climate Change: Livelihoods in the REDD?* Cheltenham: Edward Elgar.

Tavoni, A., Dannenberg, A., Kallis, G. & Löschel, A. (2011). Inequality, communication, and the avoidance of disastrous climate change in a public goods game. *Proceedings of the National Academy of Sciences* 108(29): 11825–11829.

Temper, L., del Bene, D. and Martínez Alier, J. (2015). Mapping the frontiers and front lines of global environmental justice: the EJAtlas. *Journal of Political Ecology* 22: 256.

Terborgh, J. (1999). *Requiem for Nature*. Washington DC: Island Press.

Thompson, I. D., Ferreira, J., Gardner, T., Guariguata, M. Koh, L. P. et al. (2012). Forest biodiversity, carbon and other ecosystem services: relationships and impacts of deforestation and forest degradation. In *Understanding Relationships between Biodiversity, Carbon, Forests and People: The Key to Achieving REDD+ Objectives*. IUFRO World Series Vol. 31.

Thoreau, H. D. (2001). *Wild Fruits: Thoreau's Rediscovered Last Manuscript*. New York: W.W. Norton & Company.

Tilman, D., Knops, J., Wedin, D., Reich, P., Ritchie, M. and Siemann, E. (1997). The influence of functional diversity and composition on ecosystem processes. *Science* 277(29) (August): 1300–1302.

Torras, M. & Boyce, J. K. (1998). Income, inequality, and pollution: a reassessment of the environmental Kuznets curve. *Ecological Economics* 25: 147–160.

Toulmin, S. (2007). Preface: how reason lost its balance. In De Sousa Santos, B. (ed.) (2007). *Cognitive Justice in a Global World: Prudent Knowledges for a Decent Life*. Lanham, MD: Lexington Books.

UN (2015). https://sustainabledevelopment.un.org/post2015/transformingourworld Accessed 29/08/16.

UNCED (2012). *The Future We Want*. Resolution adopted by the General Assembly on 27 July 2012 66/288. http://www.un.org/ga/search/view_doc.asp?symbol=A/RES/66/288&Lang=E Accessed 28/08/2016.

UNDP (2015). *Human Development Report 2015*. New York: United Nations Development Program.

UNEP (2016). *Global Material Flows and Resource Productivity*: Assessment Report for the UNEP International Resource Panel. http://unep.org/documents/irp/16-00169_LW_GlobalMaterialFlowsUNEReport_FINAL_160701.pdf Accessed 30/08/2016.

UNICEF/WHO (2012). *Progress on Drinking Water and Sanitation: 2102 Update*. UNICEF and World Health Organization 2012. http://www.unicef.org/media/files/JMPreport2012.pdf Accessed 30/08/2016.

United Church of Christ Commission for Racial Justice (1987). Toxic Wastes and Race in the United States: A National Report on the Racial and Socio-Economic Characteristics of Communities with Hazardous Waste Sites. New York: Public Data Access Inc.

Van der Toorn, J., Tyler, T. R. & Jost, J. T. (2011). More than fair: Outcome dependence, system justification, and the perceived legitimacy of authority figures. *Journal of Experimental Social Psychology* 47(1): 127–138.

Vermeylen, S. & Walker, G. (2011). Environmental Justice, Values, and Biological Diversity: The San and the Hoodia benefit-sharing agreement. In Carmin, J. and Agyeman, J. (eds) *Environmental Inequalities Beyond Borders: Local Perspectives on Global Injustices*. Cambridge, MA: MIT Press, pp. 105–128.

Vidal, J. (2014). Conservationists split over 'biodiversity offsetting' plans. *Guardian*, 03/06/2014. https://www.theguardian.com/environment/2014/jun/03/conservationists-split-over-biodiversity-offsetting-plans Accessed 31/08/2016.

Villarroya, A., Barros, A. C. and Kiesecker, J. (2014). Policy development for environmental licensing and biodiversity offsets in Latin America. *PloS ONE* 9(9): e107144.

Vincent, A. (1998). Is environmental justice a misnomer? In Boucher, D. & Kelly, P. (eds) *Social Justice: From Hume to Walzer*. New York: Routledge.

Visvanathan, S. (2007). An invitation to a science war. In De Sousa Santos, B. (ed.) *Cognitive Justice in a Global World: Prudent Knowledges for a Decent Life*. Lanham, MD: Lexington Books.

Vornovytskyy, M. S. & Boyce, J. K. (2010). *Economic Inequality and Environmental Quality: Evidence of Pollution Shifting in Russia.* Working Paper, PERI Working Paper Series No. 217. Amherst: University of Massachusetts.

Vyamana, V. G. (2009). Participatory forest management in the Eastern Arc Mountains of Tanzania: Who benefits? *International Forestry Review* 11(2): 239–253.

Wake, D. B. & Vredenburg, V. T. (2008). Are we in the midst of the sixth mass extinction? A view from the world of amphibians. *Proceedings of the National Academy of Sciences* 105(Supplement 1): 11466–11473.

Walker, W. (2012). *Environmental Justice: Concepts, Evidence and Politics.* London: Routledge.

Wallerstein, I. (1984). *The Politics of the World-Economy: The States, the Movements and the Civilizations.* Cambridge: Cambridge University Press.

Warren, K. J. (1999). Environmental justice: some ecofeminist worries about a distributive model. *Environmental Ethics* 21(2)(Summer): 151–161.

WCED (1987). *Our Common Future.* Oxford: Oxford University Press.

Wells, M. Guggenheim, S. Khan, A. Wardojo, W. and Jepson, P. (1999). *Investing in Biodiversity: A REVIEW of Indonesia's Integrated Conservation and Development Projects.* Directions in Development. Washington DC: World Bank.

West, P. (2006a). *Conservation Is Our Government Now: The Politics of Ecology in Papua New Guinea.* New Ecologies for the Twenty-first Century. Durham, NC: Duke University Press.

West, P. (2006b). *Dispossession and the Environment: Rhetoric and Inequality in Papua New Guinea.* New York: Columbia University Press.

West, P. and Brockington, D. (2006). An anthropological perspective on some unexpected consequences of protected areas. *Conservation Biology* 20: 609–616.

West, P., Igoe, J. and Brockington, D. (2006). Parks and peoples: the social impact of protected areas. *Annual Review of Anthropology* 35: 251–277.

Westhoek, H., Lesschen, J. P., Rood, T., Wagner, S., De Marco, A., Murphy-Bokern, D., Leip, A., van Grinsven, H., Sutton, M. A. and Oenema, O. (2014). Food choices, health and environment: effects of cutting Europe's meat and dairy intake. *Global Environmental Change* 26: 196–205.

Westman, W. E. (1977). How much are nature's services worth? *Science* 197(4307) (2 September): 960–964 doi:10.1126/science.197.4307.960.

Whiteman, G. (2009). All my relations: understanding perceptions of justice and conflict between companies and indigenous peoples. *Organization Studies* 30: 101–120.

Wilkinson, R. & Pickett, K. (2010). *The Spirit Level: Why Equality is Better for Everyone.* London: Penguin.

Wilmers, C. C., Estes, J. A., Edwards, M., Laidre, K. L. & Konar, B. (2012). Do trophic cascades affect the storage and flux of atmospheric carbon? An analysis of sea otters and kelp forests. *Frontiers in Ecology and the Environment* 10: 409–415.

Wilshusen, P. R., Brechein, S. R., Fortwangler, C. L. & West, P. C (2002). Reinventing a square wheel: critique of a resurgent 'protection paradigm' in international biodiversity conservation. *Society and Natural Resources* 1: 17–40.

Wilson, E. O. (1989). Threats to biodiversity. *Scientific American* 261(3) (September): 108–116.

Wilson, E. O. (1988). The current state of biological diversity. In Wilson, E. O. & Peter, F. M. (eds) *BioDiversity.* New York: National Academy Press, pp. 3–18.

World Bank (2013). *World Development Indicators and Global Development Finance.* Washington DC: World Bank.

World Bank (1992). *World Development Report 1992: Development and the Environment.* Washington DC: World Bank.

Worthy, K. (2013). *Invisible Nature: Healing the Destructive Divide between People and the Environment*. Amherst, MA: Prometheus Books

Wunder, S. (2013). When payments for environmental services will work for conservation. *Conservation Letters* 6(4): 230–237.

Wunder, S. (2005). Payments for environmental services: Some nuts and bolts. CIFOR Occasional Paper No. 42, Bogor: Center for International Forestry Research

Wunder, S. (2001). Poverty alleviation and tropical forests—what scope for synergies? *World Development* 29(11): 1817–1833.

WWAP (2012). *The United Nations World Water Development Report 4: Managing Water under Uncertainty and Risk*. World Water Assessment Programme. Paris: UNESCO.

WWF (2000). Indigenous and Traditional Peoples of the World and Ecoregion-Based Conservation. http://terralingua.org/indigenous/ Accessed 13/09/16.

Young, I. M. (2011). *Justice and the Politics of Difference*. Princeton: Princeton University Press.

Zbinden, S. & Lee, D. R. (2005). Paying for environmental services: an analysis of participation in Costa Rica's PSA program. *World Development* 33(2): 255–272.

INDEX